IRAN AT WAR

IRAN AT WAR

Interactions with the Modern World and the Struggle with Imperial Russia

Maziar Behrooz

I.B. TAURIS
LONDON • NEW YORK • OXFORD • NEW DELHI • SYDNEY

I.B. TAURIS
Bloomsbury Publishing Plc
50 Bedford Square, London, WC1B 3DP, UK
1385 Broadway, New York, NY 10018, USA
29 Earlsfort Terrace, Dublin 2, Ireland

BLOOMSBURY, I.B. TAURIS and the I.B. Tauris logo are trademarks of
Bloomsbury Publishing Plc

First published in Great Britain 2023

Copyright © Maziar Behrooz 2023

Maziar Behrooz has asserted his right under the Copyright, Designs and Patents Act, 1988, to be identified as Author of this work.

Cover design by www.paulsmithdesign.com
Cover image: Military Review with Fath Ali Shah and Abbas Mirza, Qajar Dynasty, Iran, circa 1815/16. (© State Hermitage Museum/ Album/Alamy Stock Photo)

All rights reserved. No part of this publication may be reproduced or transmitted in any form or by any means, electronic or mechanical, including photocopying, recording, or any information storage or retrieval system, without prior permission in writing from the publishers.

Bloomsbury Publishing Plc does not have any control over, or responsibility for, any third-party websites referred to or in this book. All internet addresses given in this book were correct at the time of going to press. The author and publisher regret any inconvenience caused if addresses have changed or sites have ceased to exist, but can accept no responsibility for any such changes.

A catalogue record for this book is available from the British Library.

A catalog record for this book is available from the Library of Congress.

ISBN:	HB:	978-1-7807-6627-0
	PB:	978-0-7556-3737-9
	ePDF:	978-0-7556-3738-6
	eBook:	978-0-7556-3739-3

Typeset by RefineCatch Limited, Bungay, Suffolk
Printed and bound in Great Britain

To find out more about our authors and books visit www.bloomsbury.com and sign up for our newsletters.

To the memory of my parents, Jahangir and Sara.

CONTENTS

Preface ix

INTRODUCTION 1

Chapter 1
QAJAR REUNIFICATION 7
  The Eunuch King and reunification of Iran 7
  Aqa Muhammad Shah 8
  Defeat of the Zand 14
  Conquest of the Caucasus 15

Chapter 2
IRAN: STATE AND SOCIETY IN THE EARLY
NINETEENTH CENTURY 27
  Fath Ali Shah Qavanllu-Qajar 27
  Early Qajar state 29
  Social classes and land tenure 35
  Ulama–state relations 36
  Early nineteenth-century society 38
  The Qajar military 40

Chapter 3
DIPLOMACY AND WAR: THE FIRST RUSSO-IRANIAN
WAR, 1804–1813 49
  Prelude to war, 1801–1803 49
  Abbas Mirza Qavanllu-Qajar 51
  Fall of Ganjeh, 1804 57
  First siege of Iravan, summer 1804 60
  The Battle of Qarabagh and the siege of Ganjeh
    and Badkubeh, 1805 67
  Diplomacy and intrigue 76
  Battles of 1806 80
  The Peaceful 1807 85
  The Gardane mission, 1807–1809 87

    Second siege of Iravan and the Battle of Nakhjavan,
        October–December 1808   91
    The Jones Brydges mission, 1809–1810   95

Chapter 4
INTERWAR YEARS AND THE SECOND
RUSSO-IRANIAN WAR   103
    The interwar years   103
    Prelude to war   105
    Russian policy toward the southeastern Caucasus   108
    Council of Sultanieh   118
    The Battlefield   125
    Causes of the Second Russo-Iranian War   128
    The aftermath   130

CONCLUSION: SEVEN POINTS   133

Chronology   139
Appendix Biographies   159
Notes   175
Bibliography   193
Index   207

PREFACE

I was in the ninth grade in Tehran when, in my history class, I received the first real dose of Iranian history regarding the early Qajar period and the two wars with Russia. Although I was aware of the history of this period, my knowledge was limited. I was already showing much interest in the history of Iran and beyond, but in the spirit of the Pahlavi period, the focus of my attention was on the more glorious parts. Our teacher in that class was a great storyteller with a strong voice which demanded attention; I no longer remember his name, but do remember that when it came to going to the blackboard and standing before the class to explain what happened during the First Russo-Iranian War, I enthusiastically volunteered, something I never did for any of my other classes. I was already shocked, as I was preparing for the class presentation, at the defeats Iran suffered during those two wars. Using a map, I presented the standard Pahlavi era narrative of the period: that the evil and brutal eunuch Aqa Muhammad had killed the young, handsome Lutf Ali Khan Zand and massacred Tiflis. That the brave young Crown Prince Abbas Mirza fought the two wars against all odds, that his avaricious, womanizing father, Fath Ali Shah, failed to provide him with adequate support, and that the corrupt Qajar court failed to defend Iran. I remember thinking, how did this happen? After all the glories of the past, the pre-Islamic Iranian empires, the mighty Safavid Empire under Shah Abbas (that year during Noruz I had visited Isfahan with my family for the first time), the smashing victories of Nader Shah Afshar, how could Iran have been in such a vulnerable shape? Ironically, years later, I watched a TV series made after the 1979 revolution named *Tabriz in Fog* (*Tabriz dar meh*), that presented a similar Pahlavi era narrative of this period. I received a good grade for my history class that year, but questions remained.

As my interest in pursuing my higher education in the field of history grew, I always had an eye on visiting this period again and making it a subject of research. However, the 1979 revolution diverted my attention elsewhere, and to more contemporary, twentieth-century subjects. My writings on the history of the left movement, and other subjects of post-WWII history in Iran, were the result. Finally, after receiving a permanent position at my current institution, I was able to focus on my young days' subject of interest, and this book is the result. This project began as a biography of Crown Prince Abbas Mirza, but as time went by it became clear that a broader approach was in order. Focusing on a key personality would not have resulted in a more comprehensive understanding of the period. I do not claim that this study has managed to produce a comprehensive picture, but hopefully it has established a broad narrative and details on areas it has committed itself to focus on.

I would like to thank the anonymous readers of the first draft of my manuscript for their constructive comments.

INTRODUCTION

> Nothing is more concrete than history, nothing less interested in theories or in abstract ideas. The great historians have fewer ideas about history than amateurs do; they merely have a way of ordering their facts to tell their story. It isn't theories they look for, but information, documents, and ideas about how to find and handle them.
>
> Eugen Weber[1]

The eighteenth century was a difficult one for Iran—or "Persia," as the Western world called the country until the 1930s.[i] In 1722, the Safavid state (1501–1722), already in decline for the previous forty years, collapsed after an internal rebellion by the Ghilzai tribe of Qandahar, under Malik Mahmud Hotak who captured Isfahan after a long siege. Thus began a period of bloody civil war and foreign occupation (1722–36) which devastated the former Safavid dominion and only

---

1. The name "Persia" is a variation on the Greek pronunciation of *Parsa* or *Pars*, which Arabs pronounce *Fars*. Iranian/Muslim geographers and historians sometimes referred to Fars as Farsistan. Today, the province of Fars (the ancient Pars) is located in south-central Iran with Shiraz as its largest city and administrative center. Iranians never called their own empire/country by any name other than "Iran." In their encounters with the rising Achaemenid Empire (550–330 BCE) from the east, Greek city-states began to refer to it as the "Persian Empire," on account of the dynasty having risen from central Iran—i.e., Pars. The name "Iran" came into prominence during the Sasanian Empire (224–651 CE) and is mentioned in the *Shahnameh* of Abu al-Qasem Ferdowsi written in the tenth century. The Safavid state (1501–1722), and other state formations after the sixteenth century, referred to their dominion as "Iran." The name "Persia" was never used by Iran-based states to refer to their dominion. In 1934, Reza Shah Pahlavi (r.1926–41) asked Western governments to refer to Iran by its correct historical name.

ended with the consolidation of power and ascension to the throne of Nader Shah Afshar (r.1736–47).

Nader Shah belonged to the Shi'a Turkic Afshar tribe of Khorasan in eastern Iran. The Afshar tribe, as well as a number of other Turkic tribes, were collectively known as the Qezelbash (or "redheads") and together they comprised the muscle behind the early Safavid road to power. However, Nader did not belong to tribal nobility, coming from humble origins—but what he lacked in "noble blood," he compensated for with his military genius, which made it possible for him to reunify the former Safavid dominion and take the throne in 1736. Nevertheless, his brief reign did not much benefit the rehabilitation of his empire, devastated by years of economic neglect and warfare. Not even his conquest of Timurid (Mughal) India in 1739 and looting of treasures of India did much to improve Iran's economic decline.[ii] While in India, he declared a three-year remission of taxation, but once back in Iran and because of costly wars, he cancelled it. Nader's continued wars demanded the maintenance of a large and expensive army. When these wars were unsuccessful, such as in Daghestan and against the Ottoman Empire in central Iraq, the cost became even more burdensome. During his 1743 campaign against the Ottoman Empire, Nader's army is estimated to have been 375,000 strong, not including provincial forces.[iii] In other words, while Nader Shah's wars of conquest reestablished and even expanded the former Safavid dominion, these conquests did little to restore his empire. A key shortcoming of Nader's military forces which prevented him from capturing Baghdad from the Ottomans was its lack of effective and modern artillery. Although he seems to have been aware of the importance of artillery, especially for siege purposes, a lack of technology prevented him from casting up-to-date cannons, which in turn worked against his ambitions against the Ottoman Empire. His reliance on ineffective but mobile *zamburaks* (little wasps) as field guns is just one example. A *zamburak* was a small cannon mounted on a camel and was fired by the rider with limited effect in the battlefield. Nevertheless, in a terrain with few roads where carrying heavy artillery proved difficult, *zamburaks* provided some portable firepower.

Another aspect of Nader's reign was his attempt to reconcile the Shi'a–Sunni divide, which ultimately was unsuccessful. His scheme involved negotiations with the Ottoman sultan and Sunni ulama in the hope of recognition of Shi'i–Ja'fari jurisprudence as the fifth legitimate school alongside the existing four schools of Sunni Islam. In return, Nader promised peace and an end to hostile Shi'i rituals that involved insulting the first three rightly guided caliphs respected by the Sunni Muslims.[iv] Nader was not a particularly religious man but hostility between his Shi'a and Sunni soldiers often caused bloody conflicts, which he needed to address. In addition, it seems he viewed his Sunni soldiers, especially those from among Sunni Pashtun tribes, to be better fighters—hence the need to address their religious sensitivities. Nader Shah's loss of his faculties during the last years of his reign, a condition perhaps close to what is known today as schizophrenia, only made a bad situation worse. The climax of his condition was marked by the blinding of his son Reza Qoli Mirza (who was a capable military commander and his heir-apparent), on suspicion of participating in an attempt on Nader's life after his return from India. Nader's assassination in 1747 resulted in the disintegration of his army, the looting of the treasure he had collected over years of conquest, and the start of another round of civil war.

Nader's grand army was essentially a seasonal force recruited from various tribes plus some sedentary populations from around his vast empire. Loyalty in his army was to the shah and to the tribal leader. Soldiers were provided for primarily with the promise of a share in the spoils of victory. After Nader's assassination his military camp began to disintegrate along tribal lines, with various elements attacking each other and others leaving the camp. Soon there emerged five major contending tribal groupings, with each dominating a geographical area while continuing to fight each other for supremacy. The five contenders were as follows:

- Nader's grandson Shahrokh, who controlled much of Khorasan.
- Ahmad Khan Abdali, a commander in Nader's army who gained control of what is today Afghanistan and established the Durani dynasty in Qandahar.
- Azad Khan, a Pashtun chieftain who gained control of Azarbaijan and its vicinity.
- Muhammad Hasan Khan of the Qavanllu-Qajar tribe, who established himself in Astarabad and Mazandaran in the north.
- Karim Khan of the Zand tribe, who established himself in Shiraz and the central region of Fars.

By 1759 Karim Khan had become the dominant ruler, with both Muhammad Hasan Khan and Azad Khan killed and their dominions annexed to the Zand territory, while the Afshar were allowed to rule Khorasan unmolested and Ahmad Khan Abdali remained busy consolidating his power in what is today Afghanistan and Pakistan. Hence, Karim Khan's dominion did not include all the Safavid–Afshar terrain or even the territory of Iran today. Nevertheless, Karim Khan's reign was relatively peaceful, which allowed for a rejuvenation in trade and agriculture after a long period of civil war and economic decline. He did not claim a royal title for himself and preferred to rule as "deputy of the people" (وکیل الرعیا). Karim Khan named an infant member of the Safavid House as nominal king and ruled as his regent.[v]

The prosperity of the Zand period is evident in the revival of many towns, especially Karim Khan's seat of power, Shiraz. Here, many buildings, mosques, and the grand bazaar attest to Karim Khan's patronage. Karim Khan's main shortcoming was, similarly to Nader Shah, his failure to establish an orderly system of succession. As a result, upon his death in 1779, another round of civil war ensued. Karim Khan's own relatives were most responsible for the new round of fighting—his sons, brothers, and nephews ignited a long and destructive period of conflict which included numerous backstabbings within the Zand clan, as well as warfare between the Zand and other tribal contenders, namely the Qajar of Astarabad. During this period, seven Zand contenders claimed the throne, with the last one, Lutf Ali Khan, captured and killed by Aqa Muhammad Khan, the chief of the Qajar tribe of Astarabad and founder of the Qajar dynasty.[vi]

While the eighteenth century was a period of civil war and economic contraction for Iran, much of the European world was poised to make a great leap forward. Here, four key developments need to be mentioned, namely the Enlightenment, the Industrial Revolution, the age of democratic revolutions, and "military revolution." Of the above, "military revolution" would find an important place in Iran's interaction with the West as the eighteenth century ended. Michael Roberts has suggested that "military revolution" in European armies began during Europe's wars of religion, 1562–1648. According to him, it entailed a "revolution in tactics," where the lance and pike were replaced by the arrow and musket. Furthermore, armies grew in size and new tactics were developed to lead them in the field. Finally, military revolution "dramatically accentuated the impact of war on society: the greater costs incurred, the greater damage inflicted, and the greater administrative challenges posed by the augmented armies made waging war far more of a burden. Both for civilians and for their rulers."[vii] By the end of the eighteenth century, one may add better drills, more and better precision artillery, better fortification, and better-trained officer corps—all of which placed further distance between European armies and their opponents.

A good example of the "military revolution" may be seen in the development of the Russian military during the eighteenth and early nineteenth centuries, which went through major reorganization. Already under Peter I (d.1725), Russia's nobility, which provided the Russian army with its officer corps, were mandated to receive an up-to-date education. The establishment of the Russian War College was to provide the military with trained officers. Peter's reforms resulted in Russian victories against its chief rivals, namely Sweden, Poland, and the Ottoman Empire.[viii] These reforms continued during the reign of Catherine II (d. 1796). Between the reign of Peter I and Catherine II, Russia had become a gigantic land empire with a powerful military. By the end of the 1700s, Russia had gained some 500,000 square miles of territory, and had a population of about 36,000,000 to 40,000,000 and an army some 500,000 strong.[ix] In this context, by the late eighteenth century the southeastern Caucasus had become a focus of Russia's imperial ambition, hence making it a major menace to the newly-established Qajar state in terms of hegemony over that region. During the reign of Alexander I (d.1825), and on the eve of war with France, Russian military command was reorganized and a ministerial system took over the military, establishing the Ministry of War.[x]

Before the Qavanllu-Qajar became a ruling dynasty, it was a tribal nobility. As such, the Qajar dynasty was different from the neighboring House of Osman (Ottoman Empire), the Timurids (Mughals) of India, and the Qing of China. These were established ruling houses with centuries of experience in managing vast empires and dealing with foreign powers. In the case of the Ottoman Empire, it was a major European power which had for centuries interacted with the rest of Europe. In contrast, time was needed for the Qajar dynasty to transform itself from tribal nobility to a ruling royal house. The Qajar had to start from scratch and build up its dominion with very little knowledge and experience in statecraft, diplomacy, or the outside world and developments in Europe. Although the services of a class of Persian-speaking bureaucrats or *divan* was available to the Qajar court once it had established its empire, it proved inadequate in facing the challenges of the nineteenth century.

This study covers the history of Qajar Iran during the late eighteenth and early nineteenth centuries, which encompasses the reign of Aqa Muhammad Shah (r.1796–7) and Fath Ali Shah (r.1797–1834). This period is still an understudied one despite some serious research done by capable historians, especially Muriel Atkin and Abbas Amanat, whose research is cited in this study. This book adopts the approach of the late Professor Eugen Weber, whom I had the pleasure of studying with at University of California, Los Angeles (UCLA). The main goal of this study is to create a narrative and historical context for the period. As such, this work is not about "theory," but about ordering facts and telling the story of the period based on available documents and data. The emphasis is on the military, diplomatic, and political history of the period, although cultural and economic aspects are examined as well.

Extensive primary and secondary sources in both English and Persian have been utilized. These include primary archival documents, firsthand observations, and historical chronicles. French and Russian sources were accessed either through translation of primary sources (in Persian or English) or through secondary research available in English or Persian. The extensive English translation of Russian documents by George Bournoutian, as well as his in-depth study of the First Russo-Iranian War, has been a tremendous help and is cited in this study. This book may read as revisionist to some readers—and at points, it is. The organization of the chapters is chronological and intended to make the research easier to read to appeal to a wider audience.

Chapter 1 explains the reunification of Iran under the Qajar and after a difficult and destructive century. This process, which started in 1779 under Aqa Muhammad Shah, was not complete when he was assassinated in Shusha in 1797. Aqa Muhammad's personality, contributions, and legacy are thoroughly examined. Chapter 2 examines late eighteenth- and early nineteenth-century Iranian society on the eve of imperialist onslaught during the reign of Fath Ali Shah. Here, special attention is paid to the condition of the Qajar military and state organization, rooted in the tradition of the Perso-Islamic and nomadic heritage of the region. Chapter 3 examines the First Russo-Iranian War in light of intense diplomatic activity, international intrigue, and reform after initial military confrontations. Chapter 4 examines the interwar period and the Second Russo-Iranian War. It argues that, similar to the first war, it was Russia and not Iran that ignited the conflict, and that again similar to the first war, Iran was defending its territory. The concluding chapter consists of seven key analytical observations on the period under study.

Chapter 1

QAJAR REUNIFICATION

Can a man of your wisdom believe I will ever run my head against their walls of steel, or expose my irregular army to be destroyed by their cannon and disciplined troops? ... their shots shall never reach me; but they shall possess no country beyond its range. They shall not sleep ... let them march where they choose, I will surround them with a desert.

Aqa Muhammad Shah Qajar to his chief minister
about facing off against the Russian army[i]

The Eunuch King and reunification of Iran

The Qajar were a Turkman pastoral-nomadic people whose origins began in Central Asia.[ii] In 1265, when Mongol conqueror and Genghis Khan's grandson Hulagu Khan set about conquering the western dominion of what remained of the Kharazmshah Empire, and the seat of the Caliphate in Baghdad, one of the tribes that accompanied his army from Central Asia was the Qajar. The tribe soon proved to be a reliable and effective fighting force in support of the Mongol Il-Khan state and converted to Islam alongside the Il-Khans. Toward the end of the Il-Khan period (1336) the Qajar were given land to settle in the Sham (Syria today). The region of Sham was conquered by Amir Timur Gorkan (Timur-e Lang/Tamerlane) in 1401, and he forced the Qajar to migrate to Turkistan (east of the Caspian Sea) via Iran. The migration was slow, and by the time the tribe reached Azarbaijan and the southern Caucasus, Timur had died (1405) and his empire had begun to disintegrate. Hence, the bulk of the Qajar settled in the southern Caucasus around Ganjeh and Iravan. The Qajar thrived in the new location and grew in numbers and power. Sometime in the middle of the fifteenth century, the Qajar became followers of the Shi'a sufi Sheikh Haidar (1460–80), the master of the Safavi Sufi Order, and converted to Shi'ism. Tribal supporters of the Safavi Sufi Order were known as the

Qezelbash.[1] In 1587, during the reign of Shah Abbas I, the growing power of the Qajar became a problem. The shah's centralizing policies required the weakening of the Qezelbash tribes. Hence, the shah ordered the breakup of the Qajar into three branches. One branch remained in place in the southern Caucasus. The second was settled in Astarabad (today Gorgan, southeast of the Caspian Sea) to guard against Sunni Turkman tribes (in what is today the Republic of Turkmenistan) who raided the region for loot and slaves. The third moved to Marv (today in Turkmenistan), to guard against Uzbek raids from beyond the Amu Darya River (Jayhun or Oxus). The Qajar of Astarabad consisted of two branches along the Gorgan River. Groups of clans using pasture on the lower side of the river were known as the Ashaqeh-bash, with the Qavanllu (also known as Quyunllu) as the most prominent clan. Groups of clans using pasture on the upper side of the river were called the Yukhari-bash, with Devellu as the most prominent clan. Competition between the Devellu and the Qavanllu helped weaken the Qajar contest for power during the 1700s.

Aqa Muhammad Shah

Aqa Muhammad Shah was born in March 1743 while his father, the khan of Qavanllu-Qajar Muhammad Hasan, was in hiding from Nader Shah Afshar. Following Nader's assassination in 1747, Muhammad Hasan Khan entered contention for political power, which eventually cost him his life in 1759. This would make him the second Qavanllu-Qajar tribal chief who had lost his life in a struggle for power after the fall of the Safavid dynasty in 1722. His father, Aqa Muhammad's grandfather, was murdered in 1726 by the order of Safavid pretender Tahmasp II in a conspiracy involving the future Nader Shah. While Aqa Muhammad's father was busy fighting, following the breakup of Nader's empire, one of his nemeses, Adel Shah Afshar (born Ali Qoli Khan), a nephew of Nader, got his hands on Muhammad Hasan's family. Adel

---

1. They were known by this name because as followers of the Imami or Twelver Shi'a Safavi Sufi Order, they wore a distinctive headgear with either twelve red stripes or other forms of red coloring. The Sunni opponents of the Safavids began to use the term as a derogatory adjective, which the Qezelbash gradually turned into a badge of honor, beginning to use it in a positive light.

Shah ordered the castration of his six-year-old and firstborn son in order to eliminate him from royal contention by visibly scarring him without killing him. Eliminating royalty from political contention by harming them in a visible manner was not an unusual act at this point in history. Besides the use of castration, blinding and the cutting of ears, noses, or tongues were also popular forms of punishment. However, this brutal act did not prevent the future shah from entering the power struggle for the throne of Iran, which makes Aqa Muhammad unique in the annals of history. While eunuchs have reached powerful positions in different political cultures, including in the Islamic world and China, rarely if at all has a eunuch in history been able to claim royal power.

There are a number of controversies surrounding the personality, achievements, and legacy of the first Qajar shah. The first one has to do with his temperament. History has recorded him as a short-tempered, cruel, and ruthless leader. Certainly, his 1794 treatment of the people of Kerman who had backed his main rival, Lutf Ali Khan Zand, his sack of Tiflis in 1795, and other instances of violent behavior point to the validity of this observation. Perhaps the cruelty done to him as a child had something to do with his aggressive manner. However, other factors have to be considered as well. His behavior was not much different from that of Shah Isma'il I, the founder of the Safavid Empire, or Nader Shah. The eighteenth century was a violent and devastating period in Iranian history. This historical context has to be taken into account while assessing his actions. Furthermore, the empire he was trying to reassemble was a fractured society dominated by very many tribal groups, each having gotten used to their autonomy in the absence of a strong central state for so many years. Even the Zand state under Karim Khan was only in partial control of the former Safavid dominion and even there, Karim's authority was only nominal in many areas. Unification of this fractured population was a monumental task and one of his key achievements, pointing to his willpower and determination, without which one cannot see how the reunification could have occurred. Aqa Muhammad was not a particularly brilliant military leader compared to Nader Shah or Amir Timur or other military greats in history. Yet his ability to combine the use of force alongside diplomacy and co-optation to achieve his goals speaks to his leadership. John Malcolm described him as one who looked like a fourteen-year-old boy from a distance but as "an aged and wrinkled woman" in close-up, with a scary face when angry. One historian has described him as having deep facial wrinkles, small stature, and a high-pitched voice.[iii] Malcolm continues to describe him as being a good judge of character with the ability to keep his own intensions hidden, which enabled him to subdue his enemies and unify the country. Malcolm never met the Qajar shah but recorded these impressions from the courtiers who knew him. Finally, he observed that the shah did not employ force until diplomacy proved futile.[iv] Other observers have pointed out his love of power, wealth, and revenge, all of which seems to be true.[v] However, without a desire for power it is hard to see how unification could have occurred. Power and violence went hand in hand during this phase of history in Iran. During the previous rounds of fighting (1722–36 and 1747–59), the struggle for power had taken the lives of his grandfather and father and had done severe bodily harm to him. This phase of conflict was no different, to the point that Aqa Muhammad even had several of his half-brothers killed in order to make sure his heir-apparent would succeed him smoothly. After ordering the blinding of one brother (Mustafa Quli Khan) and the murder of his loyal brother Ja'far Qoli Khan, Aqa Muhammad is recorded as saying, "I have shed all this blood, that the boy Baba Khan [future Fath Ali Shah], may reign in peace."[vi]

It is also true that he loved jewelry and carried parts of his treasure with him on his military campaigns, and that he loved to play with his collection of valuable stones. However, he lived a simple life, ate modestly and simply, preferred life on the go, with his troops, and had no desire for luxury.[vii] Furthermore, Aqa Muhammad collected most of the scattered treasure of Nader Shah and left his successor a full treasury chest and contemporary Iran with its imperial jewelry collection.[2]

Another controversy surrounding the shah relates to the most important aspect of his legacy, namely the unification of the core dominion of Iran and the creation of a durable dynastic reign. His legacy has been overshadowed by less relevant factors such as his tendency toward violence or his visible disability. Perhaps his first significant achievement was to unite the Qajar of Astarabad. The animosity between two important clans of the Qajar of Astarabad had proven deadly to the fortunes of his family. The two, his own Qavanllu (Quyunllu) clan of Ashaqeh-bash and the Devellu of Yukhari-bash, had been feuding and competing for most of the eighteenth century.[viii] Indeed, one of the

---

2. Today, that collection is in a vault in Iran's central bank in Tehran. Two of the most valuable diamonds in this collection are the famous Sea of Light (*Darya-e Nur*) and Crown of Moon (*Taj-e Mah*), both captured from Lutf Ali Khan Zand in 1794.

reasons for Muhammad Hasan Khan's eventual defeat and death was his competition with the Devellu clan, which actively aided Karim Khan Zand. After humbling the Devellu, Aqa Muhammad made them a partner in the new order by decreeing only the marriage between a Qavanllu heir-apparent and a Devellu bride eligible for succession to the throne.[ix] This project was so successful that according to one historian, from this point on Devellu members would form part of the court functionary personnel and would provide many military commanders to the shah's army.[x] As a eunuch, Aqa Muhammad had no children but was adamant that only the firstborn son of his deceased younger full brother, Hosein Qoli Khan Jahansuz, would be his heir. This arrangement made the first male born to his nephew and heir-apparent Fath Ali Khan (Baba Khan Jahanbani) and his bride Asia Khanum (the daughter of Fath Ali Khan Devellu) the legitimate future crown prince.[xi] Hence after claiming the throne in 1796, he named Baba Khan his heir-apparent with the lofty title "Jahanbani" (world protector), a more unifying appellation compared to his father's title, "Jahansuz" (world burner). Furthermore, Aqa Muhammad managed to humble or co-opt many other tribes and create a network of alliances under Qajar leadership, which made the unification of Iran and future continuity of his dynasty possible.

A final controversy surrounding the founder of the Qajar dynasty was his pre-coronation tribal title *aqa*, spelled with a *qaf* (آقا), which changed spelling to *ghayn* as *agha* (اغا) during the Pahlavi period. This was probably a continuation of the use of his disability as a weapon to humiliate him and his dynasty by the successor Pahlavi dynasty. Both terms are of Turkic-language origin but their use as titles are for different purposes. The title *aqa* is for males and means a master, elder, older brother, etc. In contemporary Persian, it is used mostly to mean "mister"[xii]—hence such court titles as *ishik aqassi bashi* (chief chamberlain) or *qolaler aqassi bashi* (chief of royal guards/slaves). The title *agha*, however, is a respectful reference to a female, and it may mean a lady, sister, queen, or grandmother. It was also used as a title for a castrated man in charge of the royal duties. Hence the term *aghassi bashi* (chief eunuch) for one in charge of the royal harem.[xiii] It is true that Aqa Muhammad was a eunuch, but the feminine title was never used to refer to him during his lifetime, or later by Qajar era historians.[3]

---

3. Some Western historians and observers have also used both titles interchangeably for the Qajar shah, but that is probably from lack of attention to the above points.

During his lifetime, however, his enemies used many derogatory terms to refer to his lack of manhood. The change in the spelling of his title during the Pahlavi period was a means of humiliating him and his dynasty. For example, in a 1794 letter to Ottoman Sultan Salim III, written in Ottoman Turkish, Irakli II, the ruler of eastern Georgia, asked for the sultan's help against Aqa Muhammad. However, in a post-Qajar Persian translation of the letter, the spelling of the shah's title changed to "Agha Muhammad." Similarly, in a 1796 letter written to the Grand Vazir of the Ottoman Empire by the ruler of Darband, the same change of spelling occurred in its Persian translation.[xiv]

After the death of Muhammad Hasan Khan, Karim Khan ordered the arrest of much of his family and transferred them to Shiraz as "guests" at his court. In reality, the sixteen-year-old Aqa Muhammad, his younger full brother, the eight-year-old Hosein Qoli Mirza, and the rest of the family were hostages so that the Qavanllu clan would remain obedient and behave properly. Karim married Aqa Muhammad's paternal aunt, treated the Qavanllu guests with respect, and provided them with proper education and support. As time went by, Aqa Muhammad gained the trust of Karim Khan, who often called him by the mythical name "Piran Viseh." Piran son of Viseh was a mythical minister and advisor to Afrasiab in the *Shahnameh* of Abu al-Qasem Ferdowsi.[xv] Karim Khan's trust in Aqa Muhammad grew to the point that he even discussed important state-related issues with him and relied on his advice. Nevertheless, apparently Aqa Muhammad maintained a deep hidden anger toward the Zand. One famous story has it that he would damage the expensive carpet he would sit on before Karim Khan with a small knife, out of spite for the khan.[xvi] Karim Khan's relationship with the two sons of Muhammad Hasan Khan improved to the point that in 1773 he agreed to send Hosein Qoli Mirza to become governor of Damghan in western Khorasan. Hosein Qoli Mirza, however, proved to be rebellious, unreliable, and a violent ruler, to the point that he was known by the self-awarded title "Jahansuz" (world burner). From his base in Damghan he attacked and subdued the Yukhari-bash in Astarabad and its Sunni Turkman confederates. He was assassinated in 1777, fighting Turkman tribes and embroiled in a plot involving Yukhari-bash chieftain Faghan Ali Khan while still in rebellion against Shiraz.[xvii] One historian has described Jahansuz as "an audacious brute."[xviii]

Jahansuz's rebellion and death did not diminish Aqa Muhammad's status at the Zand court. He still had enough freedom of movement to leave the city for hunting sorties. In 1779, sensing the end of Karim

Khan was near, he and a small group of relatives left Shiraz for hunting. Karim Khan fell ill and lay on his deathbed in his harem in Shiraz in January. He passed away in March 1779. Through younger members of his family, Aqa Muhammad had adequate access to the Shiraz harem and was informed about Karim Khan's health. Once news of the khan's passing reached him, his small party rushed toward Astarabad, as a new round of civil war was about to start. After reaching his destination, he overcame the challenge of two of his half-brothers and established himself as the chieftain of the Ashaqeh-bash.

By this time, a new round of conflict had already begun in the central and southern regions of former Zand dominion. The incompetent and greedy successors to Karim Khan had begun fighting with each other as his kingdom crumbled, which provided an opening for their enemies, primarily Aqa Muhammad, to challenge the Zand.[xix] Aqa Muhammad initially concentrated his efforts in consolidating his position in the north, first in his own tribe of Astarabad, then in Mazandaran, Gilan, and Azarbaijan. Once he secured his power in the north, he chose Tehran, a small garrison town south of the Alborz range and close to his home base of Astarabad, as his center of power.

During this period, initial encounters with Russia occurred in the southern Caspian region, as Aqa Muhammad Khan was engaged in a tough struggle for supremacy over Iran. The first encounter occurred in 1781 in the Mazandaran region, where a Russian force was establishing a military fort to protect Russian commercial interests. Russia's ultimate goal was to turn the outpost into a link between Astrakhan–Iran–India and Central Asia. Lacking adequate firepower to dislodge the Russians, Aqa Muhammad tricked the Russian commander into approaching for negotiations, at which point he was put under arrest until he agreed to dismantle the fort and leave the area.[xx] The second encounter occurred in 1782 in the Gilan region. This was when Aqa Muhammad was attempting to dislodge the local ruler and the Russian collaborator Hedayatollah Khan Fumeni, son of Haji Jamal Fumeni Gilani.[4] After Hedayatollah Khan was defeated by a Qajar force, the Russians betrayed him, preferring to deal with the new power in the neighborhood. He was killed in the port of Enzeli while trying to flee to an offshore Russian ship that refused him passage.[xxi] Hence, in both cases, Aqa Muhammad Khan forced the Russians to back down and leave the area. Both involved the presence of Russian consular interests intertwined with commercial

---

4. In some sources, Hedayatollah Khan is referred to as "Rashti."

interests. Because of the civil war and the chaos engulfing Iran, Russia attempted to strengthen its military presence south of the Caspian Sea by trying to establish military forts. In this context, the Russians also had started to interfere in the ongoing struggle for supremacy within Iran that involved various tribal and local factions, including the Qajar. These encounters seem to have given the first Qajar ruler an assessment of Russian ambition in Iran, leaving a negative impression on him and making him distrust the Russians for the rest of his life.[xxii]

In Azarbaijan, in 1792, Aqa Muhammad combined conquest and co-optation to win over the region.[xxiii] His trusted commander and maternal uncle, Suleiman Khan Qavanllu-Qajar, secured northeastern Azarbaijan while Sadeq Khan Shaqaqi of the Kurdish Shakak tribe was defeated and co-opted. The same happened to the Donboli tribe. Those who either resisted or betrayed him were defeated and blinded. However, his attempt at subduing the khans of the southeastern Caucasus was less successful at this point. He tried and failed to gain the submission of Mustafa Khan of Talesh. On the other hand, Aqa Muhammad sent Suleiman Khan to Qarabagh and received the submission of the khan, Ibrahim Javanshir, who delivered two hostages to him—as was the tradition, to make sure he would behave properly.[xxiv]

Defeat of the Zand

Aqa Muhammad's biggest challenge, however, was the Zand. His struggle against the Zand ended in 1794, when the last Zand pretender, Lutf Ali Khan Zand (a nephew of Karim Khan), was defeated and killed. Karim Khan's successors proved to be their own worst enemy by fighting and backstabbing each other between 1779 and 1794. As noted, during this period seven Zand pretenders claimed the mantle of Karim Khan, in effect exhausting the population in the former Zand dominion. Ali Murad Khan, a brother of Karim Khan and one of the pretenders, "generously" offered Russia the southeastern Caucasus region in exchange for Russian aid to his cause. This was while he had no actual control over the region he was offering.[xxv] In 1791, Ibrahim Khan Kalantar, the governor of Shiraz, shut the gates of the city to Lutf Ali Khan and refused him entry. Lutf Ali then put the fortified city under siege, hoping to force it open. In June 1792, Aqa Muhammad arrived in Shiraz to force the lifting of the siege. Once Lutf Ali retreated, Kalantar opened the city to Aqa Muhammad who entered Shiraz in July 1792.[xxvi] After losing Shiraz, Lutf Ali's situation deteriorated rapidly. By June

1794, he was under siege in Kerman by the Qajar army, where the population rallied behind his cause. As the town was about to fall in October, the Zand pretender fled to the town of Bam, while the Qajar army sacked Kerman. Reportedly, Aqa Muhammad ordered 20,000 men blinded in retribution for supporting the Zand cause, but it is not clear whether this account is historically accurate.[xxvii] What is clear is that Kerman was subjected to three days of sack and, some reports suggest, in the tradition of Mongol military tactics, head towers were raised.[xxviii] Finally, a few days later, the commander of Bam arrested and delivered Lutf Ali Khan Zand to Aqa Muhammad Khan, who had him blinded, tortured, and killed. After this victory, Aqa Muhammad named his 23-year-old nephew Baba Khan (Fath Ali) governor of Fars, Yazd, and Kerman, and appointed Ibrahim Khan Kalantar his chief minister.

Conquest of the Caucasus

Next, Aqa Muhammad's attention turned to the southeastern Caucasus, part of the Iran-based state formation since the Safavid period. The region Aqa Muhammad claimed as his to conquer makes up the modern-day Republic of Armenia; the eastern part of the Republic of Georgia, including Tiflis (Tbilisi); and the Republic of Azerbaijan, including Nakhjavan. It also included the region north of the Republic of Azerbaijan, which today is part of the Russian Federation, including the area of Darband, Daghestan, and the Lezgi-inhabited region all the way to Chechnya.

Historically, the Persian-language name *Azerbaijan* (آذربایجان), pronunciation *Azerbaijan* (آذربایجان) in the Turkic dialect of the Caucasus region, refers to the northwest provinces of Iran, south of the River Aras, and on the southern border of the former Soviet Republics of Azerbaijan and Armenia. Both areas to the north and south of the River Aras were part of Qajar Iran until the Russo-Iranian wars of the early nineteenth century, when the Russian Empire conquered the northern part in two phases in 1813 and 1828 via the treaties of Golestan and Turkmanchay respectively. Neither of the treaties mention the name "Azerbaijan" for the areas occupied by Russia. When identifying the northern provinces, Qajar era historian Mirza Fazlollah Khavarishirazi notes that there are four provinces in the north, two of which are north of Azerbaijan, namely Gorjestanat (Georgia) and Shirvanat. He clearly did not consider the area north of the Aras River as being Azerbaijan.[xxix]

The name Azarbaijan is a pre-Islamic Persian name for a pre-Islamic province south of the River Aras. "Azarbaijan" was not used in any definite or clear manner for the area north of the River Aras in the pre-modern period. In some instances, the name Azarbaijan was used in a manner that included the Aran region immediately to the north of the River Aras, but this was rather an exception. The adoption of this name for the area north of the River Aras was by the nationalist, Baku-based Mosavat government (1918–20) and was later retained by the Soviet Union.[5] Nevertheless, the majority Turkic Azari-speaking people of the Republic of Azerbaijan share many historical and cultural similarities with millions of Iranian Azarbaijanis south of their border.[xxx]

The absence of central authority due to civil war in Iran had created a vacuum in the region. Local rulers, mostly Shi'a Muslim petty dynasties known as khans, filled the vacuum. These khans ruled over principalities known as *velayats* or *khanates* (خانات) or sub-principalities or districts. The only exception was the ruler of Kartli-Kakheti (eastern Georgia, known as "Gorgestan" to Iranians). During the second half of the eighteenth century, the ruler of Gorgestan was Irakli/Erekli II (also known as Heraclius II) of the Bagration dynasty. While Irakli considered himself the king of Gorgestan, to the Iranians he was merely the *vali* (governor, ruler). A majority of people in Irakli's kingdom belonged to the Georgian Orthodox Church.

The khans of the northern highlands were mostly Sunni Muslim. These were Surkhay Khan the shamkhal of Daghestan and his son Nuh Beg, and Umm Khan of Avar. Further south, the population was mostly Shi'a Muslim and included: the khan of Darband and Qobbeh under Fath Ali Khan and his son Shaikh Ali Khan; Javad Khan Ziyadughlu-Qajar, the khan of Ganjeh; Hosein Khan of Shakki and his successor Salim Khan; Mustafa Khan of Shirvan; Hosein Qoli Khan Badkubeh, the khan of Baku; Ibrahim Khalil Khan Javanshir, the khan of Qarabagh; Mir Mustafa Khan of Talesh; Muhammad Hosein Khan Qavanllu-Qajar of Iravan; Kalb Ali Khan Kangarllu of Nakhjavan; and Ali Khan of Saliyan. One interesting observation on the character of the khans of the Caucasus suggests, "The most common characteristic of these khanates was their desire to maintain their independence and safeguard their rule, and they would have taken any step in this regard."[xxxi]

---

5. To avoid confusion, the region north of the modern Iranian border will be referred to as the southeastern Caucasus.

Ganjeh, Georgia, Qarabagh, and Iravan also had substantial Christian populations belonging to the Armenian Orthodox Church. The area of Iravan (today approximately the Republic of Armenia) has been known as Eastern Armenia to historians. Western Armenia was part of the Ottoman Empire at this point. When Russian aggression started against both Iran and the Ottoman Empire, the Armenian population for the most part sided with the Russians, trying to free themselves from Muslim rule. Armenian landowners known as *melik* were for the most part in charge of the Christian community in the region. In Qarabagh, the Armenian population mostly lived in the highlands of that province ruled by five *meliks* and were a source of lucrative tax. During the reign of Nader Shah, to weaken the power of the local Qajar ruler of Qarabagh who still showed loyalty toward the former Safavid dynasty, he empowered the five *meliks* by giving them a degree of economic autonomy.[xxxii] The center of Armenian Christianity was (and is) located in the Khanate of Iravan, in the village of Etchmiadzin in Armenian or Uch Kelisa (Three Churches) in local Turkic dialect. Armenians were not treated well by the Muslim rulers in Iran and the Ottoman Empire. They had to pay high taxes and had to endure other discriminations. However, a report suggests that while the assertion of maltreatment is correct in both cases, the Armenian population of Iran were freer than Ottoman Armenians in practicing their religion and did not have to wear the humiliating distinctive clothing they were forced to wear in the Ottoman Empire.[xxxiii] Furthermore, Fath Ali Shah made decrees favoring the Armenian population. In September 1800, he issued a decree granting a tax exemption to Christians, Jews, and Zoroastrians of his dominion.[xxxiv] In 1801, he issued another decree granting tax-free status to the church of Etchmiadzin, forbidding forced conversion, granting water rights, and exempting toll tax on the trade of its inhabitants.[xxxv] Abbas Mirza was also respectful of the Christian population. In one instance, after a commander in his army had raped an Armenian girl, the prince had him executed.[xxxvi] However, the sardar of Iravan, Hosein Qoli Khan Qavanllu-Qajar, continued the policy of mistreatment. He became the semi-autonomous ruler of Iravan in 1805, where the largest number of Armenians lived. There are reports that he mistreated the Christian population with over-taxation—in effect disobeying the shah, an act that created friction between him and the crown prince.[xxxvii] To sum up, according to one historian, "Sources are clear that the majority of Armenians, unlike the Georgians and especially the Tatars, welcomed the Russians and viewed them as rescuing their people from centuries of Muslim rule." However, the same source observes that the majority of the Armenian population did not take arms against Iran but did provide spying and other services to the Russians.[xxxviii]

In the absence of Iranian power, these local rulers controlled small territories and fought each other while attempting to enlist the support of the Ottomans for their cause. However, by the 1780s the above equation was changing rapidly. Expansion of Imperial Russia to the north of the Caucasus, and the unification of Iran under the Qajar, brought more powerful players into the competition for control of the southeastern Caucasus region. In this context, the ambitions of the local rulers were overwhelmed by the ambitions of more influential individuals.

A good example of an ambitious ruler aiming for goals beyond his resources is the case of Irakli II Bagration, the ruler of Georgia. Even before Karim Khan's death in 1779, he had approached the Ottomans to help him secure the region against Karim Khan. He received a cool reception form the empire that was aware of his earlier attempt at the same policy with the Russians against the Ottoman Empire. When that did not get him anywhere, he approached the Russians to help him to prevent Iran from reclaiming its lost territories. The Russian scheme resulted in a Faustian deal known as the Treaty of Georgievsk (July 1783), which turned his little kingdom into a protectorate of the Russian Empire. Accordingly, Irakli accepted Russian "super authority" over Kartli-Kakheti, in exchange for protection against Iran and a Russian guarantee of the continuation of the dynastic rule of Bagration House.[xxxix] As we shall see, he would get none of the above.

Russian policy toward Iran and the southeastern Caucasus was developed during the reign of Catherine II and was influenced by both military and commercial interests. Militarily, the Russians had become interested in dominating the region, in order to be in a better position to confront the Ottoman Empire in the western Caucasus. Commercially, the region presented Russia with the potential opportunity to dominate trade with Iran and expand beyond into India.[xl]

Russia did not show much interest in the southeastern Caucasus until the end of the 1770s. The architect of the new policy was Prince Grigory A. Potemkin (1739–91), a favorite of Russian Tsarina Catherine II.[xli] He advocated creating client states in Georgia, "Persian Armenia" (Iravan), and Albania (south of the River Kor), and putting a client on the throne of Iran. In 1778, following Potemkin's policy, Catherine ordered the building of a naval force on the Caspian Sea, which eventually numbered thirty-eight warships of different sizes.[xlii] After

Karim Khan's death in 1779, Catherine ordered General Alexander Suvorov to prepare to lead an invasion of the region.

In this scheme, the Russians had the support of key Armenian leaders, who advocated establishing a Russian protectorate–Armenian state in the region.[xliii] Because Armenians on both side of the Ottoman–Iranian border had to pay heavy taxes as non-Muslim subjects of Muslim rulers, many families had moved to areas controlled by Russia or Georgia.[xliv] Potemkin believed he had the support of the Armenian *meliks*, who promised him 30,000 Armenian families would rise up and support a Russian invasion force. It seems he envisioned establishing a "Christian" state not only on the Caucasus but also in northern Iran, from Urumiyeh to Mazandaran.[xlv] The Russian scheme for the region did not come to fruition because of Russian preoccupation in Europe, and war with the Ottoman Empire. After Potemkin's death in 1791, the plan lost its chief advocate.

By the summer of 1795, Aqa Muhammad was ready to bring the southeastern Caucasus back under Iranian rule. Neither the Treaty of Georgievsk nor Russian interest in the southeastern Caucasus deterred Aqa Muhammad, which seems to point to his self-confidence in confronting the Russians, a characteristic he maintained throughout. In the summer of that year, his 60,000-strong, mostly cavalry force moved toward the region.[xlvi] He spent the initial months gaining the submission of the Muslim rulers. Upon hearing about the coming of the Qajar army, Irakli II sent emissaries to the Russian court, informing them of the upcoming invasion and requesting help. Three other khans, namely Ibrahim Khalil Javanshir of Qarabagh, Mir Mustafa of Talesh, and Muhammad Khan Qavanllu-Qajar of Iravan, also sent emissaries to the Russians and received positive news, which convinced them they could resist the Iranian army.[xlvii]

Aqa Muhammad arrived at Adineh Bazaar (halfway between Talesh and the Mughan plain) with an army of 60,000, one sixth of which were infantry, and the rest tribal cavalry. Next, he ordered a column of 10,000 men of his army under the command of Mustafa Khan Qavanllu-Qajar to move on Talesh and secure that khanate, a task accomplished swiftly.[xlviii] Soon, news came in that the khan of Qarabagh was mobilizing to confront him. Upon the Iranian army nearing the Aras River, Javanshir ordered his troops to destroy the bridge at Khoda Afarin, the primary passage point from Azarbaijan into Qarabagh and the Caucasus. Nevertheless, the Qajar army crossed the river on boats and Aqa Muhammad ordered the bridge to be rebuilt. The vanguard of the Qajar army met the rearguard of Javanshir's army and defeated it as it retreated into the fort of Shusha. The siege of Shusha began on July 7, 1795 and lasted for thirty-three days. Aqa Muhammad sent a 5,000-man military unit under Mustafa Khan Qavanllu-Qajar to secure the fort of Askaran to the north of Shusha, and another unit to secure Takht-e Tavus, both designed to close off retreat routes to Javanshir. Nevertheless, a lack of effective artillery, the most daunting deficiency in the Qajar military, became evident during this siege. Shusha Was built by Ibrahim Khalil's father, Panah Ali Khan, and was a well-fortified garrison town, inhabited by both Muslims and Armenian Christians. Lacking effective heavy cannons, and with sappers failing to bring down the wall of the fortress, Aqa Muhammad settled for a siege and attempt to starve the population while he ordered his army to lay waste to the surrounding area. A lack of modern artillery was a problem which would continue to undermine Qajar war efforts against Russia in the coming years.[xlix]

Meanwhile, his commanders gained the submission of the khans of Iravan, Ganjeh, and Shirvan. As for Javanshir, when the siege became unbearable, and as two of his nephews were taken prisoner by the Qajar army, he sued for peace and sent presents and hostages with a promise of submission and paying tribute, but he refused to open the gates of Shusha. Aqa Muhammad accepted this arrangement, at least temporarily, and moved his army toward Ganjeh where Javad Khan Ziyadllu-Qajar had already submitted and played host to him. From Ganjeh, he began to correspond with Irakli II, hoping to receive his submission without a major conflict. Irakli, however, still hoping to receive help from the Russian army, refused. The following correspondence between Irakli and Aqa Muhammad is telling, regarding Iran's claim on Georgia and Irakli's refusal to submit. In his letter to Irakli, Aqa Muhammad Khan described, in general terms, his victories and the process of unification of Iran. He then addressed Irakli directly and wrote:

> According to the old principles and laws, Gorjestan [Georgia] belonged to the dominion of Iran since the time of Shah Isma'il the Safavid until the beginning of our august (*Homayoun*) reign. Therefore, tradition and the path of reason suggests that you realize the situation and submit and return to your sovereign.[l]

Irakli's refusal resulted in the Qajar army of 40,000 men moving toward Tiflis. With no Russian help materializing, Irakli had to face the much stronger Qajar army alone. The Georgian army was routed in the Battle of Rustavi (southeast of Tiflis) on September 10, and the siege of Tiflis began on September 11. Tiflis fell on September 13 as the royal house fled to the mountains. The city was sacked during the next nine days and some 15,000 slaves were taken away. Having humbled the strongest of the local rulers of the region, Aqa Muhammad was ready to dismiss his military for the fall and winter. However, Aqa Muhammad failed to consolidate his position and began to move southward toward the Mughan plain (near the Caspian Sea, today between the Republic of Azerbaijan and the Islamic Republic of Iran), where he spent the winter. It may seem surprising that a military leader such as Aqa Muhammad did not consolidate his position. However, looting and creating fear as a substitute for garrisoning the conquered territory was in line with the Turko-Mongol military tradition to which the Qajar belonged. According to this tradition, going back to the time of Genghis Khan, the upkeep of Aqa Muhammad's large force relied on the local population for materials and other logistical support. Also in line with tradition, those who defied the Qajar ruler and resisted were subject to looting or slavery, or both. In this context, the movement of the Qajar army in the region brought much devastation and hardship to the local Muslim and Christian populations alike and, of course, the sack of Tiflis devastated Georgia. Such acts were considered adequate for the short-term deterrence of future trouble. As noted, in the case of the people of Kerman who resisted him, retaliation against the civilian population was used in order to maintain submission and prevent future rebellions.

There are a number of theories as to why the Russians failed to come to Irakli's defense. One theory suggests that General Ivan Gudovich, the commander of Russian forces in the region, underestimated Aqa Muhammad and the imminent danger he posed. According to this view, the Russian commander saw the Russian presence in the region as deterrence enough for the Qajar leader not to attack. Another theory suggests that his forces were too scattered in operations against the Ottomans, and therefore he was not able to react promptly. Whichever was the case, the Russian response finally came in 1796 with a full ground and naval invasion.[li] Russian archival sources suggest that after the death of Potemkin in 1791, Russian policy toward the region became a little confused as the focus shifted to dealing with the Ottoman Empire on the western Caucasus and the northern Black Sea. In May 1793, Irakli conveyed a message to St. Petersburg warning Catherine and his new favorite, Platon Zubov, about Aqa Muhammad's emerging threat. In November 1793, Gudovich informed the Russian foreign ministry that Aqa Muhammad had sent 20,000 troops to Tabriz, and in December of that year, he reported that the Qajar ruler intended to take Tiflis.

Finally, on August 2, 1795, a few weeks before the arrival of the Qajar army, he reported that Aqa Muhammad was about to attack Tiflis.[lii]

After the fall of Tiflis, Aqa Muhammad was ready to dismiss his army for a fall and winter retreat. He settled in the Mughan plain and, in the tradition of Nader Shah, he agreed to become the *shahanshah* (king of kings) or *padeshah* (king) in winter 1796. As March 21, the beginning of the Iranian New Year or Noruz, fell in the fasting month of Ramadan on the Islamic lunar calendar, the shah's coronation had to be postponed until after Ramadan. Aqa Muhammad Shah arrived in Tehran on April 26, 1796, which was also the beginning of the Russian punitive invasion of the southeastern Caucasus. He held his coronation in Tehran, on May 6, two days after the fall of Darband to the Russian army.[liii] It is not clear why he did not immediately mobilize his army and go to the Caucasus to face off against the Russians. Perhaps Malcolm's quotation of him regarding direct confrontation with the Russian army can give us a window into his state of mind. It certainly shows that the shah was aware of the scale of the Russian firepower and the limitations of his own army. However, he may not have been aware of the full extent of the Russian invasion and may have assumed it to be merely a punitive expedition. Whatever the reason, the shah headed for Khorasan, where Shahrokh, the old grandson of Nader Shah, was the nominal ruler.

Meanwhile Catherine II ordered Platon Zubov to prepare to invade. General Gudovich had over 20,000 troops plus 512 sailors on the Caspian Sea under his command. He ordered 2,000 troops plus six artillery pieces to go to Tiflis, which arrived in December 1795.[liv] Platon Zubov gave overall command of the invading force to his younger brother, Valerian Zubov, known to the locals as the Qezel Iyagh.[6] In spring 1796, Russia had committed a 50,000-man force (other estimates suggest 30,000 to 40,000) under Valerian Zubov to occupy the region, with the ultimate goal of toppling Aqa Muhammad Shah and replacing him with a half-brother, Morteza Qoli, who had defected to Russia.[lv] The Russian army attacked Darband-Qobbeh, where Sheikh Ali Khan resisted but was overwhelmed by Russian firepower and his dominion occupied on May 4, 1796. Zubov arrested Sheikh Ali and humiliated him by having him publicly denounce himself for resisting the Russian Empire. However, he proved to be a daring and resilient fighter among the region's local rulers,

---

6. "*Qezel iyagh*" literally means "golden leg" in Turkish, and was a name by which Valerian Zubov was known in the region. He had lost a leg in Poland and apparently walked with an artificial leg which the locals believed to be made of gold.

and unlike his father who collaborated with the Russians, he sided with the Iranians. A few days after his public humiliation, Sheikh Ali fled Russian captivity and began to organize resistance to Russian occupation. At one point, he annihilated a Russian detachment under the nose of the Russian occupation force.[lvi] By mid-June, the fall of Darband-Qobbeh was followed by the submission of the khans of Ganjeh, Shamakhi/Shirvan, Nokha/Shakki, Shusha/Qarabagh, Lankaran/Talesh, Saliyan, and Badkubeh (Baku). The other khanates of the southeastern Caucasus, namely Iravan and Nakhjavan, were not occupied during this round of fighting but submitted to Zubov. However, the expedition faced numerous problems; as one historian has put it, "the campaign bogged down near the Caspian coast because of opposition from local Muslims and overall Russian bungling. Preparations to supply the expedition were sluggish and poorly coordinated."[lvii]

By August 1796, Aqa Muhammad Shah had occupied Mashhad in Khorasan, and had gotten his hands on the remaining stash of Nader Shah's treasure by forcing Shahrokh into delivering it. He then demanded the return of Herat and Balkh from the ruler of Afghanistan and the return of Marv and release of Iranian prisoners from the Uzbek ruler of Bukhara.[lviii] However, when the news of Russian invasion reached him, he rushed back to Tehran to prepare the army for a counterattack. Meanwhile, Catherine II died in November 1796 and by the order of the new Tsar Paul, the Russian army began to withdraw. Aqa Muhammad moved toward the region in May 1797, at a time when the Russian army had completely evacuated the area (with the exception of Georgia) and the local rulers were back in charge of their khanates. The brief Russian occupation of the southeastern Caucasus, less than a year after Aqa Muhammad Shah's conquest, was both less repressive and less destructive compared to the shah's occupation and the future Russian occupation after 1804. In this context, it seems that the Russians left a positive impression on the local population. Valerian Zubov's ability to maintain strict discipline of his troops projected an impression of justice, as Malcolm noted:

> The countries through which it [the Russian army] marched were friendly ... and its commander [Zubov] had observed so strict a discipline, that he left in the provinces he had invaded as strong an impression of justice as of the power of his sovereign.[lix]

Furthermore, the region's merchants had also been interacting with the Russians and had developed a positive attitude toward them, particularly owing to the fact that their female ruler had successfully defeated the Ottoman Empire.[lx]

Before leaving for the Caucasus, Aqa Muhammad Shah gave strict orders to the governor of Tehran to open the gates of the city only to Jahanbani, his heir-apparent, should something happen to him. Accompanying him on this last campaign were two young royal princes, Jahanbani's sons—Abbas Mirza, the future crown prince, and his older brother Muhammad Ali Mirza Dowlatshah—and Ibrahim Khan I'timad Dowleh, his chief minister. The shah sent 10,000 troops to subdue Talesh, left the bulk of his army and his companions in Ardabil, and rushed to Shusha with 8,000 troops. One of his commanders captured Nakhjavan and arrested its khan, Kalb Ali Kangarllu, who was subsequently blinded. Aqa Muhammad Shah's first aim was to retaliate against Ibrahim Khalil Khan Javanshir who had backstabbed him yet one more time. News of the shah's approaching army and the memory of the devastation he had caused during the siege of Shusha the previous year caused the population of the fortress to expel Javanshir and open Shusha to the shah. The shah resided in the house of Muhammad Hasan Khan Javanshir, the eldest son of Ibrahim Khalil.[lxi] Aqa Muhammad Shah was assassinated in Shusha-Qarabagh on June 16, 1797, eight days after his arrival; he was fifty-eight years old. He was killed by three of his own attendants, who had made him angry the previous night for fighting over food. Aqa Muhammad Shah had promised to execute them the next morning but allowed them to go about their duties. Having nothing to lose, the assassins attacked and mutilated the shah while sleeping, stole the royal jewels in his possession and fled to Sadeq Khan Shaqaqi, delivering the treasure to him and asking for protection. Sadeq Khan was from the Shakak Kurdish tribe and one of those who had been co-opted by the shah in his Azarbaijan campaign. With the shah dead, and his royal jewelry in his possession, he extended the men his protection and left Shusha for his tribe. Once news of the shah's assassination spread, the local population attacked his army outside the fortress as it began to disintegrate due to various tribal units heading home.[lxii] Within a year, all those involved in the assassination would be caught and killed.[lxiii] In Ardabil, upon hearing the news of the assassination, Ibrahim Khan I'timad Dowleh sent messengers to Jahanbani in Shiraz, and rushed to Tehran with the royal princes.

Interesting observations can be made on Iranian attitudes toward the Russians at this early stage. Starting at the top, Aqa Muhammad Shah did not trust the Russians and was confident he could rise to their challenge. While history has judged the shah as a brutal conqueror, he has also been judged a pragmatic, calculating, and shrewd military and political leader. Aqa Muhammad's conversation with his chief minister regarding the Russians reveals a number of interesting facts about the shah's military strategy against Russian aggression. First, it shows that even without having had a major encounter with Russian military power, the shah was acutely aware of his opponent's strength and his own shortcomings as far as the military was concerned. Perhaps brief encounters in the Caspian region a decade earlier had given him enough experience. Second, the shah's strategy for facing the Russians seems to have been a classic Iranian response to a stronger enemy, especially one with modern artillery. Iranians had been using this strategy since the time of the Parthian Empire's wars with Rome, up to the early Safavid wars with the Ottoman Empire. This strategy included not giving direct battle, retreating and attacking in guerrilla style where the shah's army had an advantage, and conducting a scorched-earth policy, hence denying the invading force the ability to sustain itself on occupied land. While the shah was not a great military leader, he was a pragmatic one both in military and political matters. The shah was renowned for his dedication to the military, spending much of his time with the troops, making sure they were well armed, fed and paid, and that discipline was maintained.[lxiv]

Baba Khan Jahanbani (Fath Ali Shah), the heir-apparent, arrived in Tehran on July 17, 1797. The governor of Tehran had carried out his orders to the letter and had not allowed anyone into the city, not even the royal princes and the chief minister, who were camping outside the city walls when the new shah arrived. On July 29, the 27-year-old Fath Ali Shah Qajar ascended to the throne, but postponed his coronation in order to deal with challenges to his reign. His first challenge was Sadeq Khan Shaqaqi, who had given protection to the assassins, was in possession of part of the royal jewels, and had gathered an army to capture Tehran and declare himself shah. The shah's army defeated him at the Battle of Khak-e Ali, near Qazvin (west of Tehran) in August. Another challenge came from Ali Qoli Khan, the only half-brother of Aqa Muhammad who was left alive. However, the force he had gathered dispersed once the decree of the new shah arrived asking for their loyalty. Ali Qoli Khan was arrested and blinded. In August, Hosein Qoli Khan, the new shah's half-brother and governor of Fars, rebelled and was defeated. He was given a smaller governorship but rebelled again and was captured and blinded in 1801.

The shah held his coronation on Noruz (March 21) 1798 in Tehran but challenges to his reign continued. In June, his army defeated a challenge by Muhammad Khan Zand, and in September Ja'far Qoli Khan of the Donboli tribe was defeated at Khoy. A rebellion by Suleiman Khan Qavanllu-Qajar, a maternal uncle of Aqa Muhammad Shah and one of his able and trusted commanders, was preempted and Suleiman Khan was forgiven once he delivered his accomplices.[lxv]

On Noruz of 1799 (March 21), the ten-year-old Abbas Mirza, the shah's son from a Devellu mother, was appointed prince regent (*na'eb saltaneh*) and crown prince (*vali'ahd*) in accordance with Aqa Muhammad Shah's will. In May, Nader Mirza Afshar, a grandson of Nader Shah, rebelled against the shah. It took Fath Ali Shah three major campaigns to Khorasan to put down this and other rebellions as well as challenges by the Afghan ruler, Zaman Shah Durani, during 1799–1803. By December 1803, while Khorasan was pacified, the Russian invasion of the Caucasus had begun in full force.

Chapter 2

IRAN: STATE AND SOCIETY IN THE EARLY NINETEENTH CENTURY

[On the dominion of Iran; longitude:] From the Caucasus Mountain range, Georgia (Gorjestan) and Daghestan on the Russian border, to the southern tip of Kerman bordering the Sea of Hindustan [India-Sea of Oman]. The length of this distance is three hundred and thirty *farsang* [each farsang is about seven kilometers]. The latitude of this country from the bank of the Jayhun River [Amu Darya/Oxus] to the bank of Dejleh [River Tigris] in Baghdad is a distance of two hundred and thirteen *farsakh* [Arabic for "farsang"].

Mirza Fazollah Khavari-shirazi[i]

Fath Ali Shah Qavanllu-Qajar

Fath Ali Shah was born in 1769, the firstborn of Hosein Qoli Mirza Jahansuz, Aqa Muhammad's only full brother. As such, he was chosen by the shah to succeed him. Aqa Muhammad appointed him governor of Shiraz, Yazd, and Kerman, and gave him the title "Jahanbani," in order to prepare him to take the throne. His style of reign proved to be different from his uncle's in a number of ways. Aqa Muhammad Shah's reign can be characterized as that of a tribal king, while Fath Ali Shah's may be called the imperial reign. He had a mild manner, was much less violent than his uncle, and loved luxury, dressing eloquently, and women. John Malcolm noted "he [the shah] is from six to seven hours in public, during which he is not only seen but accessible to a great number of persons of all ranks."[ii] Europeans who met him described him as tall and robust, with Turko-Mongol features.[iii] Another visitor noted the shah's large eyes, arched eyebrows, and "face ... obscured by an immense beard and mustachios."[iv] Many existing paintings of Fath Ali Shah attest to the accuracy of these observations. The new shah turned his uncle's tribal-oriented monarchy into an imperial monarchy with complex court procedures, including on how to address the shah and how to approach him. One observer recorded the court procedures of Fath Ali Shah, whether in the palace or on the move, as follows: "In no court is more rigid attention paid to ceremony. Looks, words, the motion of the body, are all regulated by the strictest forms."[v] New court positions were created to manage the rapidly growing royal household. Hence, *ishik aqassi bashi* (chief chamberlain), *qolaler aqassi bashi* (chief of royal guards/slaves or *gholaman*), *ishik aghassi bashi* (chief eunuch of royal harem), *nasaqchi bashi* (chief enforcer of royal punishment), etc. The contrast between Fath Ali Shah's court at Golestan Palace—and many other palaces he ordered built—and his uncle's court can be seen in other areas as well. The shah's long beard, down to his waist, was a stark contrast to his beardless eunuch uncle. Malcolm described his appearance and personality as follows: "The king has elegant manners and many accomplishments. Among others, he is a poet, and has written a book of odes, of merits of which the critics of Persia speak in perfect raptures."[vi]

His large harem of 158 known wives and concubines, his forty-eight sons and forty-nine daughters, were all designed to project the masculinity and stamina of the new monarch, challenging any who may have assumed, because of his eunuch uncle, that those attributes were missing.[vii] Furthermore, as tradition had it, a large harem by a tribal chief turned king provided the new state with relationships and alliances with other influential families, which helped create stability. Finally, it also provided the new monarchy with a large dynasty and line of succession that separated it from other Qajar clans.

The second Kayanid crown and the shah's full use of the imperial jewelry available to him completed the picture. It is not clear what happened to the original crown, which was with Aqa Muhammad when he was assassinated in Shusha. One historian suggests the most plausible explanation, that Fath Ali Shah, in his "thirst for extravagance and majestic grandeur," may have used its material and replaced it with the new Kayanid crown.[viii] Fath Ali Shah also ordered three thrones built by the artisans of Isfahan. The most famous was the Peacock Throne (*takht-e tavus*). As large as a king-size bed, this is often mistaken for a throne by the same name brought back from India by Nader. Nader's Peacock Throne was dismantled for its valuables after his assassination. Fath Ali Shah's throne was originally called the Sun Throne (*takht-e khorshid*) and in fact, a golden sun is attached to it and hovers over it. However, since the shah spent much time on this throne accompanied by his then harem favorite, Tavous (Peacock) Khanum, titled Taj al-Dowleh (crown of the state), the throne came to be called the Peacock Throne.[ix] The other throne is called the Marble Throne (*takht-e marmar*). Located in Golestan Palace, it is about the same size as the previous throne and is attached to the *eyvan*, or porch. It was used when the shah appeared before his audience outdoors, weather permitting. The third throne is the Naderi Throne and it is more like a gilded chair than a bed.[1] Because of Fath Ali Shah's innovations, the Qajar absolute monarchy began a metamorphosis from a tribal monarchy to an imperial one.

Early Qajar state

The above quotation by an early Qajar historian shows the early nineteenth-century perception of the Iranian ruling class, as to where the historical borders of the shah's guarded domain (*mamalek-e mahruseh*) of Iran were. It also shows that, at least among the ruling class, "Iran" was the name of the shah's dominion. A close examination of the geographical locations demarking the borders of Iran shows that not only do they correspond with the borders of the Safavid Empire at its height, and those of the empire of Nader Shah Afshar, but also those of the pre-Islamic Sasanian Empire (224–651 CE). In addition, early Qajar rulers expected the appointment of governors of Sulaymaniyah and Baghdad in Ottoman Iraq to be made after consultation with Iran and a payment of tribute. Ottoman sultans of this period usually observed this arrangement and when they did not, war broke out on a number of occasions.[x]

The Qajar state was an absolute monarchy. However, the Qavanllu-Qajar dynasty was a newcomer with much tribal-nomadic culture carried over to the newly created royal court. The Qajar tribe traced its roots to the Turkic communities of Central Asia. In order to help create legitimacy and continuity, the ruling house embraced three sets of symbols and concepts: pre-Islamic Iranian, Turko-Mongol, and Islamic. Early Qajar shahs were addressed with such imperial Iranian titles as *shah* (king), *shahanshah-e zarrin taj* (the golden-crowned king of kings), *zilollah* (shadow of God, in Arabic format), *khedive-e zaman*

---

1. The Peacock and the Naderi thrones are kept in the central bank vault in Tehran, and the Marble Throne is kept in Golestan Palace in Tehran.

(ruler of the age), etc. The Mongolian title *khaqan* (sovereign) was frequently used during the reign of Aqa Muhammad Shah and Fath Ali Shah, as was the title *padeshah-e Islam panah* (king protector of Islam). The Qajar were early supporters of the Safavid cause and along with other tribes provided the muscle behind the call of Shah Isma'il, the founder of the Safavid Empire. As such, the Qajar were part of the Qezelbash, those tribes that followed the Safavid House, adhered to Shi'ism, and wore a distinct headgear with pronounced use of the color red.

Having lived in Shiraz in the court of Karim Khan Zand, both Aqa Muhammad and his nephew were exposed to proper education in Persian language and literature, with a good knowledge of Abu al-Qasem Ferdowsi Tusi's *Shahnameh* (book of kings). Aqa Muhammad had verses of the epic read to him before sleep, and Fath Ali Shah did the same during horseback riding.[xi] The *Shahnameh* is a collection of mythical epic stories, and historical narratives, which were converted from texts of pre-Islamic origin into modern Persian by Ferdowsi in the tenth and eleventh centuries. It provides the reader with a good dose of imaginative images and narratives of how Iranian kingship looked in a different age. Pre-Islamic carvings of images or writings praising certain rulers on hills and mountains throughout Iran, and the remains of buildings and palaces such as Persepolis (Takht-e Jamshid), Pasargad (the location of King Cyrus's tomb), and the Firuzabad palace of Sasanian Ardeshir Babakan have been in plain view for centuries. These symbols had been providing ruling dynasties in Iran with concepts and images on what imperial reign could look like, though their real origins were a mystery until later in the nineteenth century. One European observer noted in 1812 that when visiting the necropolis of Naqsh-e Rostam near Shiraz, Qajar courtiers mistook the rock relief of Sasanian Shahanshah Shahpur I for the mythical Rostam of the *Shahnameh*.[xii] In addition, while most of the dynasties from the eleventh century on were Turkic, all gradually associated their reign with this pre-Islamic Iranian culture.

In this context, the services of a Persian-speaking scribal class or *divansalaran* played a significant role. This class had been providing bureaucratic services to the ruling dynasties for centuries and played a crucial role in giving them an Iranian outlook. Two groups of bureaucrats provided services to the first two Qajar shahs. The group from Shiraz, headed by Ibrahim Khan I'timad Dowleh, had been providing the same type of services to the Zand until Ibrahim Khan switched sides in support of Aqa Muhammad, whom he assessed as being the eventual winner. He became the shah's chief minister and later served Fath Ali Shah in the same position until his execution in 1801. Another influential member of the Shiraz Persian-speaking bureaucrats was Mirza Isa (Bozorg) Farahani, who later received a royal title and became the first *qa'em maqam-e sedarat-e uzma* (deputy to the grand chancellor, Qa'em Maqam I for short), and the chief minister to the crown prince and the real force behind the modernizing reforms of Abbas Mirza in Tabriz. The second group of Persian-speaking bureaucrats were from Mazandaran in the Caspian region. The most prominent among this group was Mirza Muhammad Shafi' Mazandarani, who served Aqa Muhammad before being replaced by Ibrahim Khan, and Fath Ali Shah as chief minister until his death in 1818. However, as "nobles of the robe," the status of the scribal class (those who carried the prefix *mirza*) in the Qajar royal court was considered lower than that of the tribal chiefs—especially those of the Qajar tribe, who were considered "nobles of the sword."[xiii]

The use of a crown became a prominent fixture of Qajar royalty early on. While Safavid shahs did not wear a crown, during Nader Shah's short reign, a type of hat resembling a crown was used. Aqa Muhammad was the first shah who used headgear resembling a crown in the post-Islamic period. It was named the Kayanid crown and can be seen in portraits of Aqa Muhammad. One historian described it as: "Aqa Muhammad's self-styled Kayanid crown, named after the mythical dynasty of the *Shahnameh* was inspired by the new shah's keen interest in Iran's ancient legends. [The crown] was [a] dome-shaped structure inspired by the Qezelbash cap."[xiv]

As noted before, Aqa Muhammad lived a simple life with little need for luxury. Tent was preferred to palace, company of troops to the company of courtiers, simple food to royal feasts. He maintained a small harem, which he did not have much use for, probably for projecting an image of masculinity.[xv] Tribal-nomadic culture and habits were visible aspects of the early Qajar state's overall organization of the dominion of Iran, the royal court, and most importantly, the military.

As a tribal absolute monarch, Aqa Muhammad Shah saw little use for an elaborate state apparatus, as he was a hands-on type of ruler. Besides his chief minister, Ibrahim Khan I'timad Dowleh, his government had a simple organization. There were two more state functionaries—namely, the revenue officer (*mostofi*) and the army revenue officer (*Lashkar nevis*), both of whom usually accompanied the shah in his campaigns. Aqa Muhammad even carried part of his royal treasure with him, and that is how his assassins got their hands on it. As one historian has put it, "Agha Muhammad had no official secretary, no minister of justice, no minister of court. He ran a highly personal administration and, finances aside, paper work was almost non-existent."[xvi]

Under Fath Ali Shah, reforms were implemented to accommodate the expanding responsibilities of the state. In 1806, a new expansive division of labor was introduced. The office of chief minister, titled *i'timad dowleh* (the trusted of government) as it was during the Safavid period, was renamed *sadr-e 'azam sedarat-e uzma* (the grand chief of grand chancellery), or *sadr-e 'azam* for short, and its authority expanded. Mirza Shafi' Mazandarani, from the northern faction of Persian-speaking bureaucrats, who was appointed chief minister in 1801, continued in the new post. Under him, new ministries were created, namely *mostofi al-mamalek* (the chief accountant of the realm), and Haji Muhammad Hosein Khan Sadr-e Isafahani was put in charge. The ministry of army/war (*vazir Lashkar*) was headed by Mirza Asadollah Khan Nuri. The position of *monshi al-mamalek* (chief secretary of the realm), went to Mirza Reza Qoli Nava'i. The *sahib divankhaneh* (master of mint in charge of paying civilian and military salaries) was another new ministry. The chief minister of the court of the crown prince, at this time Mirza Isa (Bozorg) Farahani, was given a more authoritative title of *qa'em maqam*.[xvii] Years later, in 1825, a ministry of foreign affairs was also created. Tehran and Tabriz were the most important cities in the shah's realm. Tehran was referred to as *dar al-khelafeh* (Arabic for "abode of the caliphate") which pointed to the shah's claim as being the protector of (Shi'a) Islam. Tabriz, the seat of the crown prince, was referred to as *dar al-saltaneh* (Arabic for "abode of the monarchy"). Both titles were a bit odd, as the Shi'a never accepted the Sunni caliphate and viewed the caliphate as exclusively belonging to the House of the Prophet through the House of Ali b. Abi Talib, the first Shi'a Imam. To call the seat of the crown prince the abode of the monarchy, while the monarch resided in Tehran, was to elevate Tabriz and the crown prince's prestige, but it was also unusual.

Information on the outside world was limited among both the general population and the ruling class, but as time went on and Iran came out of a long period of chaos and instability, interaction with the outside world increased, as did knowledge of developments outside Iran. Information on *yengeh donya* (a Turkic-Arabic composite term meaning "the new world") was scarce. Fath Ali Shah was especially curious about the new world when he asked the British mission how one got there and whether people there lived over the ground or under it.^xviii An English officer observed in 1808, "the Persians in general, however, live in the profoundest ignorance of other countries." However, the same officer found Mirza Shafi', the chief minister, to be "sufficiently acquainted with all the different courts of Europe, and knew perfectly the name of every minister employed."^xix His impression of Qa'em Maqam I was even more positive, as he was described as "the most superior man whom I saw in Persia."^xx In an exchange between Fath Ali Shah and John Malcolm, a British officer visiting Iran in 1801, the shah asked him about King George III, his life and the extent of his power. The shah was surprised to hear that the British king had only one wife and not even a concubine (*kanizak*), and that with parliamentary limits to his power, he was more like a first magistrate (*kadkhoda aval*) than a monarch. The shah's conclusion was that the British king has "permanence" but no "enjoyment."^xxi When European visitors asked to be seated before the shah, they had to resort to evidence from the Safavid period to convince court officials that it was allowed then, and thus it should be allowed now.^xxii Once chairs were provided, one British observer noted that their design was outdated by a few hundred years.^xxiii Iranians were also surprised at the British dress code and expected them to be dressed in the fashion of Safavid period European visitors. In 1808, the British mission brought a royal carriage as a gift for Fath Ali Shah. It had to be dismantled, as there was no carriage-worthy road from the Persian Gulf to Tehran. Similarly, lack of carriageways inside the city prevented its use within Tehran. Once reassembled inside the *arg* (or ark-royal palace), the shah sat in it and smoked a water pipe, and it was not used again.^xxiv

As for nomadic and tribal habits and cultural traits, a lack of secrecy in running state and military affairs was a major shortcoming. As we shall see, open discussion of political, diplomatic, and military policy allowed spies and informants to leak important information to the enemy. An absence of effective security awareness, especially during the reign of Aqa Muhammad Shah, but also during the campaigns of Abbas Mirza against the Russians, led to disaster a number of times. Aqa Muhammad's murder in 1797 closely resembled Nader Shah's assassination in 1747. Similarly to Nader Shah, he promised punishment by death to his attendants in Shusha, for minor misbehavior, but allowed them to continue with their duties. Knowing very well the shah was a man of his word, and that their demise was imminent, they murdered the shah that evening.

Another such cultural trait was eliminating a certain political, military, or tribal figure, deemed dangerous or disloyal, and yet employing his close relatives for state functions. A case in point is the fate of Ibrahim Khan Shirazi (Kalantar) I'timad Dowleh, the chief minister of Aqa Muhammad and Fath Ali Shah. Aqa Muhammad Khan was known to value loyalty above all else, even when it involved his enemies, and was suspicious of disloyalty. When Karim Khan offered Aqa Muhammad a governorship post, Karim's advisor, Mirza Ja'far Isfahani, viewed it as a major mistake and convinced the Zand ruler to cancel the offer. When Aqa Muhammad became shah, he spared Mirza Ja'far's life and allowed him to retire with his possessions because of his loyalty to Karim Khan, despite the fact that he had plotted against him.[xxv] However, when Ibrahim Khan switched sides and betrayed the Zand, the shah elevated him to become his chief minister, but warned Jahanbani to remember this betrayal. Ibrahim Khan served Fath Ali Shah as chief minister for four years, during which he became a powerful and rich man. He appointed his own relatives to important state posts, which provided his enemies with ammunition to undermine him. Led by Mirza Shafi' Mazandarani, his main rival from the northern group of bureaucrats, the shah finally turned against Ibrahim Khan and ordered him and his family killed. Many members of his family were murdered and one of his sons was castrated, and the family property was confiscated.[xxvi] However, once the shah's rage subsided, he forgave his survivors and restored their property. One such relative, a nephew of the fallen Ibrahim Khan, was Mirza Abu al-Hasan Khan the *ilchi* (a Turkish word meaning "ambassador"), who fled to Hyderabad in India. Back in Iran, in 1809 he became the shah's ambassador to Britain and later, in 1825, his foreign minister. While in Britain, he became a Freemason and was put on the payroll of the British government through the East India Company. Hence, Britain had a trusted agent in the highest echelons of Iranian government.[xxvii] Another example is the case of Fath Ali Khan Fumeni, son of Hedayatollah Khan Fumeni, the *biglerbeigi* (governor) of Tabriz. His father was the local ruler of Gilan and an ally of Russia during the civil war that followed the death of Karim Khan. Aqa Muhammad Khan captured Gilan and killed Hedayatollah Khan in 1786. In the run-up to the second war with Russia, Abbas Mirza chose Fath Ali Khan to conduct negotiations with the Russians in Tiflis, and he eventually signed a treaty favorable to Russia, which—as will be discussed later—played an important role in triggering the second war. In both cases, and numerous others, the descendants of murdered former officials and rivals were trusted to be loyal to the state and let bygones be bygones. These examples, and other similar cases, were not simple oversights of security protocol by the shah or the prince regent, but a much more deeply rooted nomadic cultural trait.

Beginning with Aqa Muhammad Shah, "The Qajars revived the Seljuq practice of assigning governorships to the ruler's sons."[xxviii] During the reign of Fath Ali Shah most but not all provincial governorships were given to the shah's numerous sons. When still underage, each son was assigned a *laleh* or teacher-caretaker.[xxix] Once the royal prince was older and ready to assume responsibility, but still in his teens, he was assigned a *pishakar* (teacher-advisor to the prince) and sent off to his governorship. Each prince, then, established his own court in the province under his control and modeled it on the shah court in Tehran, creating his own local military and collecting taxes on behalf of the shah and for his own local expenses. For example, Abbas Mirza, who was named heir-apparent in 1798 and was given governorship of Azarbaijan, was made chief commander in the war with Russia in 1805 when he was sixteen. The shah also appointed high-ranking tribal dignitaries as provincial rulers, as *hokam* and *biglerbegs* (rulers and governors) in charge of some provinces and major cities respectively. They in turn appointed *darughehs* (or security chiefs). The shah also chose, from among local dignitaries, *kalantars* (chief magistrates of a city), and *katkhodas* (magistrates of city wards or villages).[xxx] In this context, the early Qajar state was not highly centralized, and its control over distance provinces was limited and much depended on the shah's ability to manipulate local rivalries.[xxxi]

Social classes and land tenure

Ervand Abrahamian's study of this period, relying on Karl Marx and others, describes Iran's social classes in the early nineteenth century as "a simple sociological category" of groups who have "similar sources of income, similar amounts of revenue, similar degrees of influence, and similar styles of life." This, according to Marx, is a class "in itself" but not yet "for itself."[xxxii] Abrahamian organizes social classes of this period into four major categories. First, the landed upper class, which included the Qajar dynasty, royal princes, influential court officials, and large land grant holders (*tuyuldars*). To this class should be added provincial notables, aristocrats, tribal chiefs, urban administrators, and state-appointed members of ulama. Second, the commercial middle class, which included the urban merchants, shopkeepers and small workshop owners. Third, urban wage-earners such as hired labor, household servants, and construction workers. Fourth, the vast majority of the population—peasants, and the tribal community.[xxxiii]

Land was the main source of income, and thanks to European missions visiting Iran beginning in 1800, there is some data available on ownership of land and state revenue. These missions were ordered to gather detailed information on Iran's population, the shah's revenue, the state of the economy, and the shah's military. Land ownership was divided into four categories, namely: royal land; land given out by *tuyul* or land grant and considered "private property"; endowment land under the control of the religious establishment; and *mavat*, land out of cultivation with no owner.[xxxiv] This arrangement was inherited from the Safavid period. Those who supported the Qajar state were rewarded with land grants and expected to support the center with tax revenue and troops. There were two types of taxes, namely fixed and extra levy taxes, for the upkeep of the court and the army. Fixed taxation included tax on land, animals, flocks, herds, shopkeepers, trade, revenue from crown land, customs, rents, and leases.[xxxv] Land tax was paid in cash or kind, and it was ten percent in the early nineteenth century and rose to twenty percent later, probably because of wars with Russia.[xxxvi] Malcolm estimated the state revenue from taxes in the early 1800s to be three million pounds sterling, which an 1807 estimate puts as two million tumans (40 million francs).[xxxvii]

Ulama–state relations

Education and the administration of justice was primarily the responsibility of the Shi'a ulama. The state–ulama relationship had gone through much change since the fall of the Safavid state in 1722. The Safavid shahs considered their position to be above that of the ulama establishment. As such, the office/ministry of Sadr al-Sodur was established to oversee and manage the ulama. By the end of the Safavid era, the ulama establishment had pushed back and had managed to free itself from court interference and even influence the royal court. During the eighteenth century, with civil wars making life in the former Safavid dominion hazardous, many members of the ulama migrated to the 'atebat al-aliyat (the sublime threshold) or holy Shi'a shrines in Ottoman Iraq. Nader Shah abolished the office of Sadr as he attempted and failed to reconcile Shi'as and Sunnis. By the time of Qajar reunification, the ulama establishment had gone through a significant doctrinal and organizational change.

According to the Imami Shi'a ulama (the branch of Shi'ism dominant in Iran), the only legitimate ruler is the twelfth Imam or the Mahdi, who is in occultation. The temporal state (the royal court), according to this religious doctrine, is tolerated but not legitimate. Qajar shahs, unlike Safavid rulers, did not claim to be the head of the ulama establishment. Hence, the two institutions began to develop a working relationship once unification and stability returned.[xxxviii] By the end of the 1700s, a conflict between two contending schools of Shi'i jurisprudence (*fiqh*) was resolved. The conflict dated back to the Safavid era and involved two schools among the ulama in Iran and the *'atebat*, and therefore did not concern the public. The two schools were the Usuli and the Akhbari. This development sharply increased the independent power of the ulama.

The Akhbaris argued that in the absence of the Mahdi, each Shi'a individual could interpret the traditions (*akhbar* or *hadith*) of the Prophet and the Imams; hence, this school saw a less active and determining role for the ulama. According to one scholar:

> In the absence of the Hidden Imam it was not permissible for a religious scholar (alim) to engage in the use of his reason to enact a certain judgment, to apply the principles of the law to a specific problem or situation. What had to be done was merely to have recourse to hadith [*akhbar*] and on [this] basis ... to arrive at a conclusion, given any particular problem.[xxxix]

The Usulis, the victorious school, held that religious scholars or *mujtahids* were needed to interpret the foundations or principles (*usul*) of the faith for the faithful. According to this school: "The mujtahid is not merely a legal authority, one who gives an expression of opinion concerning a problem of Islamic law; he is also a person whose view must be followed."[xl] The victory of the Usuli school strengthened the tie between the ulama and the ordinary faithful and increased the power of religious scholars. The resulting independence of the ulama from the royal court increased the influence of the ulama on policymaking.

While the ulama dominated education, people's spirituality, and justice, one aspect of law that remained the prerogative of the court was *urf* or customary law, which the royal court managed in Tehran and the shah's representatives managed in the provinces.[xli] In 1809, during the first war with Russia, and again during the second war with Russia, the state solicited ulama support as a way of bringing public opinion behind the cause. In order to boost Iran's war effort, Qa'em Maqam I approached key high-ranking members of the ulama and asked for their support. The result was a collection titled *Risalayi Jahadiya*. According to one scholar, the initiative was Qa'im Maqam's, and: "He dispatched Hajji Mulla Baqir Salmasi and Sadr ud-Din Muhammad Tabrizi to the 'atabat and Isfahan to produce fatvas declaring the war against Russia to be Jihad."[xlii]

By all accounts, both Aqa Muhammad Shah and Fath Ali Shah were considered religious men, and maintained a respectful and cordial relationship with the ulama.[xliii] One report stated that Aqa Muhammad Shah "allowed them [the ulama] to approach him when no other dared." Fath Ali Shah patronized the religious class and lavishly spent on rebuilding and refurbishing religious shrines (both in Iran and at the *'atabat*) and building new mosques, most notably the Shah Mosque of Tehran. However, there is ample evidence that during the reign of both shahs, the consumption of alcohol was allowed at the royal court and in the provinces. A report on the coronation ceremony of Aqa Muhammad Shah mentions consumption of wine during the ceremony in Tehran.[xliv] During his visit to Iran, French officer Auguste Bontems noted that his host, the sardar of Iravan, Hosein Qoli Khan Qavanllu-Qajar, and his brother drank a good amount of wine during dinner. Furthermore, he noted his surprise at such high-ranking officials openly consuming wine. In comparison, Bontems noted, Ottoman high officials never acted as such. He assumed such behavior must be rooted in the conduct of Safavid era rulers who were known to have consumed alcohol.[xlv]

Early nineteenth-century society

The population of the shah's guarded dominion (*mamalek-e mahruseh*) is estimated to be around six million in 1800 and nine million by 1812.[xlvi] This population included a small number of Jews (70,000), Armenian Christians (170,000), and Zoroastrians (20,000). An economic historian's assessment of the state of Iran's economy and people suggests: "the account of all travelers visiting Iran at the beginning of the nineteenth century agree in depicting a country suffering from depopulation, poverty, and economic exhaustion and largely isolated from the mainstream of world politics, trade, science, and culture."[xlvii]

A breakdown of some of the provincial and urban populations based on available estimates provides a clearer picture. Starting from south and central Iran, Shiraz was a city of about 50,000, and Isfahan the largest city at about 200,000.[xlviii] Tehran, which was more of a garrison town until Aqa Muhammad made it his capital in 1786, was a city in the making with a population of 40,000 to 50,000 while the royal court was in residence. Because of the summer heat, the royal court moved to a cooler area of pasture at Sultaniyeh, near Khamseh (Zanjan), or the pasture of Ujan near Tabriz in Azarbaijan, while other residents moved to the cooler high ground of Shemiran north of the city. This reduced the population of the city to few thousand.[xlix] In the east, the shrine city of Mashhad, the former capital of the Afshar Empire, is estimated to have had a population of less than 20,000 by 1800.[l] In Azarbaijan, Tabriz—the largest city and the seat of a Qajar crown prince—was once a flourishing city, but it was hit by a massive earthquake in 1770. An 1809 estimate puts the number of households at 50,000, with 200 Armenian households living in their own city quarter. The total population, according to an 1806 estimate, was between 500,000 and 550,000.[li] In 1806, Khoy's population is estimated to have been 25,000, and Marand's (back then a collection of villages) 10,000.[lii] In the Caucasus, Nakhjavan City had a population of 5,000 in 1807, and the population of the Khanate of Iravan in 1811 was 100,000, not including migrant Kurdish tribes.[liii] According to a Russian estimate, the Pambak region of northern Iravan, under Russian occupation after 1804, had a total population of 2,832 (1,529 Muslims, 1,303 Armenian Christians).[liv] According to an 1823 Russian survey of the Khanate of Qarabagh, Shusha, its largest city, had 371 households divided in four quarters or parishes (*mahaleh*). The province was divided into twenty-one districts, with nine large estates belonging to Muslims and Armenians, twenty-two Armenian villages, ninety Muslim villages (both settled and nomadic), and it is estimated that Armenians were a minority.[lv] In the Khanate of Ganjeh, the population of the city was 10,425 when the Russian army occupied it in 1804.[lvi]

Historically, any Iran-based empire had to extend its territory to include more revenue-yielding regions. These included Mesopotamia (Iraq); greater Khorasan, all the way to Amu Darya; and the region in the southeast all the way to the Sind River (today in Pakistan). This was because the resources of the Iranian plateau were simply not vast enough to support an imperial state. The poverty of the land continued to keep the population low and the state poor throughout the nineteenth century. Only the discovery of oil in the twentieth century gradually changed this situation. In this context, the Qajar state was not in a position to engage in any type of prolonged war, or maintain a professional military to defend itself. Such a proposition was simply too expensive and beyond its means.

The Qajar military[lvii]

Similar problems may be seen in the organization and conduct of both the traditional military and the European-modeled military force, the organizing of which began in 1805. There were two key defects in the Qajar imperial or royal army (*urdu-ye homayoun*), which were never overcome. These were a lack of systematic intelligence-gathering ability, and an absence of a chain of command.

According to the tradition of military campaigns in the east, the upkeep of Aqa Muhammad Shah's army relied on the local population, who provided materials and other logistical support. Also in line with tradition, those who defied the Qajar shah and resisted were subject to looting or slavery, or both. In this context, the movement of the Qajar army in a given region brought much devastation and hardship to the local Muslim and Christian populations alike.[lviii]

By the time of his death in 1797, the size of Aqa Muhammad Shah's military had reached its peak and stood at 60,000 men.[lix] One estimation of Aqa Muhammad's army as having been over 200,000 strong is probably an overcalculation and is not supported by available information.[lx] The organization of the military was based on the tradition of Turko-Mongol military concepts and on the decimal system. As such, the commander of ten soldiers was a *unbashi*, of fifty *elibashi*, of 100 *yuzbashi*, of 1,000 *minbashi*, of 10,000 or *tuman*, a *soltan*. Tribal khans provided the shah with a force in accordance with the size of their tribe, and would lead it into battle. This type of military was the best of its kind within Iran's eighteenth-century military technology and culture. It was essentially a tribal and seasonal force organized around centuries-old organizational methods and tactics. As such, it was made up of around 50,000 tribal cavalry (*savar*) and 10,000 infantry (*tofangchi*), recruited from various sedentary populations. Command of each unit was based not on the merit of the officer (although good commanders were rewarded) but on the ability of the officer to assemble the number of soldiers which would allow him to acquire the rank. On some occasions, particularly during the reign of Fath Ali Shah, independent commands were given to officers, with the title *sardar* (general), who did not command military units based on their tribal credentials but on their military capability and loyalty. Hosein Qoli Khan Qajar Sardar Iravani and Isma'il Khan Sardar Damghani were two such prominent commanders in Fath Ali Shah's army.

The early Qajar army was a seasonal force, in that it fought during summer time and dispersed with cold weather approaching. It would be called to assemble when ordered by the shah and once assembled, it made up the royal army. Hence, there was no standing army in this traditional tribal setting. In the absence of a standing army, for his short-term and immediate needs, the shah relied on his royal bodyguards (*gholaman khaseh*), which by 1809 numbered 12,000.[lxi] The royal guard was made up of volunteers from ruling-class families.

The seasonal nature of the army was one of its most significant shortcomings when faced with a professional European army that was trained to fight in all weathers. However, for a state faced with revenue shortfall, maintaining a standing army was an expensive proposition, which made a seasonal army more attractive. The 50,000-strong cavalry force during the last years of Aqa Muhammad included light, mobile camel-mounted *zamburak* (little wasp) artillery.

In terms of military technology, one major shortcoming of the army was its lack of modern weapons, especially modern artillery. Typically, a cavalryman carried a variety of cold weapons, including a high-quality saber, bows and arrows, lances, and daggers. Locally produced muskets and sidearms were also in use but their flintlock (and even matchlock) technology was either outdated or inferior to standard European weapons. Similarly, the quality of gunpowder, lead bullets, and cannonballs produced locally was low and often damaged the device. On the positive side, tribal cavalrymen impressed European observers with their quick movement, mobility, and agility. A tactic known as *qi-qaj* (where the rider rapidly retreated in a zigzag manner while he turned 180 degrees and fired at the pursuing enemy) was most impressive to many European observers.[lxii] This is why many Europeans compared this essentially Turko-Mongol force to the pre-Islamic Parthian army in its confrontation with Roman legions.

Jaubert's 1806 assessment of the traditional Qajar military provides a clear picture of its performance: He observed that it moved with much noise, and that the commanders did not appoint watch-guards. Furthermore, he saw that it attacked with much disorganization, and if the first attack wave did not result in victory, it retreated. He noted, "Their lack of organization is unimaginable, as there is no commander and soldier, but much chaos where individuals fire their weapons aimlessly."[lxiii] He also stated that the army did not have a garrison, or recreation for soldiers, or depot for arms and provisions.[lxiv]

The more important shortfall was the lack of effective artillery. As noted, the most popular artillery was the camel-mounted *zamburak* that by all accounts was inaccurate and obsolete. However, in a terrain with few passible roads, where horses and camels were the main method of moving armies, the *zamburak* provided a degree of mobile firepower against an enemy that also lacked effective artillery. By 1797, the shah's army had also acquired some forty- to fifty-year-old, Nader Shah era heavy artillery pieces, or poor-quality ones casted in Isfahan and Tabriz. These were difficult to move around and were used either for siege purposes or for fixed defensive positions.

Aqa Muhammad Shah's 10,000-man infantry was comprised of recruits from among the settled peasants of Mazandaran in the Caspian region or Arak-Hamadan region, in west-central Iran. The best infantry in the shah's army were the *jalayer tofangchi*, known by this name because of a type of heavy matchlock musket they carried which at times needed to be mounted on a stool to be effective. Overall, the infantry was considered even less of a threat to a modern European army. Overreliance on light, mobile cavalry had its disadvantages. European armies with more disciplined soldiers had already discovered the use of cavalry forces to be a marginal part of military operations in modern warfare. In another words, the cavalry charge had already lost its military value in a day and age when infantry and cannon fire had created a strong firewall in the battlefield.

As mentioned above, Aqa Muhammad Shah was not known to be a brilliant military leader of the caliber of Nader Shah. However, he was an adequate leader in his wars to unify Iran. While he had many major setbacks in the battlefield, he eventually prevailed against strong adversaries through perseverance and sober leadership rather than any superior military talent. The shah was a calculating and pragmatic leader and had the proper understanding of human character to be able to recruit talented officers for his army. His army seem to have been more disciplined than his successor's—he did not allow women to follow the army, which added to its mobility and focus. He employed traditional Turko-Mongol military tactics to subdue a region and its population, which included scorched-earth policies and even head towers to terrorize and discourage the local population from rising up again, and thus do away with the need to garrison the region for a long duration. He seemed to have been aware of the advantages and disadvantages of the military available to him. He used his mobile force to quickly move against Irakli in Georgia in 1795 and conquer Tiflis, but also in the same year had much difficulty capturing the well-defended fort of Panahabad or Shusha in Qarabagh because of a lack of effective artillery. When it came to confrontation with Russia, he showed a good sense of understanding the enemy and had already developed a strategy in confronting the invading Russian army in 1796–7. The shah seems to have shown good awareness of the Russian army's firepower but was confident in his own ability to face off against them. His strategy, in light of lacking adequate firepower, was to conduct asymmetric warfare by using his mobile force to retreat and attack the advancing Russian army, and to use scorched-earth tactics to deny the enemy the possibility of living off the land, thus stretching its supply lines. Hence, the shah's answer to the superior Russian army was the age-old Iranian tactic going back to the Parthian period.

After the first Battle of Iravan in the summer of 1804 (see Chapter 3), although the Qajar army was able to force the Russian invasion army to retreat, it was badly bruised, with heavy loss of life. Hence, the first attempt at modernizing the military started after that battle and by employing Russian deserters. This was the beginning of Nezam-e Jadid[2] (new order), an attempt to reform the military based on the European model.[lxv] One scholar considered the harsh treatment of Russian soldiers a prime reason for these desertions by suggesting, "Given the reality that the only route out of the Russian army for the conscript was death, and that the regime inside the army was brutal, desertion is not surprising."[lxvi] The officer corps of the Russian military was drafted from the landed nobility, but the enlisted men and conscripts came mostly from among the Russian peasantry. Russian deserters were from among the second group. In this context, the quality of training they could offer was not high, as European observers noted in 1806, 1807, and 1809. However, when organized as a separate fighting unit, the Russians fought well and hard. Their numbers in 1822 are estimated at 800 to 1,000.[lxvii] Abbas Mirza took the Russian deserters under his wing and employed them, first as trainers and later as his bodyguards. The most famous among the Russians was Samson Y. Makintsev, or Samson Khan as he was known in Iran. He became a trusted officer in Abbas Mirza's army of Azarbaijan, and reached the rank of general.

With the Nezam reforms, new concepts and organizational methods were introduced. Nezam soldiers began to wear uniforms, first in a color resembling Russian green, and later French blue. The soldiers were called *sarbaz* (one who is willing to sacrifice his head), a term still used to this day in the Iranian military. As the training and buildup of the

---

2. One may see the influence of Ottoman reforms on Iran, as under Sultan Selim III (r. 1789–1807) similar military reforms were initiated under the same name.

Nezam units progressed, a second group of trainees named *janbaz* (one who is willing to sacrifice his soul), was created to serve the shah and some other royal princes in the provinces. By all account, the quality of the *sarbaz* in the Nezam and under Abbas Mirza's command was superior to the *janbaz* and the traditional army units. In 1806, Jaubert's assessment of Abbas Mirza's Nezam units in Tabriz was that they were disorganized but dressed well and had good horses. This goes to show the limited success of the Russian deserters' training. When Jaubert was asked by the prince regent to explain how European armies fought, he described the changing role of cavalry and the prominent role of infantry and artillery. Training of the Nezam units passed on to the French in 1807, and then to the British from 1808 on (see Chapter 3).

Nevertheless, even after attempts were made to incorporate European discipline into the Nezam force, some nomadic cultural habits were carried over to the new military. These tribal-military habits were partially responsible for neutralizing the effectiveness of the Nezam forces in the upcoming struggle, particularly against Russia. A lack of effective firearms and the tribal nature of what stood for an "officer corps" have already been mentioned. Related to the latter point was a clear lack of a chain of command within the traditional army, a shortcoming that was not overcome by the introduction of European-disciplined units. As the most ardent advocate of modernizing reforms in the military and as commander of the army of Azarbaijan and the effective commander of war with Russia, Abbas Mirza's conversation with James Morier is telling in this regard. After listening to Morier's long lecture on the need for discipline and chain of command in a modern army, Abbas Mirza was still baffled and was quoted as saying, "This discipline is a most difficult thing."[lxviii] The central command of the army during a conflict sat with a Tribal Council, made up of the overall commander and his tribal officers. In times of conflict, key decisions were made by such a council, which meant much time was wasted as the commander-in-chief struggled to make sense of the various advice he received and bring in line various interested parties. However, even then, an order given by the overall commander may or may not have been followed by the unit commanders.

Another tribal-military habit was the amount of time individual units spent in looting the enemy camp, known as *chapavol*. This act was considered a right and part of the pay for the individual fighter in any victorious conflict. However, the result was a collapse of what little discipline existed. Russians used this shortcoming repeatedly to flee a losing battle scene or regroup and attack by offering the Qajar army the opportunity to conduct *chapavol*. Related to this habit was the decapitation of dead enemy soldiers or even POWs, for reward money. This act was encouraged from the shah down and was considered a morale-boosting act, but it too resulted in wastage of time during a conflict, as soldiers would start to decapitate opponents rather than pursue a defeated enemy and finish it off. These two put together often made it difficult for the army to take advantage of a given battlefield victory, and gave the enemy time to retreat and regroup. Another negative aspect of the Iranian army's cavalry movement, which hampered Iran's efforts during the early years of war with Russia, was that during march individual units would get separated in an attempt to reach the enemy first. This would sometimes put a distance of two days between units in the back of the army and the ones in a forward position. Also, individual units would commence attack in order to outdo other units and during retreat would do the same to the point where, at times, it was impossible to have as many as 100 soldiers in one location. All this caused much confusion, loss of war material, and disorderly retreat.[lxix]

Another tribal-military habit was the sacking of conquered regions to discourage the local populations from rebelling and thus make garrisoning the area less of a burden on the army. This act, as well as the army living off the land when they moved through an area, put much burden on the local population and did not do much to make them friendly toward the military.

A lack of security and proper intelligence-gathering was another major shortcoming on all levels of the early Qajar state, and was rooted in the tribal-military culture of the time.[lxx] Repeatedly Qajar commanders, from Abbas Mirza down, failed to post adequate watchguards to protect military camps and repeatedly, Russian commanders took advantage of this and conducted raids with devastating effects. The most famous of such raids was one conducted during the Battle of Aslanduz in 1812 where Abbas Mirza's army was routed by a much smaller Russian force. Foreign visitors were astonished by state secrets, secret correspondence, military planning, etc., being discussed in the open where many attendants could hear the details. Harford Jones Brydges, the British ambassador to the court of Tehran, provided the following observation in 1809 after complaining about the lack of security and organization in the shah's military camp:

> In addition to all this, I found, when I was desired to attend a council in the King's tent, the information which the Persian Ministers

possessed of the nature and real force of the Russians on the frontier, and particularly of the position in which the force, whatever it was, was placed, of its power of motion, of its supplies, and of its character, to be so vague, so imperfect, and on many points, so contradictory, as not only to cause me great surprise, but also well-grounded alarm.[lxxi]

Military camps were poorly organized even at the shah's level. One observer, describing the shah's military camp at Sultanieh in 1806, was astonished as to how the royal camp was organized and suggested a trained European force could easily penetrate and disperse the shah's army.[lxxii] Another assessment in 1807 suggested that the shah's army was more disorganized than that of Abbas Mirza, and that at Sultanieh a "30,000 man force was spread out in a field that in European armies can take 300,000 men."[lxxiii]

Another well-established military tradition was assigning underaged royal princes to military commands or to individual military units in times of war. The purpose of this was to boost the morale of the army by showing that members of the royal house were willing to stand next to them in battle, and to provide the young men with battlefield experience. Abbas Mirza was only fifteen years old in the summer of 1804, when he was given the command of the army that confronted the invading Russians, with near catastrophic results.[3] Again in 1826, during the Battle of Ganjeh against the invading Russian army, Abbas Mirza appointed two of his minor sons, accompanied by their teachers, to his army during the battle. As we shall see, it had catastrophic consequences for the Iranian war effort.

Finally, mention should be made of the slow pace of mobilization due to a lack of military organization in taking care of provisions, logistical support, and resupplying an army in conflict. Hence, while the traditional Qajar army was very mobile because it was mainly a cavalry force, its mobility was effective only for a short-distance conflict of a limited nature. For example, when Aqa Muhammad Khan was set to conquer Tiflis in 1795 he managed to move 60,000 soldiers through the region after he made preparations. However, in 1797, when he had to move to the region again but without time to prepare, he had to leave the bulk of his force behind and move toward Shusha with minimal numbers of 5,000. Similarly, in 1804 when Abbas Mirza was preparing

---

3. The shah appointed seasoned military commanders and civilian advisors to guide him, but he was the overall commander.

his army to confront General Tsitsianov in Iravan, much valuable time was wasted in preparing the army to move, giving the Russians time to occupy strategic points before the actual battle started.

Fath Ali Shah's army was much larger than his royal uncle's, and from 1805 on had started to experiment with European-trained units. The organization of the army had changed but not substantially. By General Gardane's estimate, the shah's army by 1808 numbered 180,000, substantially larger than that of Aqa Muhammad. Other estimates roughly match this number but as the French officer and his team were put in charge of training, his assessment was the first complete overview of the Qajar army. In Gardane's assessment, around 144,000 were tribal cavalry, 40,000 infantry (including those trained on the European model), and 2,500 belonged to artillery (including *zamburakchis*). Roughly half of the cavalry force, 70,000 to 75,000, were *rekabi*, which meant they were paid by the shah's treasury when mobilized; the rest were *velayati*, which meant they were paid for and were under the command of provincial rulers and governors, and were called upon to join the royal army when needed. Tribes were expected to provide troops according to their size, and soldiers were expected for the most part to take care of their own provisions after they were paid by the state. Abbas Mirza was in command of the army of Azarbaijan which was the principal force defending against the Russians. As such, its organization and proficiency was different and superior to the rest of the imperial army. Soldiers were furnished from the villages of Azarbaijan and according to quotas in accordance with the rent each village was responsible for. Abbas Mirza paid for the clothing and arms of his troops. Morier's assessment of this force in his 1808–9 visit estimated it to total 40,000 men. Of this, 22,000 were cavalry, 12,000 infantry that included an artillery force, and 6,000 Nezam infantry.[lxxiv]

Chapter 3

DIPLOMACY AND WAR: THE FIRST RUSSO-IRANIAN WAR, 1804-1813

It is vain to tell a Persian his country is not worth our holding; he believes it the best in the world, and the object of envy of all nations.

John McNeill, British physician and diplomat appointed by the English East India Company to serve in Iran[i]

Prelude to war, 1801-1803

Among the colonial powers showing up on Iran's doorstep, Russia stood out as the most territorially aggressive, and was Iran's closest European neighbor and the one which Iranians had had the most interaction with during the 1700s. Unlike Iran, Russia in the eighteenth century had gone through significant military, administrative, educational and, to some extent, economic transformation. Between the reigns of Peter I (d.1725) and Catherine II (d.1796), Russia had become a gigantic land empire with a powerful military defeating all its traditional rivals, namely Sweden, Poland, and the Ottoman Empire. By the end of the 1700s, Russia had gained some 500,000 square miles of territory, had a population of about 36 million to 40 million, and boasted an army some 500,000 strong.[ii] In this context, by the late eighteenth century the southeastern Caucasus had become a focus of Russia's imperial ambition, hence making it a major menace to the newly established Qajar state for hegemony over that region.

Studies of this period show that both Iranian and Russian elites had a low view of the other before Qajar unification and through the early nineteenth century. These negative impressions centered on each viewing the other as uncivilized and backward, hence viewing one another with contempt. The common derogatory adjective used for the Russians in Iran was *rus-e manhus* (inauspicious Russia). Morier noted in 1808 that Iranians talked of Russians with the utmost disdain, and that one officer told him, "they fear us like dogs, we have everything better than they have, they will never dare to show their faces again."[iii] In his 1801 observation, Malcolm noted the hostile attitude toward Russia at the court of Tehran, at a time when Russia was preparing to invade Iran a second time. An Iranian court official, named Cheragh Ali Khan, had the following negative view on Russians: "They delight in nothing but strong liquor and hogs' flesh … they are so fond of the vile animal on which they live, that they actually tie their hair in a form which resembles its tail."[iv] Malcolm must have smiled at such comments, as the British consumption of liquor and pork, and fancying of a ponytail, was not much different from the Russians at this point in history. However, as recent research suggests, the Qajar elite had developed a degree of respect for Peter I as a forceful and successful reformer.[v] Valerian Zubov's invasion of the southeastern Caucasus halted with the death of Catherine II, and an early direct encounter with Russia was averted. The period 1797–1803 was one of disengagement between Russia and Iran while two new rulers took over.

In Russia, Tsar Paul's approach of distancing Russia from his mother's policies, as well as his more anti-British foreign policy and attempts to accommodate France, translated into less Russian attention paid to the southeastern Caucasus.[vi] Another perspective on Russia's change of policy after the death of Catherine II suggests that Paul wanted to gain influence in the southeastern Caucasus through winning hearts and minds and not just forcing the submission of the region. He wanted to win allies, and unite Georgian and Muslim rulers against both Iranians and Ottomans.

In the southeastern Caucasus during the run-up to the war, local rulers, with the exception of Georgia, went back to their old ways of maintaining their autonomy while paying lip service to either Russia or Iran. The period of calm, it seems, gave these rulers a false sense of security, which would allow them to regain their relative independence.

In Iran, this was a period when Fath Ali Shah was attempting to consolidate his power and therefore Tehran was also paying less attention to the disputed region.[vii] The shah wanted to improve relations with Russia, and sent several friendly messages to the Russian tsar, leading to Paul concluding that he was neither as strong a leader nor as formidable an enemy as his royal uncle. The tsar attempted to lessen tension with Iran but refused to recognize Fath Ali Shah as a royal ruler, and referred to him with his pre-coronation title of Baba Khan.[viii] Fath

Ali Shah appointed his nine-year-old son, Abbas Mirza, as prince regent (na'eb al-saltaneh) in 1799.[1] Abbas Mirza was appointed overall commander of the army fighting he Russians in 1804, and governor of Azarbaijan in 1805.[ix]

Abbas Mirza Qavanllu-Qajar

Abbas Mirza was born in 1789, and in accordance with the testament of Aqa Muhammad Shah, was named the heir to the Qajar throne in 1799. Each of Fath Ali Shah's children (girls and boys) had a royal title bestowed upon them by the shah, similarly to his royal uncle bestowing him with the title Jahanbani. Abbas Mirza's title was *dorr-e darya-e khosravy* (The Pearl of the Sea of Royalty). In 1806, a French officer who met the seventeen-year-old in Ardabil described him as tall with a sharp gaze, and a sweet and kind smile.[x] He described him as wearing simple clothes made of common cotton (*karbas*), as avoiding wearing jewelry, as brave, and said that in war with Russia he had put his own life on the line. The French officer also noted that Abbas Mirza was sincere, asked many questions, and had a large library of European-language books which he could not read.[xi] Abbas Mirza was the favorite of the shah, who admired his son's dedication and lack of interest in luxury and jewelry, although the shah himself was very fond of both. Fath Ali Shah would admonish his other sons who took after him in their extravagant expenditure, while Abbas Mirza asked for nothing but more guns and ammunition for the army.[xii] The crown prince and his chief minister Qa'em Maqam I were attacked by his jealous brothers, particularly Muhammad Ali Mirza Dowlatshah, and conservative elements in the court for their reforming ideas for the military based on the European model. Qa'em Maqam I, who was the real brain behind the modernizing effort, was even accused of being Christian.[xiii] Abbas Mirza would wear

---

1. Various documents refer to Abbas Mirza as both prince regent (*na'eb al-saltaneh*) and crown prince (*vali'ahd*). The two titles had different responsibilities during the Qajar period. Prince regent took the responsibilities of the shah when he was away from the capital for a long period, while crown prince meant the holder of the title would reside in Tabriz and succeed the reigning monarch. In the case of Abbas Mirza, it seems he carried both titles because of the importance of his position as commander of war with Russia, and the ruler of Azarbaijan.

boots and take note from European instructors, drills from Russian deserters in 1805, mathematics lessons from the French Major Lamy, and he had ordered European military texts to be translated into Persian. He observed his religious rituals, did not drink alcohol, and was an excellent rider and hunter.

By 1806, three main battles had been fought between Iran and Russia, and Jaubert, the French officer, could sense a crisis of confidence among the Qajar ruling class. He made a number of interesting observations on Qajar political leaders' attitude toward the Russians. He captured Abbas Mirza's frustration in fighting the Russians in the following words: "All my efforts and courage in confronting the Russian army have been unsuccessful. People applaud my successes while I alone am aware of my shortcomings." He then goes on to quote the prince regent famously asking about the secret of European knowledge as compared to the lack of it in Iran.[xiv] Jaubert also observed that Abbas Mirza was well aware of the firepower and discipline of the Russian artillery and infantry and had already concluded he would need a similar force to defend against Russia. Perhaps the most telling of his observations is the frank assessment given by Mirza Shafi' Mazandarani, Fath Ali Shah's chief minister:

> The Russians, whom we previously considered inferior due to their extreme lack of wit, today are in many ways ahead of us ... the Russians have extended their sphere of influence from the Neman to the Danube, to the Aras to the steppes of Crimea to the mountains of Gorjestan. Their gradual domination can to some extent show us as to what we need to do. Our resistance against this flood is futile. If our empire's northern border has been forced to recede a little, we should expand our eastern border up to and beyond Qandahar.[xv]

Of course, Qajar Iran eventually did adopt this strategy, only to be confronted with expanding British colonial interest in what is today Pakistan and Afghanistan with similar disappointing results. Mirza Shafi' is not known as having been a great statesman compared to Qa'em Maqam I, or his predecessor Haji Ibrahim Khan (Kalantar) I'timad Dowleh. Nevertheless, Jaubert's observation suggests that at least some of the civilian administrators of the Qajar state were weary of the situation and were already looking at a way to pragmatically accept the reality of Russian superiority and loss of territory.

The attitude of Mirza Shafi', as the political leader in charge of the administration of the court of Tehran, stood in contrast to that of the court of Tabriz led by Abbas Mirza and Qa'em Maqam I. Abbas Mirza continued to express self-confidence when he was quoted as saying in 1812: "With every defeat the Russians incur on me, they unwittingly teach me a lesson and by learning from these lessons I shall benefit."[xvi] Clearly, a wedge was being driven between Qajar statesmen in Tehran and those in Tabriz regarding how to deal with Russia. While one would have expected the Tabriz to be the more hesitant party, due to proximity and more interaction with Russia, the situation was quite the reverse. At this stage of conflict with Russia, it seems that Qajar statesmen in Tehran had started to advise compromise and acceptance of the reality of Russia's dominant position in the southeastern Caucasus. The statesmen in Tabriz seem to have believed that the situation could still be turned around in Iran's favor, if only a modern force could be trained.

It has been suggested that before 1804, the Qajar ruling class underestimated the Russian resolve in conquering the region and that Russian aggression was viewed as temporary raids rather than an attempt to permanently annex the region.[xvii] This conclusion seems to be based on a lack of preparedness on the part of Iran for the new round of confrontation with Russia. However, it is difficult to see how the new shah could have done more in preparing his military, in light of all the other internal problems he was facing. At any rate, with the Russian annexation of Georgia in 1801, it is hard to imagine how the Qajar could have interpreted Russian intentions as anything other than a resolve to conquer the region permanently. However, from a broader perspective, Qajar perceptions of Russia at this stage were not well informed of developments within Russia. It could not have been too difficult for the Qajar court to get a sense of Russian military might and aggression through the limited encounters they had already had with Russia. Perhaps more difficult to understand were the sheer resources and size of Russia. To have had such comprehension, the Qajar would have needed to send ambassadorial missions to Russia, accompanied by observant diplomats and translators, in order to collect intelligence on Russian society and state. None of these was available at this point.

The relationship between Iran and Russia deteriorated sharply with the accession of Alexander I in 1801. Before his assassination, Tsar Paul had issued an edict for the preparation of annexing Georgia, followed by his son and successor, Alexander, ordering the annexation of Gorjestan in September 1801. This led to the toppling of the Bagration dynasty and shipping most of the family off to Russia. Irakli's Faustian deal with Russia, made to deter Iran and safeguard Georgian sovereignty and his dynasty's continuity, had resulted in the total loss of both. In

1783, the Treaty of Georgievsk turned the kingdom of Kartel'i-Khakhet'I or eastern Georgia into a protectorate of the Russian Empire. In 1784, Russia established the fortress of Valadikafkaz on Georgian soil.[xviii] However, as noted, Russian protection did not prevent Aqa Muhammad from attacking and taking Tiflis in September 1795. Nevertheless, after the Iranian army left Georgia, by December 1795 General Gudovich had sent a military force to Tiflis to shore up its defenses.

In 1796, France sent two emissaries named Guillaume-Antoine Oliver and Jean-Guillaume Bruguieres to Iran, to tell the shah to consolidate his position in Georgia and warn him that should Russia establish itself in the region, Iran would never be secure.[xix] The French envoys never met Aqa Muhammad Shah who was on campaign in Khorasan, but they conveyed the French Republic's message to his chief minister. They delivered a letter from Raymond Verninac, French ambassador to the Ottoman Empire, who was an acquaintance of Ibrahim Khan I'timad Dowleh from his period in the service of Karim Khan Zand. In this letter, Verninac reminded Ibrahim Khan of their old friendship, informed him of major developments in France and the victories of French armies, and suggested the moment was right to reestablish relations with France. He also offered the shah an alliance with France against Russia.[xx]

Irakli II died in January 1798 and was succeeded by his firstborn son Giorgi XII (known as Gorgin in Iran), who was an ailing and weak character. In June, Fath Ali Shah wrote a letter to him demanding his submission, threatening him with reprisal, and reminding him of what had happened to Tiflis during the reign of Aqa Muhammad Shah.[xxi] Irakli's death brought the pre-existing divisions within the Bagration royal house into the open, when Russia recognized Giorgi and his firstborn, David, as Irakli's successors.[xxii] Giorgi's closeness to Russia split the royal house into factions. Three of his sons, David, Loane, and Bagrat, supported their father. By September 1799, Giorgi, whose health was deteriorating, gave instructions to his representatives in Russia to ask for the annexation of Georgia. In November, Russian envoy P. S. Kovalenskii arrived in Tiflis. Two Russian generals were also sent to Georgia, Lieutenant General K. F. Knorring II and Major General Ivan Lazarev (Lazarian). The trio were the architects of the annexation of Georgia. Kovalenskii's analysis of divisions within the Bagration royal house identified four factions. Firstly, there were those who supported conditional annexation by Russia, which would maintain privileges and a degree of autonomy for the royal house. Georgi and his heir-apparent, David, belonged to this faction. Secondly, there were those who favored independence and only a nominal protectorate status with Russia. The queen mother Darejan (known as Daria in Iran) and two of her sons belonged to this faction. Thirdly, Prince Alexander Bagration (known as Iskandar Mirza in Iran) was pro-Iran and had already fled to Iran in July 1800. Finally, there were those who favored abolishing the Georgian royal house all together.[xxiii]

Russian tsar Alexander I had a different approach to the southeastern Caucasus region. According to one scholar, "Having decided to annex Georgia, he also resolved that Russia would have to acquire all of the khanates as far south as the Aras River and as far east as the Caspian Sea."[xxiv] In September 1802, Alexander I named General Paul Tsitsianov Governor of Georgia, and gave him more authority by adding the title "Inspector of the Caucasian Line" the following year. The general's name was commonly pronounced "Sisianov" or "Zizianov" in Persian but his second title "inspector" was mischievously pronounced "*ishpokhdor*" in the Caucasian-Turkish accent of the region, and it is by this title that he was commonly referred to by most Iranians.[2] Tsitsianov presided over a new round of aggressive and brutal military aggression, which triggered the First Russo-Iranian War of 1804–13. The general was of Georgian extraction but had been raised and trained in Russia. While Russian sources praise him as a great military officer, Iranian sources refer to him in a negative light.[xxv] He apparently had a strong dislike for all Muslims in general and "Persians" in particular, and viewed with contempt everything related to Iran. He is recorded as referring to Fath Ali Shah as the "alleged Shah of Iran" and had stated that there could not be peace between the two because Russia would not address the shah with his proper royal title.[xxvi] Tsitsianov's tenure as commander and governor opened a brutal episode in the new chapter of the conflict.[xxvii]

The Qajar reunification of Iran coincided with interest in Iran on the part of European imperialist powers. As noted, for the Russian Empire, securing the domination of the southern Caucasus was a key reason for Russia's interest and conflict with Iran and the Ottoman Empire. Russia's hegemony of the region not only put it in conflict with Iran but allowed it to pursue its age-old conflict and competition with the Ottoman Empire. British interest in Iran centered on its need to protect India, a region it was gradually absorbing into its empire through the English

---

2. The title "*ishpokhdor*" consists of three Turkish words: *ish* (work or job), *pokh* (excrement), and the verb *dor* (is)—which would make it mean "he whose job is excrement."

East India Company. Protecting British interests against regional, European, and local challenges had already become a major concern of the British Empire by the beginning of 1800. Hence, newly reunified Iran became a piece of the puzzle, which came to be called the "great game." The revolutionary French Republic also became interested in Iran, mainly because of Napoleon Bonaparte's interest in India. The first general of the republic, and future emperor of France, was at war with most of Europe, and Britain was considered the republic's most formidable enemy. After the occupation of Egypt by France in 1798, and the subsequent sinking of the French naval fleet by the British, Napoleon's attention turned to a possible march to India. The idea was that with the local resources of the Ottoman Empire and Qajar Iran, as well as support from local anti-British Indian *navabs* (princely rulers), Britain could be defeated. Sending French envoys to Aqa Muhammad in 1796, encouraging him to consolidate his position in Georgia, and offering alliance with France was part of this strategy. Hence, the above quotation by McNeill, suggesting that Iranians exaggerated the worth of their country, while correct as far as Iran's lack of wealth was concerned, is incorrect in terms of its geopolitical importance.[xxviii]

British concerns over the security of their interest in India were real. Tipu Sultan, the *navab* of Mysore in central India, was already in correspondence with France and was trying to forge an anti-British alliance with Zaman Shah Durani of Afghanistan. Under pressure from the East India Company, in early 1799, Tipu sent an emissary to Iran with gifts (including three elephants), encouraging the shah to join him. However, by the end of that year, he was defeated and killed in Mysore.[xxix] In 1798, the British initially send a low-level emissary to Tehran. The emissary was Mehdi Qoli Khan, an Iran-born official working for the Company in India. His mission was to encourage the shah to attack Afghanistan in the Herat region, should Zaman Shah attack India. However, as Mehdi Qoli Khan's mission was perceived as low-level, a follow-up high-level mission was sent under John Malcolm, an officer in the Company's military. Malcolm arrived in Bushehr in February 1800 and opened negotiations with the shah's chief minister, Ibrahim Khan I'timad Dowleh. To impress the court, Malcolm had brought with him expensive gifts as a way of achieving his goal. The result of negotiations was a treaty that stipulated: the shah agreed to attack Afghanistan if Zaman Shah invaded India; Iran committed itself not to cooperate with France and to prevent the French from residing in Iran. On the commercial side, trade concessions and privileges afforded to previous British governments were reinstated. This meant Britain was given the right to trade in Iran without paying tariffs. In return, the British committed to help the shah should Afghanistan or France invade his dominion.[xxx] It is ironic that no mention is made of Russia or British aid to Iran in its conflict with that empire. Although the conflict over the Caucasus was still in its early stages in January 1801 when the treaty was signed, Russia had already occupied Tiflis and was preparing to annex Georgia. Political leaders in Tehran were at least aware of the fact that a Russian garrison has been stationed in Tiflis, and that no tax money had been arriving since 1795. The shah's threatening letter to Giorgi attests to his observation. Nevertheless, a one-sided treaty was signed which benefited the British at a time when the Company in India was still feeling vulnerable, but which contained no real benefits for Iran.

Fall of Ganjeh, 1804

General Tsitsianov arrived at his command post in early 1803 and spent much of the rest of that year consolidating Russia's hold on Georgia, by exiling the Bagration royal house to Russia,defeating the Lezgis in the Daghestan highlands, and capturing Jar and Balakau. By summer of that year, Qazzaq (Kazakh) and Shams al-Din, northwest of Ganjeh, were also under Russian occupation.[xxxi] Once the Russian position in Georgia was secure and stable, the Russian general moved against the Khanate of Ganjeh, whose khan had at some point accepted Georgian suzerainty, thus giving Tsitsianov a "legal claim" to his demand of submission. However, the khan of Ganjeh, Javad Khan Ziyadlu-Qajar (Ziyadughlu), a 48-year-old veteran of many conflicts, decided to face off against the Russian army and sent a request to the Qajar court for help. As defenders of Ganjeh prepared to defend the khanate by retreating behind the walls of the fortress of the city by the same name, a Russian force of over 5,000 divided into six battalions and three squadrons of dragoons, and eleven field guns, arrived from the northwest and surrounded the city in December 1803.[xxxii] The defenders of Ganjeh were 2,000 locals and 900 Lezgi auxiliaries plus nine field guns, three iron cast guns, and six falconets (light cannons).[xxxiii] Meanwhile, Fath Ali Shah was still busy in Khorasan and as the Qajar army was not used to winter mobilization, Javad Khan's call for help was not answered promptly and the khan of Ganjeh was left to face the Russians alone.

The siege of Ganjeh lasted about a month as Tsitsianov opened negotiations with Javad Khan to convince him to surrender. As the

Russian army had not arrived with adequate provisions for a long siege, and Javad Khan was still hopeful in receiving help from the shah, the communication between the two turned into a struggle to buy time on the part of the khan and to conclude the operation on the part of the Russian general. Tsitsianov's tone was a mixture of threat and promise of reward, telling the khan that if he did not surrender then the same misfortune that came upon Warsaw and other Russian-conquered cities would come upon him.[xxxiv] Javad Khan's response reminded the Russian general that, thanks to God, the shah's army was nearby, that if the Russians had cannons, he had cannons as well and that, "Are you sure that your troops are braver than the qezelbash?"[xxxv3]

The storming of the fortress of Ganjeh started in the early morning of January 15 from three sides, and Russia's possession of modern artillery made a big difference. The Russians battered the city's defenses throughout the day and opened a gap in one of its walls. The destructive power of modern artillery must have been surprising for the defenders. By dusk, an assault was launched from the south side of the city, which penetrated the wall and provided the invaders with a beachhead. One of Javad Khan's sons, Hosein Qoli Aqa, was the commander of defenses of this sector and was killed, failing to stop the Russians from capturing the main mosque and turning it into a fortified position. Elements from within the city helped the Russian side, including some Muslims and much of the Armenian population of Ganjeh. While fighting continued on the outskirts of the city, the conquest of Ganjeh was complete by the 17th. Tsitsianov annexed it to Georgia and renamed the city and the province Elizavetpol in honor of the tsar's wife.

Javad Khan was killed at the hands of a Russian officer by the name of Major Lisanovich, known to Iranians as *dali mayor* (crazy major), as well as many members of his family and the rest of the defenders. At one point, on January 16, 500 defenders who had retreated into a mosque inside the fortress were ordered attacked and killed by the Russian general.[xxxvi] The fighting was reported to be hard and bloody, but there is a clear discrepancy as to causes of defeat and the number of dead. The Russian general allowed Tatar troops accompanying its force to loot the city as fighting was still going on.[xxxvii]

Iranian sources suggest that the Armenian defenders of Ganjeh and a smaller number of Muslims from the Shams al-Din region switched

---

3. Iran's army and the Qajar tribe were referred to in many sources as the *qezelbash,*

sides and caused the defeat or played a significant role in the fall of Ganjeh.[xxxviii] In March 1797, in a letter to General Gudovich, Armenian archbishop Hovsep Arghutiean reminded him of Armenian help in the Russian conquest of Darband by General Zubov.[xxxix] In April of that year, the same person wrote to the Russian general, informing him of the will of Armenians of Ganjeh to become Russian subjects.[xl] In a letter, dated December 12, 1803, written from Shamkor near Ganjeh, Tsitsianov wrote to the Armenians of Ganjeh, just before the siege began, asking them to join him in ending Muslim rule. Based on the above, it seems a strong possibility that Iranian assertions about the role of Armenians in this battle are correct.

Another controversy is how many people were killed and what happened after the fall of the fortress. Tsitsianov's official report to the tsar gave low numbers and noted total enemy dead at 1,500, and total prisoners taken at 17,224 (8,585 men and 8,639 women). He gave Russian casualties as three officers and thirty-five soldiers killed, and fourteen officers and 192 soldiers wounded.[xli] Another source puts the Russians dead at about 300, and noted that many more began to die because of sickness and that the Russian general had to ask for reinforcements from Tiflis.[xlii] Russian sources later on revised the number of dead in Ganjeh to 1,756, and local and Iranian sources put the number at 3,000.[xliii] Iranian sources mention a massacre of the local population, which was very different from Tsitsianov's report to the tsar, which talks about his humane treatment of the civilians.[xliv] However, even pro-Russian primary and secondary sources mention the massacre of the civilian population by the Russian army.[xlv] Knowing what we know about Tsitsianov and his attitude toward Muslims and Iranians, and the fact that he allowed Tatar troops to attack civilians and his troops to massacre the defeated defenders in the mosque, puts a shadow of doubt on the sincerity of his official report.

Interesting parallels may be drawn between the sack of Tiflis in 1795 and the sack of Ganjeh in 1804. Ironically, historians have correctly labeled Aqa Muhammad Shah's sack of Tiflis as an atrocity but have been lenient on Tsitsianov's treatment of Ganjeh. Aqa Muhammad's sack of Tiflis is entirely based on Iranian sources. While it is true that Tiflis in 1795 was a larger city than Ganjeh in 1804, the treatment of the captured military prisoners and the civilian population by the Russian army was harsh and, similar to Aqa Muhammad, designed to create a sense of terror among the population of the region. The Russian general did not have enough troops to conquer the region and making an example of the Bagration dynasty and later Javad Khan, his family, and the civilians of Ganjeh, served as a pressure lever to bring the other regional leaders under Russian control. Russia's harsh treatment of the populace of Ganjeh was designed to sow terror in the region and put the other khanates on notice. The message was clear: submit to Russia or perish. In his communication with Tsar Alexander I, Tsitsianov's tone around how he was going to subdue the region and treat its people was violent. "Fear and greed …" he wrote to the tsar, "are the two mainsprings of everything that takes place here."[xlvi] Perhaps a major difference between the fall of Tiflis and that of Ganjeh was that slavery was still an acceptable institution in Iran, as it was in many other parts of the world at this time, but not in Russia—where serfdom kept over ninety percent of the population in a state of semi-slavery.

First siege of Iravan, summer 1804

General Tsitsianov spent the spring of 1804 preparing for an all-out invasion on three fronts, namely Iravan (west), Qarabagh (center), and the intersection of Rivers Kor and Aras near the Caspian Sea (east). For this purpose, a 50,000-man force was gathered at Ganjeh and prepared to move in the three mentioned directions. The Russian general himself took command of a force of 15,000 men (including over 5,000 infantry, 2,000 Cossacks cavalry, and 3,000 Georgian cavalry,) plus twenty mobile artillery pieces and moved from Ganjeh toward the Khanate of Iravan, entering through the plain of Shurehgol and camping east of River Arpachay, located northwest of Iravan.[xlvii] A study of Russian sources states the numbers under Tsitsianov's direct command in his invasion of Iravan to have been around 5,000 troops and between twelve and twenty cannons. The same study finds the Iranian assessment of Russian troops to be an exaggeration.[xlviii] However, based on Russian sources, the author reports that on the night of August 7, 1804, a Russian army of 10,000 strong made an unsuccessful raid on the royal camp of the shah.[xlix] The discrepancy may be resolved if one takes into account the number of non-Russian troops accompanying the main Russian invading force. In this context, the Iranian assessment of Tsitsianov's force in the summer of 1804 seems to be more accurate.

As he was preparing for his invasion of Iravan, the Russian commander wrote letters to the khans of Iravan, Qarabagh, Shirvan, Badkubeh (Baku), Qobbeh, Darband, and Shakki, demanding their submission and warning them of the calamities that could come upon them by pointing to what had happened to Ganjeh.[l] Upon hearing of the Russian victory at Ganjeh, Fath Ali Shah ordered a substantial force of 20,000 to be mobilized toward Iravan, and named Prince Regent Abbas Mirza the overall commander. In a letter to Abbas Mirza (dated April 8, 1804) appointing him the overall commander of the expedition, the shah ordered him to join with Alexander and Teimuraz (Iskandar Mirza and Tahmures Mirza), sons of Irakli who supported Iran's cause, and move toward Georgia. The crown prince was informed of the end of the Khorasan campaign and that stability had returned to that region.[li] In another letter to the people of Georgia (dated March 1804) the shah encouraged them to rebel against Russian occupation and in support of Iskandar Mirza and Tahmures Mirza, telling them Abbas Mirza was moving to liberate them with an army of 50,000 men.[lii] Abbas Mirza was fifteen years old at this point and his command would have been more symbolic than real but, as we shall see, he participated directly in the conflict and proved to be a daring military leader. In addition, the shah named seasoned commanders and tutors (*atabak*) to accompany the novice prince. Abbas Mirza's military commanders included such capable individuals as Suleiman Khan Qavanllu-Qajar (a second cousin of the shah); Ali Qoli Khan Shahsavan; Ali Qoli Khan Sartip (brigadier) Qajar; Pir Qoli Khan Shambayati-Qajar; Sadeq Khan Az al-Dinlu-Qajar, and Mehdi Qoli Khan Devellu-Qajar. Another key figure accompanying Abbas Mirza was his teacher and future chief advisor, Mirza Isa (Bozorg) Farahani (Qa'em Maqam I).

Assembling such a large force was a slow process, as the organizational shortcomings of the traditional Qajar military made it impossible for a rapid reaction force to be made ready. Indeed, the slow mobilization of the army, and the fact that it usually did not fight during wintertime, was a key factor in the shah's inability to aid Ganjeh, despite his promise to do so. While the crown prince was mobilizing his force, the shah moved the bulk of the imperial army from Sultanieh, near Tehran, to a forward position at Ahar in Azarbaijan. In March 1804, the Russian army moved toward its designated objectives in three columns. The eastern column reached its destination at Saliyan and crossed the Kor-Aras intersection, occupying northern Talesh near the Caspian Sea. The central column reached the fortress of Shusha and laid siege. The western column under Tsitsianov had stationed itself northwest of Iravan, where the initial contact with the Iranian army came about. General Tsitsianov's overall strategy was to secure all the roads to the north and then move to control all the passages in the south, from River Aras to the north.

Upon hearing of Russian victory at Ganjeh, Muhammad Khan Qavanllu-Qajar, the khan of Iravan, opened negotiations with the

Russian general and offered his submission. Although related to the Qavanllu-Qajar of Astarabad, where the royal family came from, he proved to be one of the more opportunistic and least reliable khans of the Caucasus. He constantly played the game of changing loyalty between Iran and Russia, in a desperate attempt to preserve his position. Muhammad Khan's lack of determination and fluctuation from the Russian side to the Iranian side was increasingly becoming an untenable balance to maintain. By 1804, room for maneuvering for him and other small principalities in the region was fast disappearing as two stronger powers were lining up against each other. Muhammad Khan negotiated with Tsitsianov during the month of June with the intention of offering Iravan's submission in return for his authority recognized and secured by Russia.

It was at this point that the Iranian army moved out of Nakhjavan, bypassed the fortress of Iravan, and moved to the northwest to meet the Russian army. The Iranian force had much difficulty preparing to move, particularly in terms of logistics and supplies for such a huge force. Hence its movement was slow, which gave the Russians time to occupy advantageous ground. Abbas Mirza also had some difficulty with a number of tribal leaders who did not wish to fight and were forced to do so after the intervention of the ulama. The composition of the force under Abbas Mirza's command was 20,000 of mostly cavalry tribesmen with a smaller force of infantry riflemen (*tofangchi*). The cavalry force was armed with a mixture of cold weapons and some firearms, and its artillery consisted of light, camelback *zamburak*. In anticipation of the arrival of the Russian army, and to weaken the Iranian side, the khan of Iravan had moved many local, potentially pro-Iran tribes to Ottoman territory in the western Caucasus. Before arrival, Abbas Mirza had written to the Ottoman governor of Erzurum, informing him of the imminent arrival of his army and asking his help in returning pro-Iran tribes to Iranian territory. Upon arrival in Iravan, Abbas Mirza sent a 6,000-man cavalry force under the command of Mehdi Qoli Khan Devellu-Qajar to bring the tribes back to Iranian territory and to engage the Ottoman border guards if they tried to prevent it. This mobile force was returning toward the Iranian military camp with the tribes under its protection when on June 19 it encountered the bulk of the Russian army east of Arpachay River at Pambak. During that day and the next, Mehdi Qoli Khan, a capable military commander, engaged the Russian army in skirmishes and managed to move his force and the tribes under his protection toward the Iranian military encampment west of the fort of Iravan.

After this initial engagement, the Russian army moved south toward Uch Kelisa (Etchmiadzin), the seat of the Armenian Church. On June 28, the Russian army lined up against the Iranian army at Uch Kelisa, in three square formations, separated from each other by a few hundred meters with artillery placed within the central square. Next, the Russian force launched an all-out assault on a kilometer-long front with a few hundred meters separating the two sides. The Russian general's main tactical objective in this battle was to pass through Iranian lines so that he could lay siege to Iravan, conclude his negotiations with Muhammad Khan, and storm the fortress if necessary. However, his army was now bogged down and there was no sign of the Iranian army giving way. The two armies battled fiercely for the next four days. The Russian army used its superior firepower to pound the Iranian position before launching infantry attacks, especially on the left flank of the Iranian army. Abbas Mirza countered by using his Shahsavan and Makuie cavalry to attack the Russian right flank, while under the capable command of Ali Qoli Khan Sartip Qajar, with Shaqaqi tribal cavalry and Nakhjavani infantry, the left flank withstood repeated and heavy Russian assaults. According to one account: "The Persian cavalry charged the Russian squares with great impetuosity, and even broke into the rear-guard and baggage, but suffered severely from their fire of the squares and artillery."[liii]

During the battle, Abbas Mirza wrote to the tribes of Qazzaq, north of Iravan, asking them to join the battle against the Russian army.[liv] By July 1, both sides were exhausted but the Iranians were running out of ammunition and had taken heavy casualties. At this point Tsitsianov launched a heavy all-out attack accompanied by intense bombardment—the biggest Russian advantage. This Russian attack was also unsuccessful but the Iranian army had had enough and was forced to regroup, as it needed to rest and rearm. Hence, a reluctant Abbas Mirza was convinced by his advisors to order an orderly retreat to Sadrak, southeast of the fort of Iravan in Nakhjavan, and await the arrival of the shah. The retreat was well organized and since the Russian side was also exhausted, it did not give serious chase. The Russian army then moved to lay siege on the fortress of Iravan, defended by a formidable two-layer wall, some heavy but old artillery pieces, and 4,000 defenders under the command of the unreliable Muhammad Khan Devellu-Qajar.

The Russian army laid siege on Etchmiadzin and partially occupied the town, but the bulk of the force moved toward Iravan.[lv] A byproduct of the Russian army's move into this region was resistance by the local Muslim population, which was not expected and which in turn resulted in Russian repression against the local people coming under its control. The Russian army was not kind to the Christian population either, as there were reports of Russian forces damaging the Armenian churches at Etchmiadzin, looting their treasures and books, and melting printing press lead to produce bullets. According to a French officer visiting Iran in 1807, the Russian army was not only cruel to the local Muslim population but also looted and severely damaged Armenian religious centers at Uch Kelisa. He contrasted the Russian behavior with the respectful manner with which the Qajar shah treated the local Christian subjects.[lvi]

The first siege of Iravan was in fact the third and last phase of this conflict that stood for the first stage of the First Russo-Iranian War. After witnessing the size and commitment of the Iranian army, the khan of Iravan was ready to change sides once again and refused the Russian general's overtures. Soon, he would ask Mirza Muhammad Shafi' Mazandarani, the shah's chief minister (*sadr-e'azam*), to intercede on his behalf and ask for a royal pardon. A pardon was granted but the shah was already thinking of removing him from power. However, first the Russians had to be dealt with.

The fortress of Iravan was built next to the Zangi River and protected by two walls made of brick, stone set on clay. It had eighteen towers, surrounded by a deep ditch and garrisoned by 7,000 troops, sixty cannons and two mortars.[lvii] The Russian army occupied the surrounding area of Iravan and laid siege. On July 7 the 34-year-old Fath Ali Shah arrived in Sadrak with fresh troops and supplies. At this point, the shah took a more direct role in the war, taking overall field command, the first and last time he would be this close to the actual front line in the Russo-Iranian wars. On July 8, Abbas Mirza moved with a large force (estimates are up to 50,000) to encircle the Russian army besieging Iravan. As the Russian firewall prevented the Iranian army from breaking the siege, the new strategy was to prevent reinforcement and supply reaching it, thus starving it into retreating. Hence, while the Iravani defenders would hold the Russians at bay, the bulk of the Iranian army would harass and starve the Russian force. Tsitsianov quickly understood this strategy and moved to disrupt the movement of the Iranian army by attacking it south of Iravan as it moved into position. The Russian general's plan was to deceive Abbas Mirza into believing he was retreating so that the young prince would order a chase, thus falling into a trap. However, Abbas Mirza figured out the deception and, leading a 10,000-man cavalry force and at great risk to himself, made a daring charge at the center of the Russian army and forced it to retreat.

The Russian army attempted several times to break the encirclement, both from the north with fresh troops and supply from Tiflis and from within the encirclement; all such attempts failed. The shah had appointed Pir Qoli Khan Shambayati-Qajar in charge of the north Iravan sector to make sure nothing got through, a mission he accomplished successfully. On one occasion a volunteer detachment of 150 Russians and Armenians under a colonel attempted to reach Qara Kelisa (today Vanadzor), a village sixty-four kilometers north of Iravan where the Russians had established a depot. About twenty-two kilometers short of its destination a 6,000-man cavalry force under Pir Qoli Khan fell upon it, and the colonel and 100 of his men were killed, the rest becoming prisoners of war. Pir Qoli Khan then moved to occupy Qara Kelisa.[lviii]

Tsitsianov also attempted to use the Qajar army's lack of security precautions to conduct raids. Here, the shah showed much awareness and sobriety in securing his military encampment and these attempts failed as well. On the other hand, fearing the Armenian population inside the citadel might switch sides, the shah ordered a daring reinforcement to the citadel. Here, a 2,000-man force marched right before Russian troops and entered the fort, reinforcing the defenders. By July 10, 1804, the Russian army had had enough and began to retreat in an orderly manner but harassed by the Iranians all the way to the border of Ganjeh. The first siege of Iravan and associated battles between the two armies were in fact the first real encounters between the Russian Empire and Qajar Iran, in a conflict that dated back to the 1790s. One observer likened the battle to "Mamluks of Ottoman Egypt and the French at the battle of the Pyramids" which occurred in 1798.[lix] Of course, in the case of this confrontation, the Russians were defeated and forced to retreat. The encounter exposed the shortcomings of each side. The Russians were quick to realize their points of strength and weakness in this conflict. While its modern military organization and firepower was the strength of the Russian army, overstretched supply lines and underestimating the resilience of the Iranian army were aspects that needed to improve. In this context, Russian commanders would now emphasize building new roads and improving old routes, and establishing small and large forts dotting the region, acting as supply stations and retreat sanctuaries.

For the Iranian side the lessons of this battle were even more profound. The Qajar ruling class and military commanders must have been shocked at the awesome firepower of the Russian army and the massive casualties inflicted on its army. To begin with, unlike the Russians, the Iranian side did not have a coherent overall strategy on how to deal with Russian aggression, and merely reacted to a given situation. While this battle was a victory of a sort for Iran, it was now clear how little intelligence existed on Russia and the Russian army. Also clear was difficulty of moving a large force, in terms of logistics and coordination. Such sluggish movement had given the Russian side advantages during this conflict. One would have thought that a tribal cavalry force such as the Qajar army, with camel-mounted light artillery, would be naturally more mobile than the Russian army with its reliance on infantry and heavy guns. However, a lack of proper organization together with logistical shortcomings neutralized that apparent advantage. The Qajar army also needed to learn how to become an all-season army rather than a force suited to fight only during certain periods. Perhaps the most apparent shortcoming was the lack of adequate firepower. Qajar light mobile artillery was simply ineffectual against the mobile field guns of the Russian army. The Qajar army did possess some old heavier artillery pieces, but these were mostly obsolete siege weapons rather than field guns and difficult to move around. The muskets used by the infantry *tufangchis* were also outdated compared to the standard muzzle-loading rifles used in European armies at this time. Finally, as noted before, a chain of command and competent and disciplined leadership provided by the educated officer corps of modern European armies was completely missing in the Qajar army, despite the existence of many capable and brave commanders. Harford Jones Brydges' account of a discussion on modern warfare with a young son of Fath Ali Shah in 1809 is telling. In discussing a particular battle in German lands with Prince Hosein Ali Mirza Farman Farma, the governor of Shiraz, the British emissary told the prince the story of an army of 120,000 incurring 25,000 casualties in a single battle, to which the prince reacted:

> he said, in plain terms, he did not believe either the one or the other of these things to be possible—'for this plain reason,' said the Prince, 'that the king, my father, cannot bring into the field more than 60,000 horses; how, therefore, can any European potentate bring 120,000; and as to 25,000 men being slain in a battle, that is equally impossible, because in our severest and longest battles our loss never exceeds from 50 to 100 men.[ix]

While Prince Farman Farma was not a top leader in the Qajar military establishment, and by this time Abbas Mirza and others had already realized the merits of modern European discipline, his view may be seen as a window into how modern and pre-modern military mindsets were at work. By 1812, Napoleon Bonaparte would move an army of 600,000 from central Europe to Moscow. At any rate, if there were any doubt about the lessons of the events of 1804, the Battle of Qarabagh in 1805 put an end to it and shook the foundation of the Qajar ruling elite's perception of the danger facing the guarded domain of Iran. Steps needed to be taken to remedy the situation.

The Battle of Qarabagh and the sieges of Ganjeh and Badkubeh, 1805

The shah and crown prince viewed the Russian retreat as a substantial victory and started to write letters to the khans of the Caucasus, giving the good news and asking them to stand up to the Russians. For example, in September 1804, the shah sent a letter to the northern Caucasus tribal leaders (Chechnya, Cherkess, etc.) informing them of the defeat of Tsitsianov, the capture of 1,750 POWs, and the battle in northern Iravan led by Pir Qoli Khan, stopping supply to the Russian army.[lxi] Similarly, in 1805 under the direction of Qa'em Maqam I, Abbas Mirza began to reform the military. Here Russian deserters were employed to teach modern drills and other European military tactics to Abbas Mirza and his officers. This was the beginning of the Nezam-e Jadid military reforms. However, the initial attempt of using Russian deserters to train Abbas Mirza's army of Azarbaijan did not improve its performance by much. European military officers' assessment of Abbas Mirza's military after he employed Russian deserters was negative.[lxii] Among the Tabriz leadership Qa'em Maqam I was by far the ablest, not only in Azarbaijan but also in all of Iran. Brydges found him to be a capable minister to the state and spent much time in his company discussing various issues.[lxiii] He was known to be an ardent and consistent anti-Russian high official and had developed a close relationship with the prince regent. As such, Qa'em Maqam I no doubt played a major role in developing the uncompromising anti-Russian strategy of the court of Tabriz.[lxiv]

Meanwhile, Tsitsianov began correspondence with the khans of Qarabagh and Shakki, trying to convince them to join Russia. Ibrahim Khan of Qarabagh signed the articles of submission with Russia on May 26, 1805, as a new round of fighting began. Salim Khan of Shakki followed on June 2.[lxv] Ibrahim Khalil Khan Javanshir had convinced his son-in-law, Salim Khan of Shakki, to join him in submitting to Russia as a way of defending their respective khanates against Iran. Obviously, the two khans were convinced that a deal with Russia would leave them in a better position to rule their principalities without outside interference. Both khans, as with other local rulers (Iravan, Nakhjavan, Talesh, etc.), were continuing the dangerous game of playing Iran and Russia off against each other, submitting to one or the other in the hope of gaining the type of independence that was no longer possible. It seems the lessons of the Bagratian royal house had not made much impression on either. Both khans would lose their dominion soon, and the Russians would assassinate the elderly Javanshir in 1806.[lxvi] By spring 1805 General Tsitsianov had also received reinforcements and was ready to resume the conflict. However, an important impediment for Russia in terms of committing an overwhelming force to its first war with Iran was that Russia was also at war on several other fronts. These included France (1805–7 and again 1812–15), the Ottoman Empire (1805–12), and Sweden (1808–9). The Russian command of the Caucasus changed hands four times between 1806 and 1812, with Ivan V. Gudovitch (1806–9), Alexander P. Tormezov (1809–10), Filippo Paulucci/R. N. Rtishchev (1809–11), and finally Rtishchev alone (1811–16) taking their turns succeeding Tsitsianov.

In spring 1805, the shah was in the process of removing Muhammad Khan Qavanllu-Qajar from Iravan by sending a force under Mehdi Qoli Khan Qavanllu-Qajar into Iravan and disarming the khan and his supporters, a task which was accomplished by June 1805. Muhmmad Khan was ordered to move to Tehran with his family and Mehdi Qoli became the new temporary governor. By the end of 1806, the governor of Iravan would be the famous Hosein Qoli Khan Qavanllu-Qajar Sardar Iravani, one of the best commanders of the shah's army. The Iravan front was quiet in 1805 and involved minor skirmishes. The Russian army was in possession of Gyumri at Shuregol (northwestern tip of Iravan) with a forward position at Talin just southeast of Gyumri. Iranian forces had lined up just to the south of Talin, facing the Russian encampment. The shah had ordered the forts of Iravan, Uch Kelisa, and Sardar Abad strengthened and stocked with provisions. The bulk of the army in this sector was stationed in Nakhjavan on standby.

In Qarabagh, while Javanshir and the khan of Shakki were negotiating with the Russian general, Tsitsianov had sent a 2,000-man detachment to Qarabagh and a 500-man unit to Shakki while moving his command center from Tiflis to Ganjeh. Smaller Russian military units were present at the intersection of Kor-Aras at Saliyan where a 2,000-man Iranian unit stood against them on the opposite bank. Further south an Iranian garrison of 5,000 men was stationed in the fortress of Lankaran in Talesh.

The next round of fighting began in the spring of 1805 after Noruz (New Year) celebrations in Tehran.[lxvii] Upon hearing of negotiations between the khans of Qarabagh and Shakki and the Russians, the shah ordered Abbas Mirza to cross into Qarabagh with an army of 25,000 men. In March 1805, Abbas Mirza had already moved his command center to Ahar when the royal order came to cross the Aras River at Khoda Afarin, enter Qarabagh, and either receive Javanshir's submission or remove him from power. The prince regent's plan was to engage and neutralize the Russian force stationed in Qarabagh before Tsitsianov's main force arrived, and then move toward Ganjeh. Ibrahim Khalil Khan Javanshir had dispatched one of his sons, Muhammad Hasan Aqa Javanshir, with a small force to secure the bridge of Khoda Afarin with the intention of preventing the Iranians from crossing. A Russian force from Shusha under Major Lisanovich was ordered to provide support. A 2,000-man Russian force under Colonel Paul M. Koragin and the famous major (future general) Pyoter S. Kotliaverskii, known as Qezil Mayor,[4] followed this force. Meanwhile, Abbas Mirza had already sent Pir Qoli Khan with 10,000 men to secure and cross the bridge. The vanguard unit of this force crossed to the other side on March 29, before enemy troops arrived. This unit under Isma'il Khan Sardar Damghani engaged and dispersed the Qarabaghi detachment and forced the Russians to retreat to Shusha after a brief battle. The bulk of Abbas Mirza's army of 25,000 began to cross into Qarabagh after this engagement. Abbas Mirza divided it into two columns and began marching from the west and the east, from Khoda Afarin northward to Shusha. The shah followed this force by moving his army toward Ahar and then crossed Khoda Afarin with reinforcements and supplies. On March 30, the eastern column of the Iranian army reached Aq Oghlan on the eastern approach to Shusha, and occupied it, then moved west to Chenaqchi and lined up against the Russian force to the north of Chenaqchi. By April 1, while maintaining contact with the other column further to the west, the eastern column of the Iranian army was in a good position to attack, as it could see the Russians were retreating north toward Shusha in an orderly manner. However, the commanders decided to wait until fresh supplies had arrived. By April 2, both columns had arrived south of Shusha where the Russian force was lined up some two kilometers south of the town.

4. Known by this name to Iranians because of his reddish-blond hair.

The two sides fought hard from April 2 to 9, with superior Russian firepower pitted against Iranian numbers and mobile cavalry. Here again, the Iranian side took heavy casualties but by the April 9 when the shah's reinforcements arrived, the remnant of the Russian force began an orderly retreat north toward the fort of Askaran (to the northwest of Shusha), in effect leaving Shusha to its own accord. On April 10, the Iranian army reached Shusha, surrounded it, and moved further north and laid siege on Askaran as well. During April 11–14, Iranian attempts to open Shusha or capture the remaining Russians at Askaran was unsuccessful. Ibrahim Khalil Khan had already fled Shusha and would meet Tsitsianov and sign articles of submission. The defenders of Shusha held out against the Iranian army, which lacked adequate siege guns. The remnants of the Russian army at Askaran managed to use a northern route to make a daring night escape, with the help of Armenian *meliks*, and join Tsitsianov's main army at Shah Bulaghi to the northeast, south of the River Tartar.

Russian and Iranian sources provide similar narratives up to this point of the conflict. However, the Russian narrative gives a much smaller number for the Russian invaders and a much larger number for the Iranian army. For example, for the Battle of Arkaran, Colonel Koragin's force is recorded to have been 400 plus two cannons, half of whom were wounded or killed by Pir Qoli Khan's 10,000-man force. Similarly, the total Russian force involved in the conflict of 1805 is given as 2,371 plus three cannons, while the number for the Iranian side is given as 40,000.[lxviii]

The Iranian army spent April 14 to July 3 resting near Shusha after a period of heavy fighting and high casualties.[lxix] During this period, Fath Ali Shah also crossed the Aras and set up his central command at Takht-e Tavus just northeast of Khoda Afarin. At this point news of Russian activity in the Caspian Sea and a possible attack on the port of Anzali reached the shah, as did news of Russian activities on the Iravan border. To counter, the shah sent orders for the defense of Gilan against General Zavalishin, and the strengthening of Iravan's defenses. He also arranged for Mahdi Qoli Khan to remove and replace Muhammad Khan of Iravan. In addition, to be closer to the battlegrounds of Gilan and the Caspian Sea, he moved his central command further south to Aslanduz after resupplying the army of Abbas Mirza in Qarabagh.[lxx]

On July 6, 1805, the Iranian army began to engage the Russian army at Shah Bulaghi, capturing the fortress and forcing it to retreat toward Ganjeh. The Russian narrative becomes confused and unreliable at this point. According to a study of Russian sources, Tsitsianov's force of 2,372 reached the remnants of Koragin's near the River Terter on July 28, and forced a 40,000-man Iranian army to retreat south of the River Aras. However, the narrative also reports that on July 29, Abbas Mirza was laying siege to Ganjeh. As Abbas Mirza's force had entered from the Qarabagh front, it could not have laid siege on the 29th and retreated to the south the day before.[lxxi] Hence, the Iranian narrative seems to be more reliable for the events following the fall of Shah Bulaghi.

According to Iranian sources, at this point the two armies were about the same size, with each numbering 25,000 to 30,000 as Abbas Mirza approached Ganjeh. General Tsitsianov kept 5,000 men inside the city walls and moved the rest of his force to the hilly ground to the west, between Ganjeh and the town of Shamkor. The first Iranian units under Isma'il Khan Sardar Damghani reached Ganjeh in early August and began to lay siege.[lxxii] During the early stages of the siege, for reasons not clearly explained by any source, a large number of civilians exited Ganjeh and joined Abbas Mirza's military camp, asking for protection and expressing fear that his army would leave the area to the Russians again. This could have been a Russian trick, spreading a rumor that the Iranian army was about to abandon Ganjeh. The presence of such a large civilian population complicated the task of fighting the Russians and ultimately proved to be a heavy burden.

On August 9, the Russian army launched an all-out attack from the south with heavy bombardment of the Iranians besieging Ganjeh. Artillery barrage came from both within and outside Ganjeh. However, as the defenders inside Ganjeh were not ready to attack in coordination, the Russian army stopped and resumed its attack the next day. On August 10, the Russian army concentrated its pressure on the left flank of the Iranian army as the defenders inside Ganjeh joined the battle by exiting the fort and attacking Iranian lines. Faced with heavy bombardment and the need to protect the civilian population, Abbas Mirza ordered a retreat in two columns, which were separated from each other because of heavy Russian attacks. Ultimately one column began to retreat southward under Abbas Mirza but lost all contact with the other column. With civilians in tow, this column fought its way south and reached Iravan by August 13. The other column marched east, attempting to reach Qarabagh and move south to cross the Aras, but it fell into pieces and only individual units or soldiers managed to flee to safety by August 15. Because of this retreat, all the sacrifices and gains of that spring and summer were lost in the Qarabagh and Ganjeh regions. The Russian army stopped its pursuit of the remnants of the eastern column at Shusha, probably because of exhaustion, which gave the Iranians time to regroup the forces crossing the Aras. By the end of August 1805, Abbas Mirza seemed to have recovered his force, as he reconstituted two divisions of his army, posting one at Khoda Afarin and the other in Iravan. On October 3, the central command of the army once again moved to Ahar, awaiting orders from the shah.

On October 5, Russians opened hostility by attacking the port of Anzali via the Caspian Sea with the intention of capturing Rasht, the center of Iran's Gilan province. The Russians had committed twelve naval vessels, 3,000 men and four artillery pieces, and moved against Anzali under the command of General Zavalishin. The defenders, 500 in Ghaziyan (near Anzali) and 3,000 in Rasht and under the command of Miza Musa Monajem Bashi and Mirza Yusef Monshibashi, allowed the Russian force to land and occupy the port by pulling back, but then ambushed it as it moved inland through the inhospitable marshlands of the region. The Russian force pulled out after losing 1,800 men, all its artillery, and much of its baggage.[lxxiii]

After withdrawal, General Zavalishin retreated to the island of Sari, off Talesh, awaiting orders and supplies. Once this task was accomplished, Zavalishin's reinforced detachment of 5,500 landed south of Baku (Badkubeh) and demanded its submission. Once Hosein Qoli Khan Badkubeh, the khan of Baku, refused, the Russian general ordered heavy bombardment of the city. On November 25, General Tsitsianov moved with a force of 5,000 from Ganjeh toward Shamakhi, the main city of the Khanate of Shirvan, and ordered a Russian force of 5,500 stationed at Saliyan to move north and join him at Shamakhi. The khan of Shirvan, Mustafa Khan, was already cooperating with the Russians and had submitted. Hence by the end of November 1805, General Tsitsianov may be estimated to have had around 16,000 troops plus local collaborators under his command in and around Baku, Shirvan, and Shakki—and he was ready to move on Baku, Darband, Qobbeh, and Talesh.

News of the Russians landing south of Baku prompted the khans of the region to request Iranian help by pledging loyalty. These khans were: Sheikh Ali Khan of Darband, Surkhay Khan of Lezgi, and Hosein Qoli Khan Badkubeh of Baku. Their emissary reached Tabriz in November and the prince regent asked them to cooperate with each other and not allow Baku to fall into Russian hands. In addition, he ordered Askar Khan Afshar Urumi (or Urmavi) to lead a force to help the defenders of Badkubeh. By December 1805, a severe winter had set in that made communication very difficult, to a point that the Iranians did not know where the bulk of Russian army was, and the Russian command had not been able to establish contact with General Zavalishin's force south of Badkubeh. Meanwhile, both the detachment sent by Abbas Mirza and those of the Khans of Darband and Lezgi reached Baku and broke the siege. With inadequate weapons but much resilience, this combined force fought hard (and at times negotiated with the Russians) until January 6, 1806 when Zavalishin, while praising the bravery of the defenders, ordered the Russian army to board its vessels and retreat to the Island of Sari.[lxxiv]

By the beginning of 1806, Russia had firmly established itself in Georgia, annexed Ganjeh, Qazzaq, and Shams al-Din, occupied a sliver of territory in northern Iravan, and received the submission of the khans of Qarabagh, Shirvan, and Shakki and maintained small detachments at the central cities of each of them. Iranian attempts at dislodging Russia from Ganjeh and Qarabagh had failed, but Russian control over southern Qarabagh (south of Chenaqchi) was weak at best. The Russian commander had an army of over 30,000 at his disposal. By this time, Iran had established firm control over Iravan, Talesh, and Nakhjavan, and had made alliances with the khans of Badkubeh, Qobbeh, Darband, and Talesh. Iran's attempt to recapture Ganjeh and defend Qarabagh was a failure and incurred great expense in terms of both men and materials, but it had managed to repel a Russian invading force at Anzali and Baku and deter the Russian army at Iravan.

Until 1806, Iran had been fighting with its traditional army, while with the help of Russian deserters, it had started to build up the Nezam-e Jadid force. In spring 1805, Abbas Mirza had made a request and the shah accepted, giving his seventeen-year-old heir-apparent permanent overall command of the Russian front. This appointment put the prince regent in full command of all of Azarbaijan plus overall command of Talesh, Iravan, and Nakhjavan, although the latter three remained under local khans. Hence, the court of Tabriz became the command center of war with Russia while the court of Tehran maintained overall command. In this context, Abbas Mirza's command was not an autonomous one where he could make his own decisions independent from Tehran. The shah appointed key military commanders within his army and Qa'em Maqam I was to be his resident civilian advisor. Also, from 1806 on, after Hosein Qoli Khan Qavanllu-Qajar became the governor of Iravan (thus receiving the title "Sardar Iravani"), that region acted semi-autonomously from Tabriz but always in coordination. Furthermore, Abbas Mirza's appointment exacerbated court tensions and his relations with some of his ambitious brothers. These siblings did not see him as fit to be heir to the throne and the main commander of the Russian front. They were all too aware that Abbas Mirza's new military appointment left him with a powerful army and income from some of the most lucrative taxable land in the shah's dominion. Chief among his brothers and his main rival was his half-brother Muhammad Ali Mirza Dowlatshah, the governor of Kermanshah.

Muhammad Ali Mirza Dowlatshah was the firstborn son of Fath Ali Shah, born a few months before Abbas Mirza in January 1789. His mother was a Georgian slave girl, Zibachehr Khanum. Two more brothers were born after him, namely Muhammad Qoli Mirza Mulk Ara and Muhammad Vali Mirza, before the birth of Abbas Mirza in August, and a fifth brother, Hosein Ali Mirza Farman Farma, in September. The five were of different mothers and only Abbas Mirza was of the right maternal line, which made him eligible to take the crown in accordance with Aqa Muhammad Shah's testament. In this context, there was much competition between the five brothers, but none as furious as the one between Dowlatshah and Abbas Mirza. Dowlatshah seems to have been the main source of gossip and accusations against the crown prince, Qa'em Maqam I, and their modernizing reforms. Those who met him described him as not resembling Fath Ali Shah or any of his other brothers in looks; he was described as a warrior soldier, a robust, intelligent man, but very violent and short-tempered.[lxxv]

He and his royal brothers, including Abbas Mirza, accompanied Aqa Muhammad Shah in his last campaign in the Caucasus but remained in Mughan and did not accompany the shah to Shusha in 1797. Upon the shah's assassination, Dowlatshah returned to his father and for two months became ruler of Fars. The new shah then assigned him to Qazvin and finally made him ruler of Kermanshah, Khuzestan, and Lorestan. Similarly to his other brothers, he established a court and a large army in Kermanshah and was in charge of Iran's conflict with the Ottoman Empire over Iraq. He successfully fought a number of border wars against the Ottoman governor of Iraq in 1806, 1812, and 1821.[lxxvi] By all accounts, he was a ruthless ruler but a capable military commander and a formidable rival of Abbas Mirza. In 1809, the shah ordered him to attack Russian forces in the direction of Georgia, but his campaign had minimum impact. He continued to challenge Abbas Mirza until his death by plague near Baghdad during a war with the Ottoman Empire. It is said that he almost met his death at an early age, when Aqa Muhammad asked the boy, Muhammad Ali, what he would do if he gave him the gold-plated sword he was holding in his hand. The boy replied that he would wear it and then chop off the head of the shah. The shah wanted to have him strangled right there and then. He survived only because of the intervention of court officials.[lxxvii] Harford Jones Brydges, the British ambassador to the court of Tehran, was told another incident by Mirza Shafi' attesting to Dowlatshah's violent behavior. The incident, seconded by Qa'em Maqam I who was listening to the conversation, occurred when General Gardane gave Dowlatshah a pair of rifle-barreled pistols as a gift. When the French general left, the prince ordered his secretary to stand by a wall holding out his hand, so that he could practice shooting his new guns. Luckily, he missed his target, to the relief of the secretary.[lxxviii]

The period 1806–11 was a difficult one for Russia, with a long war with the Ottoman Empire (1806–12), an on-again-off-again conflict with France, and tribal insurrections in various part of the southeastern Caucasus. Tsar Alexander's commanders in the Caucasus were therefore ordered to bring the conflict with Iran to an end but without offering any meaningful concessions. Both Gudovich and his successor, General Alexander Tormasov, wrote to Abbas Mirza and proposed peace by making the River Aras the border between Iran and Russia; both proposals were rejected.[lxxix] In reality, the Russian peace terms were demands for nothing short of total capitulation by the Iranian side at a time when Iran was not defeated. In addition, the Russians continued to insult Fath Ali Shah by addressing him by his pre-coronation name Baba Khan (Jahanbani). Each rejection by the Iranian side resulted in an escalation of conflict by the Russian army, as in the case of the second siege of Iravan conducted by Gudovich in 1808, which caused some 3,000 Russian casualties and a retreat.[lxxx]

After the 1804 confrontation, the overall conclusion among Qajar statesmen and commanders was that the traditional army establishment, with all its merits, was no match for the Russian military. The 1805 confrontation reaffirmed that the cost in men and materials was not sustainable and military reforms were in order. Only if Iranian officers and soldiers could move around in a disciplined manner like the Russians did, and, even more importantly, if Iran could match Russia's firepower, was it possible to think of victory. The idea of forming a European-style unit seems to have occurred to the team in Tabriz first but had the full support of the shah from the early days. It is doubtful that the young Abbas Mirza was the initiator and the main brain behind the idea of reform. However, as the commander of war with Russia and heir to the throne, he was in a good position to be the promoter of reforms and partner to the key person behind the idea of modernizing the army, namely Qa'em Maqam I.[lxxxi] During the 1804–5 battles, the Iranians had picked up some Russian and Polish POWs and deserters. Abbas Mirza convinced some of these to join him and provide training to his military. However, French envoy Jaubert's 1806 assessment of Abbas Mirza's military in Azarbaijan, including the new units, was still negative.[lxxxii]

Diplomacy and intrigue

Encounters with Russia had made it clear that the reform of the military was necessary and outside help was essential in this respect. The Qajar court's contact with European powers, other than Russia, was limited to some interaction with envoys of the French Republic before Fath Ali Shah took the throne, and with Britain, which had signed a treaty with Iran in 1801. This treaty, however, did not obligate Britain to help Iran against Russia. British support did not materialize for two reasons. First, in 1804 the British government was in the process of developing a policy to contain Napoleon Bonaparte's ambition to master Europe. Bonaparte, who became emperor in December of that year, had become a major challenge to the old order in Europe and stopping France could not be achieved without Russia, the largest and most populous European power. Therefore, British policy at this point concentrated on establishing an anti-French alliance and they could not allow a relatively minor affair such as the war in the Caucasus to disturb this plan. Second, and on a local level, the British government demanded unacceptable concessions from the shah of Iran before any aid was rendered. These included: handing over Khark Island to Britain, allowing the establishment of a fort in Busheher in the Persian Gulf, and allowing full British control over one of the ports of Mazandaran on the Caspian coast.[lxxxiii]

The Iranian side expected British help against Russia in the spirit of the 1801 agreement and was much disappointed with the British response. In 1804, while Fath Ali Shah was in Iravan, he met an Armenian priest from Etchmiadzin (Uch Kelis) who had traveled abroad and was relatively aware of European affairs. This person informed the shah of Napoleon and his conquests, which captured the shah's imagination. Perhaps, the shah thought, if the British refused to help, France, as mortal enemy of Russia, would be willing to do so. Already by 1803, First Consul Bonaparte had focused his attention on "Persia" as part of his larger overall scheme to reach India by land.

Furthermore, Qajar Iran and the Ottoman Empire made natural allies for France who were at war with Russia and Britain. Similarly to Iran, the Ottoman Empire's war with Russia was an on-again-off-again process and would flare up once more in 1806. Hence, Napoleon asked his diplomats to gather information on Iran and its rulers.[lxxxiv]

Meanwhile the shah decided to approach Napoleon directly by writing to him. An Armenian named Ossep Vassitovits carried the royal correspondence and delivered it to the French ambassador in Istanbul on December 17, 1804. The letter was addressed to First Consul Napoleon Bonaparte and proposed a joint attack on Russia: a French infantry attack from the west, and an Iranian cavalry attack from the south. Vassitovits also provided the French with important information on Iran and its ruling dynasty. He described the 34-year-old Fath Ali Shah as a warrior king who was loved by his subjects and lived at peace with his neighbors except for Russia. He also informed the French that Russia had taken over Georgia and had been making incursions into the shah's dominion. He provided an estimate on the strength of the Russian army in the 1804 campaign in the Caucasus. According to him, General Tsitsianov's force was 15,000 strong when it entered Iravan and 2,000 strong when he left, and the current level of his army in Georgia was 6,000. Fath Ali Shah's letter to Napoleon estimated the overall Russian invasion force in the summer of 1804 to have been 40,000, with 12,000 casualties.[lxxxv] Despite the difference in the estimates, the numbers above approximately correspond to other available estimates and shed light on the high Russian casualty rate in that year. The Armenian also told the French that the British had refused to help the shah and therefore relations between the two were at their lowest point. In addition, the French were told that the shah's attempt at modernizing his army by employing Russian deserters had not been very successful and that he was looking for French help in this area. As noted, French–Iranian relations dated back to the late eighteenth century as Aqa Muhammad was completing the unification of Iran. Revolutionary France during the period of the Directory (1795–9) approached the court of the shah to promote unity between Iran and the Ottoman Empire, against Russia and Britain, but the scheme had come to nothing.[lxxxvi]

Emperor Bonaparte's response to the developing situation was swift, as he dispatched two emissaries to the court of Tehran. His first envoy, an officer named Alexander Romieu, had an audience with the shah on September 30, 1805, but he had no concrete proposals other than delivering the French emperor's letter, and gathering intelligence on Iran. Napoleon's letter, dated March 29, 1805, did not contain anything concrete either, which must have been a disappointment for the Qajar court. It noted that Britain and Russia were not so strong and that they could be defeated if the shah's army was trained properly in modern ways, and that his envoy would determine what was needed. "Today, an army of twenty-five thousand well-disciplined foreigners might ravage and even subjugate Persia," the emperor wrote to the shah.

Romieu also had extensive conversations with the shah, with Mirza Reza Qoli Nava'i Monshi al-Mamalek, the dominion's chief scribe, and with Mirza Muhammad Shafi' Mazandarani, the chief minister. Romieu described them as the strongest supporters of Franco-Persian relations. The two statesmen bitterly complained about the inadequacies of the Iranian military, despite the bravery of its soldiers and officers, and of the destructive firepower of the Russian military, especially its dreaded howitzers. Through this interaction, the French envoy realized that even the more worldly and better-educated Persian-speaking scribal class in Qajar Iran was very much ignorant of what was going on in Europe. For example, the two ministers wanted to know where the borders between the French Empire and Russia were. He was also asked whether France's sea connection was the same as that of Constantinople, and whether it could send ships into the Black Sea. In his audience with the shah, the French envoy was told of the monarch's desire to have an alliance with Bonaparte, whom he described as a reliable ally against the other unreliable European powers.[lxxxvii]

Romieu's impression of Qajar Iran and Fath Ali Shah included some interesting observations. He reported the shah to be a despot who nevertheless consulted with his ministers on a daily basis; an honest man who kept his promises and a charitable man who was well loved by his people; a religious man but not a fanatic; and a Muslim monarch in whose dominion Christians were happy and felt protected. Furthermore, the shah was described as loving women and at this point (1805) to have had 100 legal wives and concubines in his harem, and fifty-four sons and daughters whom he loved equally. Beside women, the French envoy observed that the shah loved hunting and jewelry. As to the shah's faults, similarly to his royal uncle, his avarice was mentioned, but unlike his uncle who took care of his army, the shah neglected it and was not popular with the military. Romieu pointed to the shah's failure to reward bravery, and that he was known for not paying his soldiers on time and not feeding them properly. His assessment of the imperial army was that its loyalty and effectiveness would have been in question had it not been for the respect and loyalty toward Crown Prince Abbas Mirza, who fought hard to take care of it.[lxxxviii] Romieu's assessment of Russia was that it posed the greatest threat to Iran, that it could easily penetrate deep into the shah's guarded domain, and the reason it did not commit more troops and resources to capture all of the southeastern Caucasus was its commitment in Europe (i.e., war with France). Romieu's estimate of Russian troops in Georgia was 10,000 to 12,000, mostly locally trained and Cossacks, and his estimate of Iranian troops was 18,000 which seems to be lower than the actual numbers. After two meetings with Romieu, Fath Ali Shah decided to send an envoy to the emperor accompanying Romieu on his return trip, but the French envoy fell sick and died in Tehran on October 12, 1805.

The second French envoy, Amedee Jaubert, an orientalist and fluent in Persian, had spent eight months in an Ottoman prison and almost did not make it to Tehran. Only after the shah exerted much pressure was he finally released and made his way from Iravan to Tabriz, to Ardabil and finally to Tehran in spring/summer 1806. Jaubert was an acute observer, and his travel log has left some detailed notes on Iran in the early nineteenth century. His mission was to open preliminary negotiations to establish a context for a long-term relationship between the French Empire and Iran. As he entered Tehran and started his interaction with Iranian leaders, war with Russia flared up again and it was not going well for Iran. In Ardabil he met with the seventeen-year-old Abbas Mirza in his military camp and captured his frustration in fighting the Russians. The author noted that Abbas Mirza was well aware of the Russian firepower and the discipline of the Russian artillery and infantry, and had already concluded he would need a similar force to defend against the Russians. The prince regent also showed much interest in Napoleon and wanted to know how old he was, how his face looked, whether he had many wives, and whether he spoke Persian. Abbas Mirza also asked detailed questions about European military discipline and was told that the reason Russians were successful against his army and the French were successful against the Russian army was mobile artillery and the ability to use it most effectively.[lxxxix]

The above observations suggest that already by 1806 Iranian leaders showed better awareness of events in Europe and had become aware of French animosity toward Russian and Britain, British friendship with Russia, and French victories against Russia and its allies in the European arena. Hence, a more realistic understanding of Iran's situation in the world and in its war with Russia was taking shape. However, multi-layered factional differences were also developing around the issue of the best long-term policy. In this context, an old statesman like Mirza Shafi' was already thinking of war with Russia as a lost cause and had started to think of expansion in the direction of Afghanistan as a way of compensating for losses to Russia. In this, the *sadr-e 'azam* was opposed by the court of Tabriz and Abbas Mirza and his chief minister Qa'em Maqam I, who were not ready to concede defeat and were looking for ways to empower the military. It seems that everyone agreed that to fight the Russian threat a reliable European ally was needed and that this ally was not Britain, which had proven to be unreliable. However, a pro-British faction was also taking shape in the court, including notables such as Muhammad Hosein Khan Sadr-e Isfahani and Mirza Abu al-Hasan Shirazi (Ilchi). Both men had financial ties to Britain and their faction was not happy about the turn of events that had resulted in animosity toward Britain. At the same time, part of the Qajar ruling establishment had become convinced that France, because of the greatness of its ruler and its distance from Iran, was the preferred European power. Hence, a pro-French faction within the royal court was taking shape, which lined up against the pro-British faction. This pro-French faction included the court of Tabriz in its entirety, but also Mirza Shafi' and other notables in Tehran. Even the shah had put much hope in the developing relationship with France and dispatched Mirza Muhammad Reza Qazvini to meet the French emperor and negotiate an alliance. Both factions were obviously against Russia but differed in their opinions on who would make the best ally. The year 1806 also proved to be a setback in the conflict with Russia, despite its promising beginning.

Battles of 1806

After the failure to capture Baku, General Tsitsianov's line-up of his forces from the west to the Caspian Sea was as follows. Russian units were stationed at Gyumri (northern Iravan), and Ganjeh (General Nebolsin was stationed in Ganjeh with a reserve force). Russian detachments were stationed in the main cities of khanates that had submitted to Russia—namely, in Shusha (Qarabagh), Nokha (Shakki), Shamakhi (Shirvan), and Saliyan (at the intersection of Kor-Aras). Russia also maintained a naval force in the Caspian Sea, stationed at the Island of Sari, under General Zavalishin. The Russian force in the region of the southeastern Caucasus by the end of 1806 would have totaled 20,000 to 30,000, plus 10,000 to 15,000 local militia. In Qarabagh, the Russian contingent stationed in Shusha was led by a Colonel Dimitri T. Lisanovich (*dali mayor*). The Iranian military was lined up in Iravan south of Gyumri, in southern Qarabagh at Aq Oaghlan, and south of Saliyan in Talesh, with a contingent in Baku and a reserve force in Tabriz. The khans of Darband, Qobbeh, Talesh, and Baku remained loyal to Iran.[xc]

In February 1806, General Tsitsianov moved toward Baku from the northwest and ordered Generak Zavalishin to once again land south of the city from the Caspian. He then opened negotiations with the khan of Baku for submission of that khanate. The khan, Hosein Qoli Khan Badkubeh, one of the khans more loyal to Iran, then tricked the Russian general into meeting him outside the city walls for an official surrender. On February 20, when Tsitsianov showed up with a minimum security detail of three, the khan's nephew, Ibrahim Khan Badkubeh, ambushed and assassinated the general and killed his guards.[xci] This event was a short-lived high point for Iran, as a religious man in Tehran had predicted his death. A member of the ulama named Mirza Muhammad Akhbari Neishaburi claimed the ability to contact the world of the occult and other supernatural powers. He was asked by the shah and court officials to cast a spell to cause Tsitsianov's demise. Akhbari agreed and promised to deliver his head to the shah in forty days. After Tsitsianov's death, court officials asked him to do the same to the Russian tsar, to which he responded that that task would be much more difficult, and that due to the death of the Russian general, his own life was already in danger. Other officials feared him and worried that his power could harm people at home. Hence, they plotted to exile him to the 'atebat, but he was killed in Baghdad before reaching his destination.[xcii]

Tsitsianov's head and hands were cut off and sent to Tabriz and then Tehran, as trophy and for identification purposes, but it is worth noting that Abbas Mirza was appalled by the act.[5] Subsequently the Russian army withdrew from Baku and disengaged on all fronts. The spring of 1806 was a difficult time for Russia, with the rout of its army at Austerlitz by the French in the previous December and the defeat of its allies. Furthermore, Tsitsianov's assassination emboldened Russia's enemies in the region. The Ottomans saw a chance to push against Russia, igniting

---

5. Because Tsitsianov's head and hands were rushed to Tabriz and then Tehran, as a sign of a grand achievement, the Persian proverb *"sar-e ishpokhdor avardi"* (have brought the head of Ishpokhdor) came to life and was still in use until the mid-twentieth century. It was used to complain about someone who was in a rush. Today, the proverb *"saresh ra avardi"* is still used to refer to a person in a hurry.

a new round of hostilities by December of that year. Local rulers and Georgian princes also saw an opportunity and there were at least two anti-Russian revolts in Georgia in 1806. Hence, Russia refrained from opening hostilities in spring 1806 as General Glazenap took temporary command in Tiflis, awaiting orders from the center.

In this context, the old Ibrahim Khalil Khan Javanshir of Qarabagh was ready to switch sides once again, and sent news to the shah to that effect. The shah then ordered Abbas Mirza to move on Qarabagh and the bulk of the Iranian army moved to a forward position, arriving at Khoda Afarin on May 24 ready to cross. At this point, Abbas Mirza's plan was to maintain a defensive posture at the other fronts (Caspian, Talesh, and Iravan), and put his full effort behind capturing Qarabagh. News of an emerging anti-Russian union between the khans of Qarabagh, Shakki, Darband, Daghestan, Talesh, and Baku must have been very encouraging. Hearing of the Iranian military movement, Ibrahim Khalil moved out of Shusha, which was effectively under Russian occupation, toward the south to a location closer to the Iranian army awaiting Abbas Mirza's arrival. At this point one of his own grandsons who hoped to become the next khan of Qarabagh betrayed him. On June 2, the Russian garrison commander Major Lisanovich was informed of the khan's intentions and raided his camp with 300 of his soldiers at night, murdering the khan and much of his family and entourage.[xciii] The murder of Javanshir was perhaps not a wise decision by the Russians. The shah had married one of his daughters to the khan of Shakki, whose sister was also murdered, as was his brother-in-law. The Russian commander appointed Mehdi Qoli Khan Javanshir, a pro-Russia son of Ibrahim Khalil, as the new khan rather than the grandson who had betrayed him.

On June 8, the bulk of Abbas Mirza's army of around 20,000 began to cross the Aras and move to Aq Oghlan to the southeast of Shusha. General Nebolsin, the Russian commander in Ganjeh, countered by sending reinforcements to Shusha and moving the bulk of his regiment from Ganjeh to a location north of Shusha. Nebolsin's regiment plus two battalions stationed at Shusha totaled around 2,000, mostly infantrymen. The two armies began hostilities on June 30 at Khanshin, a location south of Shusha and northwest of Aq Oghlan. By the time Abbas Mirza's vanguard had arrived at Khanshin, the Russian general had decided to pull north and wait for reinforcements. Noticing the Russian retreat, Abbas Mirza ordered a full assault on the retreating force, which caused the Russians to turn around and give battle. The Battle of Khanshin began around noon and lasted all day and into the night. Casualties among Iranians were high and with the arrival of three Russian regiments reinforcing Nebolsin, Abbas Mirza decided to pull south and await reinforcements. On June 31, the Iranian army began to retreat south as the Russians harassed it. By July 6, reinforcements had arrived as Isma'il Khan Sardar Damghani and Hosein Qoli Khan Qajar Sardar Iravani joined Abbas Mirza's camp and immediately began to engage the Russians at Aq Oghlan. On July 7, Nebolsin ordered a retreat and regrouping of his army north of the River Tartar while skirmishes continued for the entire period of retreat. It is not clear why historical accounts based on Russian sources have judged the Battle of Khanshin as a win for Russia.[xciv] Perhaps the fact that a smaller Russian force was able to withstand a larger Qajar army for a while was the cause of such an impression. What is clear is that by July 7, 1806, General Nebolsin had abandoned Qarabagh and retreated to Ganjeh, north of the River Tartar.

Meanwhile, on June 21, Darband fell to the Russians without a fight for the fourth and last time. The khan of Darband and Qobbeh, Sheikh Ali Khan, was a daring opponent of the Russians, having fought them several times dating back to Zukov's invasion of 1796. He would continue to be a thorn in the side of Russia until his death.[xcv] However, as ruler it seems he was not popular with his own subjects and had lost his touch with his fellow Darbandis. This situation gave General Alexander P. Glazenap (temporary commander of the Russian forces) the opportunity to move on the khanate; he captured it without a fight after the locals had rebelled against the khan, and expelled him from the town.[xcvi] Later in June, the new Russian commander arrived in Tiflis. He was the former governor General Ivan Gudovich, who promptly replaced Glazenap with General Bulgakov and then began preparations to move on Baku.

The month of July proved to be an eventful one. First, news reached Abbas Mirza that on July 2 the Russian army at Saliyan had attacked and overrun the Iranian detachment guarding the bridge at the Kor-Aras intersection. Second, news came of an anti-Russian rebellion in Georgia, and finally, news emerged of the Russian army's move on Baku. These developments caused Abbas Mirza to revise his priorities and move his army to the northeast, toward Shirvan. The prince regent dispatched Pir Qoli Khan to Saliyan and the Russian force was pushed back to the north of the bridge. When the Qajar detachment attempted to move north of the Kor River toward Darband, it was attacked and harassed by local Shirvani militia sent by the collaborating Mustafa Khan. After the arrival of reinforcements led by Hosein Qoli Khan

Sardar Iravani and others, the Shirvani force was dispersed and Abbas Mirza's army began to cross into Shirvan and moved to the northeast and camped at Aq Su. There is evidence that in retaliation for the collaboration with the Russian army, the Qajar army began to plunder the region, which could not have been a good tactic for winning the hearts and minds of the locals but was a common nomadic military practice. The khan of Shirvan then attempted reconciliation and asked for a pardon and to switch sides yet again. However, because he failed to present himself in person before Abbas Mirza, the Qajar army led by Isma'il Khan Sardar Damghani and Hosein Qoli Khan Sardar Iravani began to lay siege to the khan's stronghold of Shirvan and captured it. While the conflict in Shirvan was going on, Abbas Mirza ordered some 6,000 families to be moved south to Mughan and began to turn his attention toward Baku and Darband. At this point, a major outbreak of plague hit the region from Iravan in the west to Shirvan. It is unclear how the plague affected the Russian army in the region but its toll on the Qajar army was so heavy that Abbas Mirza ordered a retreat from Aq Su. With the Qajar army retreating, the Russian force under General Nebolsin moved against Selim Khan Shakki and after defeating him, captured Nukha by storm.[xcvii] Abbas Mirza's reinforcement under the command of Farajallah Khan Shahvasan did not make a difference. The people of Nukha turned against the khan ~~and the Iranian detachment sent to help him, as a way of avoiding more des°truction during the Russian siege~~. Salim Khan Shakki and his family fled to Iran. Simultaneously, the Russian army in Darband under General Bulgakov moved against Baku from the north and captured it without resistance as the khan Hosein Qoli Khan Badkubeh and his family fled to Iran.[xcviii] Although there were some skirmishes in Iravan, the Russian army maintained a defensive posture for the remainder of this year due to uprisings in Georgia, while plague forced the Iranian army not to pursue the conflict in this sector. On October 9, Abbas Mirza, encouraged by the French, sent a cavalry force of 11,000 north of the Kor River but this attempt came to an end when the Russians landed a regiment north of Lankaran in Talesh and behind Iranian lines, which led to the withdrawal of the Iranian army from the northern Kor sector.[xcix]

The year 1806 must have been a disappointing one for the Qajar leadership in Tabriz and Tehran, and the need for modernizing reforms of the military became even more urgent. While the Battle of Khanshin should be considered another draw, the Russian army's advance was only checked at high cost to the traditional Qajar army. The conflict between the Russian army and local authorities was even more telling.

The local khans with their own limited resources were no match for the superior Russian army. Furthermore, the fall of Nukha and Darband, the strongholds of Salim Khan and Sheikh Ali Khan, pointed to another development—namely the war weariness of the local population and their willingness to accept Russian rule at the expense of betraying their own ruler. Mismanagement and the tyrannical behavior of some local rulers must have been contributing factors, as with the case of Sheikh Ali Khan of Darband. However, at the same time, anti-Russian rebellions in Georgia pointed to another pattern in this war, namely that the local occupied populations, both Muslim and Christian, were having second thoughts about Russian rule and requesting Iranian aid to free themselves. In the case of Georgia, two rebellions in the summer of 1806 gave an opening to Georgian pretender Iskandar Mirza (Alexander Bagration) to lead an army provided by the shah in an unsuccessful attempt to liberate his ancestral land. The region would witness a number of popular anti-Russian rebellions by the occupied populations throughout both Russo-Iranian wars. Meanwhile the prominence of international diplomacy and Russia's preoccupation with other conflicts turned the year 1807 into a peaceful one.

The Peaceful 1807

Twice during 1807, Abbas Mirza asked the shah for permission to commence hostilities with Russia and was turned down by him. Clearly, other more important developments overshadowed the war. Hence, the front line remained quiet as Russia consolidated its position in Darband, Shakki, Qobbeh, and Baku, as well as Qarabagh and Shirvan. The khanate of Talesh was still semi-autonomous, but the Qajar army had a strong presence in Talesh and southern Qarabagh and was in firm control of much of Iravan and Nakhjavan.

In this context, diplomatic interactions kicked into high gear. General Gudovich sent an emissary named Major Istifanov to Abbas Mirza, asking for a ceasefire for the duration of his mission and requesting the opening of negotiations. Russia in 1807 was facing challenges, from French wars in Europe, to fear of a joint Ottoman–Iran attack, to rebellions in the Caucasian occupied territories. Hence, the tsar had ordered Gudovich to request a ceasefire with Iran.[c] Abbas Mirza accepted the ceasefire offer but wrote that opening negotiations depended on the context in which they would be held.[ci] The French sent a number of missions culminating in the Gardane mission of December

1807. After Jaubert's 1806 mission was over, another French mission under Joseph Marie Jovannin arrived, followed by the 1807 missions of La Balanche, a nephew of Talleyrand, Napoleon's foreign minister, who delivered a letter from Napoleon dated January 17, 1807. These missions were followed by the arrival in June 1807 of Auguste Bontems and finally the Gardane mission. Meanwhile, in 1806 and before Jaubert's arrival, the shah had already dispatched Mirza Muhammad Reza Qazvini to negotiate with Bonaparte. By the time the shah's emissary reached Paris, the French emperor was already in Eastern Europe. Therefore, the ambassador dispatched one of his deputies to meet Napoleon in Poland. The deputy, Sayyed Muhammad Amin Vahid, signed the Treaty of Finkenstein with Napoleon on May 4 and left for Iran to have it ratified by the shah. The French emperor moved to meet the Russian army and defeated it on June 14 at the Battle of Friedland, forcing the tsar to accept the French diktat for peace, which resulted in the Treaty of Tilsit, signed on July 7, 1807.[cii]

Bontem's impression of Iran provides a window into the general political situation in Iran in 1807 and prior to the arrival of the Gardane mission. His goal was to begin training of the Nezam-e Jadid force based on French doctrine, to encourage Iran to continue its war with Russia, and to gather intelligence. Some aspects of his observations on Iran's general population make-up and economy have already been noted. When he delivered Napoleon's letter to Abbas Mirza, he was shocked to observe that the letter was read aloud in public and in a musical tone. As noted, a lack of protocol for maintaining state secrets had been observed by other visitors and was rooted in the tribal habits of the Qajar ruling class, and was repeatedly used against it by its enemies.[ciii] Besides meeting with the crown prince and later the shah, the French officer also met with key Persian-speaking bureaucrats. These included Mirza Shafi' Mazandarani, the shah's chief minister; Qa'em Maqam I, Abbas Mirza's chief minister; Mirza Qoli Khan Nava'i Monshi al-Mamalek, the shah's chief scribe; and Haji Muhammad Hosein Sadr-Isfahani Amin al-Dowleh. While he found Mirza Shafi' to be a pro-French figure in the Qajar court, Bontems noted that Sadr-Isfahani showed much interest in following and observing him and considered him to be a British agent and on their payroll.[civ] His accurate observation also gives us a glimpse into the early formation of the pro-British faction in the Qajar court.

The Treaty of Finkenstein had been signed a few months before Tilsit, but it was not yet ratified by the shah. There was no mention of Iran in the peace treaty between the French and Russian Empires. Most likely, omitting Iran had more to do with European politicking and intrigue rather than any technical problem. In the Treaty of Finkenstein, Iran committed itself to an anti-British alliance with France, which in May 1807 meant anti-Russian too.[cv] (By signing the Treaty of Tilsit, France and Russia became allies and Britain become an enemy of both.) In return, France committed itself to the defense of Iran and the return of Gorjestan to Iran. Hence, Iran cut all contact with Britain, and France began to assess the feasibility of moving an army through Iran for the conquest of India. However, the Treaty of Tilsit changed the above equation, for by the time the main body of the French mission arrived under Brigadier General Gardane in December 1807, France and Russia were allies and the French attitude toward aiding Iran had changed. In effect, France's role switched from a major power helping an ally against the common enemy (Russia), to a mediator attempting to bring peace between two allies. The new reality was not what the shah had bargained for, and the French alliance soon became a major disappointment.

The Gardane mission, 1807–1809

Brigadier General Alfred du Gardane was an aide-de-camp to the French emperor and as such was close to him and had his full confidence. In a letter to Gardane informing him of his new appointment, Napoleon outlined his mission as follows: to intensify enmity with Russia in order to encourage Iran to continue war with Russia, and to remind Fath Ali Shah that the Russian tsar did not recognize him as the king of Iran. Here Napoleon was referring to the continued official Russian reference to the shah not by his full imperial title but as "Baba Khan Jahanbani," his pre-coronation tile, thus refusing to recognize his legitimacy. Bonaparte asked his general to strengthen the Iranian military so that Russia was forced to divert more forces to that front, and reminded him that Russia's position in Georgia was vulnerable and that the local population tended to favor Iran. In this context, the French general was tasked with organizing a European-modeled army of 12,000 with adequate artillery, at the shah's expense so that he would appreciate the value of the effort. The general was also asked to encourage an anti-Russian alliance between Qajar Iran and the Ottoman Empire, both natural enemies of Russia. Finally, Gardane was reminded that such a large French mission was meant to prepare the ground for the use of Iranian territory to invade India; one of his objectives was to help lay the foundations for this.[cvi]

General Gardane's mission of fourteen military personnel and thirteen civilians arrived in Tehran on December 14, 1807. The French general arrived with the promise of delivering up to 10,000 rifles and thirty field guns, setting up munition factories, and improving existing fortifications and building new ones. Gardane had his first audience with the shah on December 17, and the Franco-Iranian treaty was signed on December 20, which stood for the ratification of Finkenstein with updated modifications.[cvii] He made detailed observations of Iranian society in 1808 and 1809, some of which have already been mentioned. But his ability to maintain a balance between Napoleon's orders and the reality of the Russo-Iranian War seemed an impossible task from the very beginning.

Gardane's letter to the shah on February 11, 1808 spelled out the change in French policy toward the Russo-Iranian War. He wrote to the shah about the reason for not mentioning Iran in the Treaty of Tilsit and informed him that the French emperor and the Russian tsar were now allies, and the shah was asked to join them in boycotting Britain. This policy was an extension of Napoleon's "Continental System," designed to choke off the British economy by preventing trade with the European continent. European powers defeated by France were forced to join this system and Russia was no exception. The shah was reminded that he was the only French ally who had not yet cut all economic ties with Britain. Fath Ali Shah responded on February 13 that Iran welcomed French mediation in the Russian war and that all ties to Britain were cut—and John Malcolm, the British envoy from India, was not allowed to proceed to Tehran and was returned to India.[cviii]

In March 1808, Gardane received a friendly letter from General Gudovich, asking him to mediate the conflict. The letter was followed by the arrival on May 6 of Lieutenant Colonel Baron de Werde, Gudovich's envoy. The Russian general's proposal was for the shah to send an emissary to Tiflis and for Iran to accept a borderline starting from the Arpachay River in the west to where the Kor River entered the Caspian Sea. This meant Iran had to give up some territories under its control and forfeit the territories already lost. According to one historian, "Gudovich, who had been instructed by the Emperor to get an armistice prior to any negotiations for peace, offered impossible conditions."[cix] The shah refused to send an envoy, rejected the proposal, and demanded Russia return the occupied territories if it wanted peace with Iran. Gardane's solution was a proposal to have the tsar's envoy, Count Tolstoy, travel to the court of Paris and negotiate peace with the shah envoy to Paris, Asgar Khan Afshar Urumi. This was a clever move by the French general, as it would have relocated the problem of making peace between Russia and Iran to Paris and would have left the general to deal with other tasks. He lobbied the shah to send an envoy to Tiflis and asked the Russian general to lobby the tsar to accept his Paris proposal. The shah agreed and dispatched Fath Ali Khan Nuri to Tiflis as Abbas Mirza's envoy, and Gudovich agreed to lobby the tsar.[cx] The fact that an Iranian representative was sent from Tabriz and not Tehran points to the shah's attempt to send an envoy equal in status to the Russian general and no more.

Hence, diplomacy was in high gear during the spring and summer of 1808. During this year, although Russia had ended its war with France it was engaged in a war with the Ottoman Empire[cxi] and Sweden (the Finish War 1808–9); diplomatic activity bought it enough time to attend to those conflicts before returning to war with Iran. As for Iran, the shah had little choice but to wait and see if the French were able to deliver through diplomacy what they had promised him—namely Russian evacuation of occupied territories. As a result of these activities, a temporary ceasefire was in place.

Meanwhile, French advisors went to work training the Nezam forces, and erecting new factories in Isfahan and Tabriz to produce modern guns and rifles for the Iranian army. French engineers also began the task of fortifying the Iranian fortress of Iravan, the fort of Sardarabad in the Khanate of Iravan, and Urdubad in Nakhjavan. In addition, a new modern fort named Abbasabad (named in honor of the prince regent) was built in Nakhjavan.[cxii] The task of training and arming the Nezam forces moved slowly and faced difficulties along the way. Part of the difficulty was the way the shah conducted business, but it was also due to the pro-British party sabotaging the French efforts. As for difficulties created by the shah, he expected each governor to pay for the cost of establishing military factories on their territory. This meant imposing a high cost on local governments, which the local authorities did their best to avoid, thus slowing down production. Furthermore, in a locale like Isfahan, where the governor, Sadr-Isfahani, was a pro-British figure, steps were taken to sabotage progress.[cxiii] The above conditions slowed down but did not prevent the French from delivering modern equipment required for the Nezam forces.

Gardane's "Paris proposal" did not go far with the Russians, as General Gudovich informed him in a letter dated July 2, 1808 that Tsar Alexander I had rejected it and had ordered Gudovich to conduct direct negotiations with Iran. Gardane reported this development to Paris without informing the Iranians.[cxiv] The Russian reaction to Gardane's proposal provides a window into how and why French schemes involving Iran were ultimately unsuccessful. The Russian request for French mediation and peace proposals were most probably disingenuous and designed to buy time so that Russia could deal with other problems. After pointing out the failure of Gardane's mediation, one observer of the time has suggested: "but it was evident from the tone adopted by both parties that peace was impossible, and that the attempt had only been made on the part of Russia for the purpose of gaining time."[cxv] By the summer of 1808 Russia's war with the Ottoman Empire had subsided but not ended, and its war with Sweden (and naval hostilities with Britain) was flaring up. If Russia's history of warfare with its neighbors (especially the Ottoman Empire) is any evidence, Russian peace overtures were usually part of an overall aggressive imperialist policy to buy time to achieve set goals. In the case of Iran, contrary to suggestions by some analysts, there is no reason to believe that Gudovich's peace overtures were anything but a delaying strategy.[cxvi] Abbas Mirza responded to Gudovich via the departing Russian envoy, Baron de Werde. He rejected all Russian demands one by one and reminded Gudovich that Iran still held territory to the north of the border demarcation he had in mind and was not ready to relinquish it.[cxvii]

In a letter to the French foreign minister dated August 18, 1808, Gardane informed him of a document presented to him by the shah's chief minister, Mirza Shafi'. According to Gardane, this document summed up Fath Ali Shah's views on the Franco-Iranian alliance and the Russian war. The shah told the French that Iran's policy toward its obligations stated in the Treaty of Finkenstein was dependent on French steps in fulfilling its obligations. The shah then explained the steps taken on his part, which included preparation for the invasion of India. Gardane doubted this claim, accused the Iranians of exaggeration, and concluded that as long as war with Russia was going on, Iran was in no position to aid "France's India plan." The shah also stated that, by respecting French concerns, Iran had not begun hostilities with Russia in 1807–8 and did not involve itself in the Russo-Ottoman war. On the other hand, the shah complained that the French had not taken any steps to help Iran take back Russian-occupied territories. Gardane's own conclusion was that the shah did not want a fight with Russia and preferred the return of lost territories through French mediation.[cxviii] In summary, what Fath Ali Shah expected from the French emperor was the pressuring of his defeated enemy-turned-reluctant-ally to hand over to Iran the territory of Gorjestan and other khanates taken by the Russian Empire. This the French were not able to deliver, as Napoleon had much bigger strategic concerns in mind and dealings with "Persia" did not occupy a prominent place in his priorities.

Second siege of Iravan and the Battle of Nakhjavan, October–December 1808

On October 11, 1808, General Gudovich wrote a seemingly undiplomatic and hostile letter to Abbas Mirza, demanding he accepted the Russian proposed border and threatening him with war. He also informed the Iranian side of the tsar's rejection of direct French mediation, which must have been a shock and probably did much to diminish Gardane's standing. Reportedly, Abbas Mirza tore the letter in anger, which points to the mood in Tabriz.[cxix] The letter also showed that the Tiflis negotiations had gone nowhere. According to Gudovich, Fath Ali Khan Nuri's request for the return of the occupied territories was unacceptable, and Russia was in a position to impose its will should Iran reject the generous offer of the Arpachay-Aras-Kor border. The Russian general reminded Abbas Mirza and Qa'em Maqam I that during the reign of Peter I, Russia was in control of the entire region and beyond, and that the current offer of border demarcation showed Tsar Alexander's generosity and limited objectives. Finally, he reminded the Iranians of their own internal challenges and further threatened them and demanded they accept the Russian offer.[cxx] By October 1808, winter was approaching and the Iranians were getting ready to dismiss the army. Abbas Mirza was against this decision, as it would have taken him much longer to mobilize should the Russians attack.[cxxi]

In late October 1808, General Gardane issued an order asking French officers to leave Iranian units they were training if hostilities with Russia commenced. However, there is evidence that at least some French engineers remained in Iravan after hostilities began.[cxxii] Already by September 1808, the Russian commander had collected a substantial force in the town of Gyumri at Shuregol and had put General Nebolsin's force in Ganjeh on high alert. According to one estimate, the total Russian force in the Caucasus at this point was between 25,000 and 35,000, but Gudovich's invading force consisted of 8,000 troops with four 24-pounder heavy artillery, two 12-pounder mobile artillery and two 8-inch mortars, which roughly corresponds to the Russian estimate.[cxxiii] Nebolsin's force included seventy-eight officers, 3,052 soldiers and nine field guns.[cxxiv] He was ordered to attack Nakhjavan to prevent a repetition of the Russian encirclement in 1804 by preventing the shah's army coming to the rescue. On October 24, the shah ordered Abbas Mirza to move from Khoy to a forward position in Nakhjavan. The main Iranian army totaled 10,000 (all cavalry) under Abbas Mirza, 3,000 in Iravan under Hasan Khan Sari Aslan, and 2,000 under Sardar Iravani who had left Iravan and camped south of the fortress. Added to this force were around 6,000 French-trained and -equipped modern Nezam infantry and artillery pieces, but no French officer or trainer was present. There was also a 10,000-man, poorly trained and armed volunteer militia (*cherik*) from Salmas, Khoy, and Maku which was dispatched to the fortress of Sardarabad, west of the fortress of Iravan.

The Russian military plan was to move on Iravan and Nakhjavan in two columns. Gudovich and his command would move south from the Arpachay River in the northwest of Iravan, and General Nebolsin and his army would move from Ganjeh to Qarabagh and then from the northeast on to Nakhjavan. Gudovich's army would then lay siege to Iravan and meet Nebolsin's column in Nakhjavan, where they would jointly take on the main Iranian army and annihilate it before opening Iravan. Gudovich sent General Semen A. Portnagene in command of a dragoon unit to harass the main Iranian force in Nakhjavan. At the same time, Abbas Mirza sent a 2,000-man cavalry force under Amanallah Khan Khamseh-Afshar to the Pambak sector in northern Iravan to harass the Russian army. In one encounter in Nakhjavan, General Portnagene's attempt to make a surprise raid on the main Iranian camp was discovered and the Iranians made a "Parthian style" retreat in front of the charging Russian dragoons before turning around and charging the Russian line, surrounding and inflicting heavy casualties on it. The Russian unit was saved by dismounting and forming squares, and using artillery fire to keep off the Qajar cavalry.[cxxv]

In late October, Gudovich moved to occupy Sardarabad and Uch Kelisa then moved to lay siege to Iravan, while inconclusively fighting a cavalry force sent by Abbas Mirza to slow him down. The second siege of Iravan began on October 31. The defenders of Iravan, 3,000 strong with eleven artillery pieces under Sardar Iravani's younger brother Sari Aslan, began to engage the Russians while, as planned, Gudovich moved with the rest of his force toward Nakhjavan. General Nebolsin had managed to push the Iranian army in southern Qarabagh toward the Khoda Afarin bridge on the Aras River. Subsequently, he split his force and sent a column toward Nakhjavan to join Gudovich. However, unknown to Gudovich, a small Iranian force had stopped Nebolsin's column while trying to pass through the highlands of Qarabagh into

Nakhjavan. The Iranian force was commanded by Amir Khan Devellu-Qajar, one of Abbas Mirza's commanders and his maternal uncle.

Gudovich's army began to engage and push back Abbas Mirza's army at Devellu, north of Nakhjavan, but its advance was stopped by the arrival of reinforcements. One report suggested that during one battle in Nakhjavan, on November 8, Abbas Mirza's horse was hit by a bullet and he fell down but continued to fight alongside his French-trained Nezam forces, personally discharging cannons, executing four deserters, and ending the battle. The sardar was reported to have engaged the Russian army in unsuccessful cavalry charges around Iravan but the fortress robustly resisted the Russian siege.[cxxvi] The Russian account of the battle in Nakhjavan reported Nebolsin defeating Abbas Mirza and capturing the town of Nakhjavan despite the Iranians' numerical superiority.[cxxvii] However, Nebolsin's army was not able to capture all of Nakhjavan and was thus unable to join Gudovich's army.

General Gudovich's rear was vulnerable in the absence of Nebolsin and while the siege of Iravan was ongoing. The defenders of Iravan had fought well and Abbas Mirza had managed to send in 5,000 fresh troops from two different directions under the command of Farajallah Khan Shahsavan and Amanallah Khan Khamseh-Afshar. Taking advantage of this vulnerability, Abbas Mirza began to march north toward Iravan, as the month of November ended. At this point Gudovich made contact with Nebolsin and lined up against the Qajar army. Abbas Mirza split his army while the Russian army intensified its attacks on Iravan. On December 10, the Russian army opened two breaches in Iravan's walls but was repulsed. Gudovich's army met Abbas Mirza's army in northern Nakhjavan on December 11 and was defeated. The retreating Russian general made one last desperate all-out attack on Iravan but was repulsed, leaving 1,500 dead. On December 18, Abbas Mirza's army defeated Nebolsin and forced him to retreat to Qarabagh. The Russian account makes no mention of Nebolsin's defeat but reports that Abbas Mirza was defeated as he attempted to pursue and harass the retreating Russian force toward Ganjeh.[cxxviii] Subsequently, Gudovich ordered a general retreat toward Gyumri at the cost of 5,000 dead to his army and an undetermined number of casualties to General Nebolsin's army.[cxxix]

The Russo-Iranian military encounter in 1808 was a setback for Russia. It was also a major setback for the old General Ivan Gudovich, who would lose his command and retire. In 1807, with impressive victories against the Ottoman Empire in the western Caucasus in his résumé, Gudovich seemed to have rejuvenated his career, as he got closer to the age of retirement. Now, because of poor judgment, lack of preparation, underestimating the enemy, and poor commandership, he asked to be retired which was accepted by the tsar.[cxxx] His replacement, General Alexander P. Tormazov, was a meticulous career military officer. He took charge of what must have been a command in crisis for the Russian Empire.

For Iran, the win at Nakhjavan and the Russian failure at Iravan were major victories and something to boast out. Abbas Mirza wrote two letters, one to Napoleon and the other to Sheikh Ali Khan of Darband. The letters were similar in content but the one to Sheikh Ali was more heroic and rhetorical in tone.[cxxxi] Here, Abbas Mirza gave a report on the battle as proof of the possibility of victory over Russia by a well-trained Iranian army. Indeed, this was the first time that an Iranian force, partially equipped and trained by European instructors, had manage to repel a major Russian invasion. The fact that the letter was addressed to Sheikh Ali Khan is of particular interest, in that he alone among former khans of the region had remained a consistent enemy of Russia, and even more importantly, had remained in the region conducting guerrilla attacks on the Russian occupation army. Abbas Mirza used this occasion to encourage him to fight on in coordination with his own efforts.

Relations with the French mission began to take a downward turn in fall 1808, which by extension weakened the pro-French party in the shah's court. General Gardane's failure to provide meaningful mediation and Paris's refusal to pressure Russia had translated into deep disappointment in Tehran and Tabriz. The withdrawal of French instructors just before Gudovich's attack had only exacerbated the situation. To his credit, Gardane did his best to deter Gudovich from opening hostilities. In an October 12 letter to the Russian commander, and concerning his threatening letter to Abbas Mirza, Gardane reminded him that the French Empire considered the Russian-occupied territories in the southeastern Caucasus as belonging to Iran and requested he refrain from any military activity until news of the result of negotiations in Paris was received.[cxxxii] In a letter to the French foreign minister dated October 24, 1808, he reported on his activities in trying to prevent the resumption of hostilities. Accordingly, one of the mission's secretaries by the name of Lazar was dispatched to Abbas Mirza's camp in Khoy, on his way to Tiflis for negotiations with Gudovich. Gardane's report continued to state that as a result of his lobbying in Tehran, Abbas Mirza was asked to facilitate Lazar's trip, and to write a cordial letter to Gudovich, as a way of decreasing tensions. He suggested that in his opinion the reason Russia was proposing a settlement with Iran was because it needed a break to pursue its war with the Ottoman Empire, and that in his view there could be no settlement between the two without French mediation. Finally, he reported that, in a November 22 conversation with Mirza Shafi', the general was informed that in Tehran only he and the shah remained optimistic about the French alliance.[cxxxiii]

On November 23, 1808, Gardane attended an audience with an apprehensive Fath Ali Shah in Golestan Palace. While his armies were engaged in heavy fighting with Russia, the shah wanted to know why his letters to the French emperor had not been answered and complained that the training of his Nezam force was not complete and that he was compelled to fight the Russians in a cold season. The shah also complained that he had dismissed his military camp at Sultanieh based on Gardane's assurances that the Russians would not attack, and that now Abbas Mirza had to fight them with limited forces. Finally, he told the French general that it looked as if Iran could not rely on French help and that he had sixty days to come up with a proper response from Paris.[cxxxiv]

The reality was that Gardane was in an impossible situation. He had received no instructions from his superiors during the late summer and fall of 1808, and did not really have much to say to the shah that would have calmed the situation. On the other hand, the British had already initiated contact with Tehran and had made promises of aid. In light of the French failure to deliver on Finkenstein, the British overture was positively received in Tehran. While Malcolm was prevented from approaching Tehran, out of respect for the French mission, he had already made firm promises of aid against the common enemy of Russia and a mission directly from London was approaching Tehran.[cxxxv] The British mission under Harford Jones Brydges was the highest-level ambassadorial mission sent by London to the court of Tehran, and prompted the French mission under General Gardane to leave.

The Jones Brydges mission, 1809–10

General Gardane had his audience of farewell at Golestan Palace on February 12, 1809 and left Tehran the next day. The British mission under Harford Jones Brydges arrived in Tehran on February 14 and the shah gave audience to the ambassador on February 17. Brydges was familiar with Iran, as he spoke Persian, had served in Basra during the Zand period, and was personally friends with some key figures in the shah's court, especially Mirza Bozorg Farahani Qa'em Maqam I. Both Brydges and a mission secretary named James Morier left detailed accounts of their impression of Qajar Iran during this period. Morier would have a second chance to visit Iran with the Ouseley mission in 1811 and would write a second volume. The difference between the two accounts is that impressions left by Brydges are in general more sympathetic toward Iranian society and statesmen, while Morier in general shows a degree of contempt for the "orient" in general and Qajar Iran in particular. An interesting and even satirical first exchange of information between the British mission and the shah's court was on the health of the British king. Before he left Iran General Gardane had informed Fath Ali Shah that the British King George III had died. This was probably a French ploy of disinformation to slow down British efforts in normalizing relations with Iran. The death of a monarch, in the Iranian mindset of the time, would entail probable internal struggle and even civil war for succession, which would make any permanent treaty doubtful. To the surprise of the shah and his court, he was assured by the British ambassador that his king was in good health.[cxxxvi]

The shah appointed his chief minister Mirza Shafi' and Muhammad Hosein Khan Sadr-Isfahani Amin al-Dowleh to negotiate a treaty with the British over a long-term alliance. The choice of the two figures was telling as the chief minister was associated with the now disgraced pro-French faction and the other was known to be a pro-British figure in the shah's court. Negotiations were long and hard, and there were moments of friction, especially between Brydges and Mirza Shafi', but the text of the preliminary agreement was made ready and signed on March 19, 1809, ready to be sent to London for ratification.[cxxxvii] While the details of the Anglo-Iranian agreement had to be worked out, the general parameters of the treaty were clear. As enemy of both the Russian and French Empires, the British promised to support the shah's war effort by providing him with military experts for continued training of the Nazam forces, supplying the shah's military with modern weapons, especially artillery, and supporting his treasury with financial aid. In effect, the British were now promising the shah what he had asked for back in 1804 and which the British had rejected, because at the time Britain had been an ally of Russia.

The British revised the agreement a few times before it was finalized. Brydges' original treaty was the most favorable to Iran. This was a time when Britain was at war with both France and Russia, and Britain made a generous offer of arming and training the Nezam force, plus financial aid to the shah to fight Russia. After the treaty returned from London in 1811, during Gore Ouseley's mission, it was revised. The signed document (June 1812) committed Britain to support Iran militarily and give financial aid of 200,000 tumans, if Iran was at war with a European power and for the duration of the conflict. At this point, Britain was an ally of Russia and at war with the United States. The British ambassador did his best to convince the shah to accept a ceasefire with Russia. He made the unrealistic, perhaps devious, promise to lobby the tsar on behalf of the shah to return some of the lost territories. The third revision made by the British was in 1814, and committed Britain to help Iran only if Iran was not the initiator of the war.

The British soon realized that Iran's assessment of the Russian threat was problematic at best. Brydges' observations upon his visit to the shah's royal military camp at the pastures of Sultanieh and Ujan in the summer of 1809 are telling. By summer 1809 a little over a year and a half had passed since the Nezam forces had been organized under French instructors. Furthermore, Iran had managed to repair and update its arsenal, and survive the siege of Iravan by General Gudovich in the autumn of 1808. The British assessment of the Nezam force and the army of Azarbaijan under the crown prince stated it consisted of 20,000 cavalry, and 6,000 infantry (Nezam) drilled by the French. The Nezam troops wore blue (the French color) uniforms. There was also a 10,000-strong militia (*cherik*) force supporting the main army. It was decided that with British subsidy and training, the Nezam force could grow to be an infantry force of 12,000.[cxxxviii] Brydges' assessment of the state of the Nezam forces was not flattering, as he found them to be poorly trained and led. In his observation, he went as far as suggesting that the traditional tribal forces under the command of Muhammad Ali Mirza Dowlatshah, Abbas Mirza's half-brother and chief rival, were more reliable than the European-trained forces of the prince regent.[cxxxix] On another occasion, at the pasture of Ujan and while present at a royal council attended by Abbas Mirza, Qa'em Maqam I, Mirza Shafi', and two Qajar noblemen, Brydges made a number of telling observations. According to him, Fath Ali Shah opened the session by praising the readiness of the Nezam force and availability of supplies in Tabriz and Iravan, and then ordered Abbas Mirza to march and attack the Russians until they were driven from Georgia. Apparently, because of the victory against Gudovich the previous fall, the shah and his commanders had recovered some confidence in their cause. When asked for his opinion, the British ambassador had to discuss at length the merits of fighting a defensive war using natural barriers (rivers and mountains) while Iran remained the weaker party. Furthermore, he suggested that Iran had no realistic assessment of Russian strength, and that an alliance with the Ottoman Empire, at this point at war with Russia, was advisable.[cxl] He then made the following remarks to the shah:

In saying this, let it not be imagined, that I undervalue the bravery of your troops; but that I only speak of them relatively, when opposed to those who have been longer disciplined, and more experienced in a species of warfare, to which Persia is at present not much accustomed. Russia possesses a large army of troops ... and I cannot contemplate an offensive war with that power, on the part of Persia ... If your majesty proposes to attack the Russians, it appears to me, the most important thing for you to be acquainted with is their means, their resources, what numbers, and what kind of forces ...[cxli]

The British ambassador, we are told, persuaded the shah who left the war to the prince regent to conduct as he saw fit. However, in reality, he ordered Abbas Mirza to attack Ganjeh to create a diversion so that Dowlatshah could attack Tiflis.[cxlii] Each prince was assigned 25,000 troops, and Sardar Iravani and Sardar Damghani were ordered to join Dowlatshah. There was a lack of coordination and as a result Abbas Mirza's advance stalled in southern Qarabagh. Dowlatshah did not even get close to Georgia, and while he captured Imamli and a few other villages in northern Iravan, it was not to last long and his attempt at capturing Hammamlu (Spartak), Bashaparan (Aparan), and Qara Kelisa (Venadzor) failed. The Russian contingent in those locations took a defensive posture and inflicted casualties on the prince's cavalry. Years later, in 1813, a British officer noticed human and horse bones still visible, left over from Dowlatshah's encounter with the Russian army.[cxliii] What the prince did accomplish was the looting of a local Muslim population left defenseless. In September, with Russian aid and encouragement, Mir Mustafa Khan of Talesh, sensing Iranian weakness, rebelled against the shah, but was quickly defeated and submitted again.[cxliv]

The new Russian commander General Tormazov wrote a letter to Abbas Mirza in August 1809, addressing him as "the heir-apparent of the dominion of Qezelbash."[cxlv] He also did not address the shah with his royal title, and informed the crown prince that the tsar had approved opening negotiations for a permanent cessation of hostilities. He complained about Dowlatshah's attack and reminded Abbas Mirza that six years of warfare had not achieved anything for Iran, and that if he accepted the Russian peace offer, Russia would recognize the shah and his position as crown prince and would help Iran against the Ottoman Empire. Finally, he warned the crown prince to be wary of the devious British, and that friendship with Britain would bring the wrath and enmity of Russia and France. General Tormazov proposed receiving a high-ranking emissary from the shah at the fort of Askaran in occupied Qarabagh. Abbas Mirza's response was that any peace between the two had to satisfy both, and that if Russia wanted peace, it should evacuate occupied territories. Meanwhile, British ambassador Brydges tried his best to prevent peace between the two. He wrote to Abbas Mirza and Qa'em Maqam I and asked to see the Russian commander's letter. Brydges also told the two leaders in Tabriz that Tormazov's request showed Russian was weak and vulnerable, that his proposal was no different than that of Gudovich, and that any ceasefire would alienate the Ottoman Empire. The British were doing their best to unit Iran and the Porte against Russia.[cxlvi]

As the battles of summer 1809 did not show much progress, Qa'em Maqam I was chosen to meet the Russian general, an encounter which took place in April 1810 at Askaran, but did not result in any agreement since the Russian commander repeated the same border demarcation of Arpachay-Aras-Kor. At this point, Russia was in a heated war with the Ottoman Empire and war with France was looming, and hence peace with Iran would have helped it face these challenges. Tormazov's attempt, therefore, was in line with Russia's previous tries at turning a two-front war into a single-front war, and preventing unity between Qajar Iran and the Ottoman Empire. Cooperation and coordination between Iran and the Ottoman Empire, against their common stronger nemesis, would have been a prudent policy. As early as 1805, both Abbas Mirza and the shah had attempted to establish an anti-Russian front with the empire. However, a number of religious, territorial, and cultural differences prevented an effective unity between the two. Cooperation between the two Turkic dynasties, which traced their roots to a common ancestry in central Asia, was difficult to come by, primarily because of the Shi'a–Sunni divide dating back to the Safavid period. Furthermore, there were territorial disputes over Iraq, which had already resulted in military confrontation on two occasions, and finally, an age-old animosity between the two, each viewing the other as inferior. Nevertheless, by 1810, and because of a deadlock in negotiations with Tormazov and British efforts to bring the two together, a treaty of alliance was signed. War flared up again in the summer of 1810.[cxlvii]

In January 1810, there were a number of anti-Russian rebellions in Russian-occupied territories. Sheikh Ali Khan of Qobbeh and Darband rebelled in lower Daghestan and Qobbeh with the aid of the Lezgis, and attempted to capture his former territory. At the same time, Iskandar Mirza led a rebellion in Georgia. This was a good opportunity for Abbas Mirza to attack Russia, but winter weather, slow mobilization, and hesitation prevented it, as the Russian army defeated both rebellions. In 1810, the Ottoman Empire was at war with Russia on two fronts: the Balkans and the Caucasus. The Ottoman army maintained a defensive posture in the Caucasus while trying to ward off Russian advances in the Balkans. In early summer, a joint Ottoman–Iranian attack on Russia from Qars was stopped; the Iranian commander, Sardar Iravani, suffered heavy losses and a Russian siege of the Ottoman fortress of Akhalsikh failed.[cxlviii] A British officer's assessment of Iran's military after five years of modern training and equipment is telling. After praising regular Iranian soldiers for their bravery and endurance, he wrote: "Unfortunately all these advantages were neutralized by the total want of military talent in Abbas Mirza and his chiefs, not one of whom was capable of commanding in action or of forming a consistent plan of operation."[cxlix]

By the summer of 1811, Major General Nicolas E. Rtishchev had taken command of Russian forces in the region. In February 1812, an 800-man Russian detachment with two cannons set up a post at Sultanabad (sometimes referred to as Sultanbout), north of the Aras. Abbas Mirza surrounded this force with a 9,000-man force of his own. The Russians did not take the Iranian threat seriously and failed to either retreat from the post or ask for help from Shusha. After heavy bombardment by the Iranian army, the Russian detachment surrendered at the cost of 300 dead and 500 captured. Interestingly, as part of the conditions for their surrender, the Russian commander asked for and received a promise from Abbas Mirza that there would not be any decapitation. All non-Iranian sources agree that Iranian sources, beginning with Abbas Mirza and Mirza Shafi', exaggerated the importance of this battle and inflated the numbers. Nevertheless, the Battle of Sultanabad was a minor victory for the crown prince.[cl] In March 1812, Russian forces briefly and unsuccessfully crossed to the south of the River Aras and their brutality gave the local population a taste of heavy-handed Russian occupation.[cli] These events started a new round of intense fighting between the two sides as war between Russia and France loomed. The British ambassador, Gore Ouseley, did his best to calm the situation for its new Russian ally. Russia also wanted to end the hostilities in the Caucasus, in order to be able to deal with the French threat. Hence, it made a hasty peace with the Ottoman Empire in May 1812, returning all captured territory. However, as negotiations between Iran and Russia were still ongoing, skirmishes and artillery duels between the two resumed in late July to October 1812, at a time when Napoleon's Grand Army was preparing to invade Russia.

Nevertheless, the First Russo-Iranian War came to an end after Iran's defeat in October 1812 at Aslanduz and in January 1813 at Lankaran. At Aslanduz, despite warnings by British officers to post guards to prevent Russian raids, Abbas Mirza neglected to do so. This gave Russian commander Kotlyarevskiithe opportunity to surprise the Iranians twice, and inflict heavy casualties and take much of Abbas Mirza's artillery. The Battle of Aslanduz forced Abbas Mirza to retreat toward Tabriz, which gave time to the Russian commander to attack Lankaran in Talesh. Lankaran had fallen to the Qajar army in September, after Mustafa Khan, its ruler, once again sided with Russia. Abbas Mirza had chased the remnants of Russian forces and khan loyalists to an island off Talesh. He then fortified the fortress of Lankaran and ordered the building of two smaller forts near the city. The Russian commander now attacked Lankaran and after a bloody battle, it fell. A 5,000-man Nezam force defending Lankaran, including its brave commander Sadeq Khan Az al-Dinllu, perished; the rest, mostly militia, fled the city and returned home.[clii]

By the time the Treaty of Golestan was signed in October 1813, a clear division had appeared between Tehran and Tabriz on the assessment and extent of the Russian threat. The court of Tehran had the final word in accepting the treaty. The shah accepted defeat in light of British pressure and promises, real financial problems, and military challenges elsewhere. Indeed, the shah, advised by Mirza Shafi' and others, reluctantly accepted this arrangement hoping, somewhat naively, that the British as mediator with the tsar could get him a better deal. As to why the shah accepted peace with Russia, one observer suggested that Iranian political leaders lacked a full understanding of the international situation and put their trust in British ambassador Ouseley's promise to lobby to get some of the occupied territories back.[cliii] There was certainly a degree of naivete involved in the decision-making process when it came to trusting the British ambassador. However, the picture is more complicated. As noted, Mirza Shafi', who advocated signing the treaty, was known to be better informed about European politics than others at the court of Tehran. He had already concluded that the war with Russia was not winnable, and in persuading the shah to accept peace with Russia, he may have wanted to prevent further loss of territory. There were a number of internal rebellions and financial problems as well.

In Tabriz, Crown Prince Abbas Mirza and his chief minister Qa'em Maqam I were against signing the treaty and voiced confidence in Iran's ability to regroup and continue the war. Indeed, between October 1812 and October 1813, the army of Azerbaijan had recovered in terms of both men and materials. A report suggests that by 1813, Abbas Mirza had more cannons than before Aslanduz, but that the morale of the army was low.[cliv] However, the shah overruled the Tabriz leaders.[clv] Abbas Mirza and Qa'em Maqam I had presided over the establishment of the modern force, which was mostly based in Azarbaijan and under Abbas Mirza's command. Although defeated in 1812 and 1813, the prince regent seems to have been confident in his own ability to continue the war. Both Tehran and Tabriz were displeased with the outcome of the war but apparently their conclusions were based on two conflicting assessments of Iran's ability to continue and more importantly of Russia's strength.

The Treaty of Golestan has eleven clauses and it confirmed the Russian annexation of occupied territories, which included: Daghiastan, Darband, Qobbeh, Shakki, Shirvan, Qarabagh, Badkubeh, Ganjeh, northern parts of Iravan (Shuregol), and the north and central part of Talesh, including Lankaran. Dispute remained between the two sides on the location of the demarcation in southern Talesh and southern Qarabagh (see Chapter 4). Russia recognized Fath Ali Shah as the legitimate ruler of Iran, something it had refused to do up to this point. Russia also accepted the line of succession in Fath Ali Shah's family, but the treaty did not make any mention of Abbas Mirza as the heir to the throne.[clvi]

Chapter 4

INTERWAR YEARS AND THE SECOND RUSSO-IRANIAN WAR

He [Ermolov] has been given the authority to declare war or maintain peace. Maybe one day he would conclude that our border with Iran is not definite and try to expand our border all the way to Aras, in which case I am not sure what will happen.
Alexander Griboyedov to Stephan Beguitchov, February 10, 1819[i]

The interwar years[ii]

The period between the First and Second Russo-Iranian Wars, 1813–25, provided more opportunity for interaction between Iran and the outside world. The first diplomatic exchange with Russia led by Mirza Abu al-Hasan Khan Shirazi the Ilchi (ambassador) was a mission to ratify the Golestan Treaty and to negotiate the return of some of the lost territories. The mission lasted three years (1813–16) due to the absence of Tsar Alexander I, who was preoccupied dealing with Napoleon. The Ilchi mission was chronicled by a younger member of the mission named Mirza Muhammad Hadi Alavi-shirazi and provided the Iranian elite with the opportunity to examine Russia more closely than ever before.

The chronicle is a mixture of everyday mundane events and detailed observation of Russian society. It presents the reader with a conflicting attitude toward Russia, which may be attributed to the different levels of understanding of Russia held by Ilchi and his younger assistant. As a seasoned diplomat and one who had been known to have pro-British views, Ilchi had developed a lifelong dislike for the Russians. Furthermore, his observations on Russia and Russians was in line with his generation's attitude: that the Russians were brutes and unclean. The chronicle complains about a variety of Russian characteristics, from Russian washroom hygiene to the "dominant" status of Russian women in society.[iii] However, the author also shows a fascination with the state of Russian cities, opera houses, factories, etc. One underlying theme in this document is the author's fascination with "order" in Russian society, and his observation that everything, from cities to governmental organizations, was properly organized.[iv]

Another visitor to Russia, a younger man, had a more positive impression. Mirza Saleh Shirazi spent some time in Moscow and St. Petersburg on his way to Britain as part of Abbas Mirza's first group of students sent abroad in 1815. Mirza Saleh's account is in general more detailed and accurate than the previous document, which points to the observant mind of its author. The author takes it upon himself to provide the reader with a detailed account of Russian history, society, and social organization. He notes similarities between Russia's despotic form of government and Iran's political system, but he was impressed with Russian efficiency in general and showed much admiration for Peter I.[v]

Most notably, and similarly to the previous document, Mirza Saleh was impressed with Russian "order," both in the organization of centers of learning (Moscow University and library) and the efficiency of the police force.[vi]

Mirza Saleh was one student of a total of eleven, sent by Abbas Mirza to learn modern technology, medicine, and languages. These students were to mainly engage in military-related education, such as weapons production, engineering, printing, etc. Upon their return, the state offered them titles and comfortable jobs.[vii] Limited as it was, sending students abroad was a follow-up to the Nezam military reforms, and the first program of its kind in Iran. Nile Green's colorful work on the cultural encounters these students had with early nineteenth-century British society contains many interesting episodes. However, perhaps none are more amusing than the cultural encounters over gender relations. While describing the many "spectacles" the first group of students encountered in England, he wrote:

> Not least among the "spectacles" that struck the students was a hall in which they saw men, women, and girls mixing gaily and freely, enjoying each another's company unashamedly in public. It was something that the students had never seen in Iran, at least among the respectable classes; the different morality of public space would be one of their earliest and least expected lessons.[viii]

The relationship between Iran and Russia began to take a turn for the worse after the 1816 appointment of General Alexis Petrovich Ermolov as commander-in-chief of Georgia with jurisdiction over all of the Russian-occupied Caucasus and ambassador-extraordinary to the court of Tehran. As such, he commanded the Independent Georgia Corps with considerable autonomy as to how to deal with the local population and with Iran. Ermolov is on the record as one of the more brutal Russian officers in charge of the Russian-occupied Caucasus and perhaps the single most instrumental figure in causing the second war between Russia and Iran. Pushkin, as well as other Russian poets, had written poems praising him and his heavy-handed rule over the Caucasus. Pushkin wrote: "Bow down thy head, oh, Caucasus: submit; Yermoloff comes."[ix] He has been described as a Spartan, an honest man, but also as rude and cruel.[x] He openly expressed his wish to unleash terror on the region in order to secure submission.[xi] Known as "Yermol" to the locals, his central strategy was to bring all of the Caucasus, both Ottoman and Iranian territories, under Russian control. Ermolov traveled to Iran in 1817 and visited both Tabriz and Tehran. His visit to Tabriz immediately created friction with Abbas Mirza and Qa'em Maqam I. Members of his entourage, such as Moritz von Kotzebue, had a negative view of Qa'em Maqam I.[xii]

Prelude to war

On June 12, 1826, when Fath Ali Shah Qajar arrived at the pasture of Sultanieh at the head of the imperial army, intense lobbying had already started for and against escalation of hostilities with Russia. The shah's move from Tehran to Sultanieh (near Zanjan, west of Tehran) usually took about twelve days and was part of the monarch's annual routine of seeking a cooler climate away from the summer heat of Tehran, and an opportunity to gather part of the army in one place for military drills. However, that year's gathering at Sultanieh (also referred to as the Council of Sultanieh) was happening at a particularly tense period in relations between Iran and Imperial Russia. Russian policy in the Russian-occupied southeastern Caucasus throughout the 1820s, Russian border incursions in 1825, and political tensions in St. Petersburg in late 1825 had caused much excitement and agitation in Iran. With the arrival of a group of top members of the ulama (*mujtaheds*) from various parts of Iran and Iraq, Crown Prince Abbas Mirza Qajar from Tabriz, and the Russian envoy Prince Alexander S. Menshikov by early July, the stage was set for making the final decision. The problem of what to do about Russia in this moment of crisis depended greatly on how serious Russian incursions into the shah's guarded domain (*mamalek-e mahruseh*) were, as well as how events in Russia were understood in Iran. How serious were Russia's provocations? This question is often either left out of studies of the second war with Russia or not given enough attention. How badly were the Russians treating the Muslim population of the occupied territories? How much difficulty did Russia face in its handling of ongoing rebellions in the Caucasus? How weak had Russia become after the accession of the new tsar Nicolas I Romanov (the Iron Tsar), followed by the Decembrist rebellion? How did various interest groups in the shah's court understand these developments? There are various, and at times conflicting, analyses by contemporary observers and later historians as to why the Second Russo-Iranian War broke out. A majority of these observers blame the Iranian side for starting the war but differ on the extent to which one or another Iranian player was responsible. This chapter will revisit the Second Russo-Iranian War and reexamine its root causes, various policy differences—both in St. Petersburg and Tehran as well as Tiflis and Tabriz—and the perceptions of each side about the motives and developments of the other. Finally, the role of actual perpetrators of the war will be discussed in detail.

In terms of the "blame game," the official Russian and pro-Russian narrative has blamed Iran for starting the war and pointed to British influence in convincing the shah to open hostilities. According to this narrative, it was Iran which had breached the arrangements of the Treaty of Golestan (1813), thus provoking Russia into occupying the Lake Gokcha (Sivan) territory leading to the crisis of 1825, which then led to war the next year. Furthermore, this genre of historiography has suggested that because of their influence over Prince Regent Abbas Mirza, British diplomats managed to influence Iranian policymakers and promote the war option.[xiii] Accounts of the two wars with Russia written by local Muslim historians of the Caucasus region follow the above narrative. These historians were those who in effect collaborated with the Russians.[xiv] Even Soviet era historical studies of this period go a long way to claim British influence in the outbreak of the war and to put the blame on the Qajar court of Tehran. One such study claims, without providing much evidence: "The English not only encouraged Iran to start a war with Russia, but also prepared the Iranians for the conflict in every way they could including with military and financial aid."[xv]

Qajar period Iranian sources, on the other hand, blame the Russians for starting the war by illegally occupying the northern shore of Lake Gokcha (Sivan) in 1825 and then trying to dictate terms to Iran during the follow-up negotiations. Mirza Abu al-Qasem Farahani, Qa'em Maqam II best captured the Iranian line of argument in his letter to an unknown British diplomat.[xvi] Here, Qa'em Maqam II explains the nature of the territorial dispute between Russia and Iran dating back to the Treaty of Golestan (1813). According to him, the ceasefire of 1813 and the subsequent Treaty of Golestan were based on *status que praesentem*, which meant that each side would remain in possession of territories under their control pending future negotiations. According to Qa'em Maqam II, the Russians broke this agreement by unilaterally occupying some territory in Talesh (south of the line of ceasefire) after signing the treaty. In addition, endless negotiations had been going on over Iranian control of a territory in the southern part of the Khanate of Qarabagh (the territory between Qapan [Kapan], toward the southwest, to Moqri [Meghri], just north of the River Aras). It was presumably in exchange for this territory that the Russians had unilaterally occupied the Gokcha territory, triggering the crisis. Other Iranian sources of the Qajar period follow Qa'em Maqam II's narrative and blame the Russians. Where these sources differ is whom to blame for the escalation of the confrontation. In this context, some blame the ulama for pressuring the shah, while others blame the deposed immigrant khans of Russian-occupied Caucasian territories, and yet others the shah and the prince regent.[xvii]

Iranian observers and historians of the Pahlavi period exclusively blame the Qajar court for the outbreak of the war. Those blamed include Fath Ali Shah, or the prince regent, or both, as well as the ulama. This genre of writings shows much disregard for historical facts and context when dealing with this subject.[xviii] In this context, Sa'id Nafisi at one point goes as far as blaming the shah and the court of Tehran for the outbreak of war while exonerating Abbas Mirza, while at another point in the same volume he blames the prince regent for the outbreak of hostilities.[xix] Homa Nateq's view on the causes of the war puts the blame entirely on the Qajar court as well. She argues that the British played a significant role in encouraging the Iranians to open hostilities. Interestingly, while the author dismisses Russian provocations, she remains unfazed by the fact that the chief British diplomat in Iran was against the war and did all he could to discourage the Iranians from responding in kind to Russian provocations. The fact that the new British representative, George Macdonald, the person Nateq accuses of promoting war between Iran and Russia, arrived at the shah's camp after hostilities had already started, does not seem to change her impression of the root causes of the conflict.[xx]

The voice of British policy in Iran before the outbreak of the second war was the chargé d'affaires in Tehran, Henry Willock. His meticulous note-taking in his diary and in the reports he sent to London has left a wealth of information on the day-to-day development of the crisis from his perspective. Willock also translated into English correspondence between various parties. These letters were either given to him by Iranian officials to view and translate or were acquired by what seems to be his extensive network of spies at the court of Tehran. It should be noted that since 1814, the British Empire had committed itself, both militarily and financially, to the defense of Iran against Russia. For British commitment to go into full effect, it was stipulated that aggression against Iran had to be started by the other side. This meant that if Iran started hostilities against Russia, the British government was free of all treaty obligations. Hence, Britain had no real interest in igniting a war between Iran and Russia and actually did its best to prevent it. In addition, in order not to adhere to its treaty commitments toward Iran, the British had real interest in pressuring the shah to give unilateral concessions and if that did not work, in accusing Iran of initiating the war, thus freeing Britain of any treaty commitment.

As representative of British government at the court of Tehran, Willock was against the war and blamed Abbas Mirza for its outbreak.[xxi] He also made it clear to the shah that British policy was against the war.[xxii] In his audience with the shah at Camp Sultanieh and in the presence of Ilchi the foreign minister, Willock advised the shah that in his opinion he should settle his border dispute with Russia in a definitive manner even if it meant some sacrifice on his part. He also noted that the Russian treatment of Muslims under their control did not warrant war and advised the shah to stop the approach of top ulama to his court. Finally, he advised the shah that he should prepare to open negotiations with the approaching Russian envoy, Prince Menshikov.[xxiii] Interestingly, Willock rather clearly admitted that Russia had initiated hostilities by "forcefully" occupying the Gokcha territory.[xxiv] In his study of the causes of Iran's second war with Russia, P. W. Avery rejects Willock's assertion that the prince regent was responsible for the outbreak of the war but then adds, "He [Abbas Mirza] tried to keep a precarious balance between peace and war, but nearer war than peace. Circumstances went beyond his control and he lost this balance."[xxv] However, as we shall see, Avery's assertion does not pass the test of available evidence.

Russian policy toward the southeastern Caucasus

After the end of the first war, St. Petersburg gave a free hand to Ermolov to pursue Russia's strategic plans for the region. As noted by Griboyedov (above), Ermolov's independent command in Tiflis put him in a powerful position to improvise policy if he wished to do so. After signing the Treaty of Golestan, the shah's hope was that with the help of the British, Russia would make some concessions and return to Iran some of the lost territories. However, any hope of Russian concession or goodwill or the ability of the British to intercede on behalf of Iran came to nothing with the ambassadorial mission of Mirza Abu al-Hasan Khan Shirazi Ilchi to the court of St. Petersburg. The mission lasted nearly three years (1814–16) and was designed to ratify the Golestan Treaty and to negotiate the return of some of the lost territories. Qa'em Maqam I's observation upon the return of the Ilchi mission was telling and provided a window into the thinking of Qajar policymakers. He observed "that not only had Persia nothing to expect from the generosity or forbearance of Russia, but that further encroachments in that quarter were to be dreaded."[xxvi] Ermolov used territorial disputes to bring about a new round of conflict, as his aggressiveness did not help settle the issue and prolonged negotiations failed to produce results.

Ermolov traveled to Iran in 1817 and visited both Tabriz and Tehran. His visit to Tabriz immediately created friction with Abbas Mirza and Qa'em Maqam I—a bitterness which was both mutual and enduring. The Russian general refused to observe court protocol, treating the crown prince with a condescending attitude and refusing to recognize him as heir-apparent while establishing contact with his half-brother and chief rival Muhammad Ali Mirza Dowlatshah. In addition, the general added more friction by demanding the return of Russian deserters employed in the Iranian military.[xxvii] Ermolov's own recollection makes clear at least one of the reasons for the mutual dislike: "The shah was generous in his praise and no one dared contradict him. Crown Prince Abbas Mirza, however, did not like me because I refused to recognize him as heir to the throne finding nothing beneficial for us, though my instructions stipulated this."[xxviii] The following exchange between him and Qa'em Maqam I is a good example of the deteriorating relationship between Russia and Iran after Ermolov's tenure began. In answering Ermolov's question as to why the prince regent was continuing to build up his military defenses, Mirza Bozorg answered: "To repel any further aggression attempted by your government, or any state."[xxix]

When visiting the shah in Tehran, Ermolov's attitude was only different in that he showed respect to Fath Ali Shah, but he displayed "limitless arrogance" toward other court officials and refused to observe court procedures.[xxx] He refused the shah's rather naive request of partial reinstatement of Iranian rule over the lost territories and only offered minor concessions, prompting Abbas Mirza to make the following remark: "Your mission appears to have had no object, except that of presenting us with some glass and china."[xxxi] The general would spend the rest of his tenure until 1827 subduing the occupied population and preparing the ground for annexation of the rest of the southeastern Caucasus. According to one observation, "Yermoloff's central idea was that the whole of the Caucasus must, and should, become an integral part of the Russian Empire."[xxxii] This view was very much in line with that of Catherine II's court when hostilities over the Caucasus began.

After the Russian mission returned to Tiflis, Alexander Griboyedov remained behind to continue to demand and arrange for the return of ex-Russian soldiers in Abbas Mirza's employment. His observations about the state of relations between Iran and Russia, as quoted above, show him as a keen observer of the developments that led to the second war. Nevertheless, his relations with Abbas Mirza in Tabriz soon deteriorated over the ex-Russian soldiers. The Russian diplomat held extensive negotiations with the crown prince as he insisted some of the ex-soldiers wanted to go back. However, when Samson Khan, Abbas Mirza's trusted commander, entered the room, Griboyedov's rude behavior prompted the crown prince to stop and ask him to leave and not return. After this incident, on their return trip to Tiflis, their Iranian hosts all the way from Tabriz to Tiflis treated the Russian party poorly.[xxxiii] On his return trip to Iran in 1820, Griboyedov made the following remarks to an acquaintance:

> Prince Abbas Mirza, of whom we have presently the honor to be guests, and I must add he is my enemy, has hired weapons and leather, and other specialists from London, and wants to establish a college. He has a minister named Mirza Bozorg Qa'em Maqam [I] who is an enemy of Russia and under no circumstance wants to see a close relation between Iran and Russia.[xxxiv]

Another reason for the worsening of relations with Russia was ambiguities in territorial demarcation in the Treaty of Golestan, a problem that was left to future negotiations. Both the Iranians and the Russians were displeased with the treaty. The Russians had accepted Golestan only as a temporary arrangement, as their strategic plan for new borders with Qajar Iran had always centered around the River Aras. On the other hand, for Aras to become the new border Russia had to annex the two remaining khanates of Iravan and Nakhjavan.

By all accounts, Ermolov was a capable administrator and military leader, but he was also brutal and cruel, especially when it came to dealing with the local population. He also dealt with Iran in a condescending manner, and held all Muslims in contempt. Perhaps the most important legacy of Ermolov was his intention from early on to prepare the ground to conquer the remaining khanates under Iranian rule and make the River Aras the border. As has been noted, this task was part of an overall Russian imperial ambition and to accomplish it, Ermolov adopted a policy of provoking conflict with Iran accompanied by employment of force if necessary. As part of this strategy, during his tenure pressure on the Muslim population of the occupied Caucasus increased. The pressure included implementing direct Russian rule on some of the khanates by removing the autonomous khans who had sided with Russia during the first war, substituting Shari'a law with Russian law and undermining the position of the Muslim ulama, and finally by favoring the Christian population over the Muslim peoples of the region.[xxxv]

There seems to have been a degree of policy disagreement between Tiflis and the court of St. Petersburg concerning how to deal with Iran during the interwar years. Correspondence between Ermolov and the Russian Foreign Ministry and with Tsar Alexander I provides a window into the depth and roots of the differences. The nature of the differences seems to have been tactical rather than strategic. The primary focus of Ermolov's strategy regarding Iran appears to have been neutralizing the court of Tabriz under Abbas Mirza and Qa'em Maqam I. This was because the court of Tabriz was in charge of governing and defending Azarbaijan and the remaining southeastern Caucasian territories of Iran, and of diplomatic dealings with Russia through Tiflis. Hence, Ermolov essentially viewed the court of Tabriz as the prime threat to Russian imperial ambition in the region and weakening Abbas Mirza's position in Iran became a key aspect of the general's policy. In his correspondence with the Russian foreign minister Count Karl Nesselrode, the general reported on his diplomatic trip to Iran in 1817 and presented Abbas Mirza as a reformer who was rapidly improving the armed forces to challenge Russian power in the region once again. He did not consider the crown prince as a progressive figure, but as one who promoted reforms to consolidate his own power against his rivals.[xxxvi]

It seems the Iranians tried their best to show off the strength and readiness of their army as a way to impress the Russian envoy and perhaps to deter Russia.[xxxvii] However, there seems to be a degree of exaggeration in Ermolov's assessment of how rapid and effective Abbas Mirza's military reforms were. Only a few years later another observer of the prince regent's military had a different impression of its state of readiness. In his observation of the military and the arsenal in Tabriz, in the middle of a war with the Ottoman Empire in 1822, James Fraser wrote about the inadequacies of weapons, disorganized state of factories and "the sorry state of pay for soldiers."[xxxviii] The exaggeration could have been because the Iranians put on a convincing show, or it could have been because Ermolov needed to impress his superiors and convince them of a more aggressive policy toward Iran as well as the allocation of more men and materials to his command. The second scenario fits well with Ermolov's desire to use his powerful position in Tiflis to steer Russian policy toward Tehran rather than being a simple executor of policy emanating from the Russian Foreign Ministry.

Ermolov also reported on how he refused to recognize Abbas Mirza as heir-apparent, and how he antagonized both the crown prince and Qa'em Maqam I on a variety of other issues including overtly and secretly making contact with Abbas Mirza's half-brother and chief rival Dowlatshah. The Russian foreign minister admonished him for his secret contact with Dowlatshah, proposed a more moderate approach, and asked Ermolov to be more accommodating toward the shah.[xxxix] Overall, it seems that as long as Alexander I was alive, Ermolov could feel safe in playing a cat and mouse game with St. Petersburg without putting his own safety and job in jeopardy.

The year 1825 was pivotal and holds a significance place in the narrative of the Second Russo-Iranian War. In 1823, Iran proposed to establish a joint commission to study the border issues between Iran and Russia in the southeastern Caucasus and to propose guidelines for a final demarcation. The commission's work was at an impasse by 1825. Hence, in early 1825 Ermolov escalated hostilities with Iran by ordering the occupation of an area in the northwest sector of Lake Gokcha (Sivan), a territory clearly on the Iranian side of the border. Some historians have wrongly suggested that the occupied territory had been under Russian control since 1813 and was a subject of negotiation between Iran and Russia over border demarcation.[xl] This was not the case, as the exchange between a Russian general and the governor of Qarabagh sometime after 1813 shows that the Russians were asking Abbas Mirza for permission to allow the tribes under their rule to spend the summers around Lake Gokcha for use of the pasture.[xli] Another observer has noted that Ermolov ordered "guards on the Persian territory at the northern and southern extremities of the Lake of Gokcha."[xlii]

The year 1825 was also when Tsar Alexander I, Ermolov's chief benefactor, died and was succeeded by his younger brother, Nicolas I, followed by the Decembrist rebellion. In his correspondence with Alexander I on July 25, 1825, Ermolov once again asked for military preparedness in the Caucasus to prepare for the presumed Iranian threat. Alexander's reply on September 12 pointed to the core policy difference between Tiflis and St. Petersburg, as the monarch told his commander that based on the information available to him, it was hard to believe that the shah was getting ready to start a war over the lost Caucasian territories.[xliii] Interestingly, at the end of the tsar's letter, he ordered Ermolov to maintain peace while at this very time the general had already commenced the occupation of the Gokcha territory. The fact that there is no mention of this occupation and the negotiations that had been going on between Tabriz and Tiflis in correspondence between the general and the tsar suggests that Ermolov did not report on all the developments, perhaps as part of his overall plan to provoke a conflict with Iran. On the other hand, the fact that Ermolov was able to carry on his own strategy despite hesitation and even direct orders from St. Petersburg opposing any provocative act, points to his special position and his relationship with Tsar Alexander I. It seems that the general had the trust of the tsar, who allowed him to maintain a high degree of autonomy in making decisions with regard to his jurisdiction. The policy of providing Ermolov with considerable independent decision-making power was clearly emanated from the court of St. Petersburg and cannot be separated from overall Russian policy toward Iran. Ermolov would lose his special relationship with the court of St. Petersburg upon Alexander's death in December 1825, and eventually his command with the accession of Nicolas I and the Decembrist rebellion.

It is clear that the north and southeast territory around Lake Gokcha came under Russian occupation in spring 1825 as a unilateral and provocative act on Ermolov's part. Despite all his differences with the court of Tehran, the British chargé d'affaires in Tehran, Henry Willock, admitted to Russian aggressive behavior in this case.[xliv] Furthermore, occupation of this territory was a clear violation of the Treaty of Golestan and was the most significant provocation to date by the Russian side. By all accounts, the occupied territory was not inhabited at this time and had no material value in terms of tax revenue or otherwise.[xlv] However, it would have given Russia access and legal claim to the lake and was seemingly a valuable military position for further incursion into the Khanate of Iravan. At any rate, the Iranian side viewed the Russian occupation as a direct threat to its territorial integrity. Initially, the court of Tabriz was in charge of negotiating with Tiflis over the new point of dispute, and as such, Abbas Mirza dispatched Fath Ali Khan Fumeni, the governor (*biglerbeigi*) of Tabriz, to negotiate with Ermolov in the spring of 1824. In a letter to Ilchi, the shah's newly appointed foreign minister, Abbas Mirza reported on the return of his envoy, and that his envoy had been received well, but that the Russians' position had hardened and that the Gokcha area was under Russian occupation. He suggested that if Tehran accepted the Russian demand on ceding Gokcha territory, negotiations would move forward. The shah rejected any such concession. Finally, Abbas Mirza reported that he (Abbas Mirza) had not breached the Treaty of Golestan, but that the Russians were threatening Iran with military action.[xlvi] The appointment of Fath Ali Khan Fumeni as chief negotiator was a problematic choice. Although he had lived most his life in Tabriz, his father was killed by Aqa Muhammad Shah during the upheavals of the 1780s, which made his loyalty suspect. Griboyedov considered him, his two sons, and the rest of his family to be pro-Russia elements in Tabriz.[xlvii] In early 1825, he returned to Tiflis and signed an accord handing over the Gokcha territory in exchange for the Qapan/Moqri territory in southwestern Qarabagh, which Iran held.[xlviii] As noted, this was a territory under Iranian control but in dispute between Iran and Russia since 1813, with no resolution in sight. The signing of the accord maybe characterized as a major diplomatic failure on the part of the Qajar state, which failed to treat relations with Russia as a most delicate matter. Hence, instead of appointing a seasoned diplomat to negotiate with Tiflis, the responsibility was given to the court of Tabriz, which then made the most unfortunate decision in appointing Fath Ali Khan. Nevertheless, as protocol had it, no negotiated settlement was final until ratified by the sovereigns of both sides. The final ratification of the Treaty of Golestan, for example (signed in 1813) was completed in 1817 after further negotiations and back-and-forth diplomatic missions. Similarly, an agreement with Britain during Harford Jones Brydges' mission in 1810 was not finalized until 1814, after going through revision. This time around, however, Ermolov contended that the agreement was final and could only be revised at the pleasure of the tsar. In his letter to the Iranian foreign minister, dated March 1825, Ermolov contended that Fath Ali Khan had negotiated with full power to resolved the border disputes, and that the territory acquired by Iran was worth much more than the Gokcha territory acquired by Russia, and finally that this agreement put an end to the territorial disputes dating back to Golestan.[xlix] This act was an unprecedented breach of diplomatic protocol and nothing short of a diktat by the Russian general to the shah of Iran. As expected, the shah did not ratify the treaty and the Russians refused to evacuate the territory, thus creating the most important crisis in Russo-Iranian relations since 1813.

Interestingly, when discussing the Qapan/Moqri territory, which the Russians had made into an important point of contention since 1813, they did not even seem to know the region and its geography well. In their correspondence the Russians kept referring to the area "between the two rivers" which were then identified as "Kapan" and "Kapanik Chay." As Qaem Maqam II's letter indicated, there was no river by the name of "Kapanik Chay" and the Russians were probably referring to a small river near the settlement of Moqri.[1]

The above developments suggest that the Russian occupation of the Gokcha territory and the follow-up negotiations were stage-managed by Ermolov in line with his policy of provoking Iran into either a war or capitulation, which would then have staged the scene for further expansion in the region. The occupation of Gokcha in spring 1825 was in fact the beginning of the second war with Russia, some year and a half before actual combat started in the summer of 1826. The Qajar court would spend this period trying to prevent an all-out war by attempting to get Ermolov to compromise. However, events in Russia and perceptions in Iran made finding a solution rather difficult.

Russian and Iranian officials spent the rest of 1825 in increasingly angry correspondence with the tone of letters becoming more undiplomatic, pointing to rapidly deteriorating relations. Fath Ali Shah took charge of the situation after the late March 1825 signing of the treaty in Tiflis. In October 1825, he dispatched a confidential officer named Safi Khan to the Gokcha region to report on the situation. His assessment was that most Russian troops had left but that the Russian pickets remained in place and the occupation had not ended.[li] Next, the shah ordered his envoy, Mirza Sadeq Khan Marvazi, to leave for Georgia. The envoy left Tabriz on October 23, arriving in Tiflis on November 23 and immediately opening negotiations. However, as General Ermolov had left Tiflis to take command of a new war in Daghestan, Sadeq Khan conducted negotiations with his next in command, General Wilhelmov, until December 1, 1825. Sadeq Khan was apparently treated poorly by the Russians, a clear insult to the shah.[lii] Negotiations did not go far, but they gave Sadeq Khan a chance to assess the situation in Tiflis, the nerve center of Russian operations in the Caucasus. For example, he reported that Ermolov was defeated in Daghestan and had lost many guns.[liii]

Negotiations came to an end in December with the news of the tsar's death and the Decembrist revolt. Willock translated the text of a letter written by General Wilhelmov to the shah in early 1826, perhaps delivered to the shah by Sadeq Khan who returned to Tehran in March 1826. This letter provides a comprehensive and definitive view of the Russian position from the vantage point of Tiflis. In the letter, the Russian general told the shah that Iran had been in illegal occupation of the Qapan/Moqri region and that the swap of land would settle a territorial dispute dating back to Golestan, and finally that if Iran wanted the Gokcha territory evacuated, he was authorized to order evacuation but only after Iran handed over the Qapan/Moqri territory.[liv] Interestingly, in January 1826, the new tsar Nicolas I wrote a letter to Ermolov emphasizing the need to maintain peace with Iran based on the Golestan Treaty. Furthermore, the tsar noted the delicate situation in Europe and problems with the Ottoman Empire (the Greek War of Independence), and asked for any dispute with Iran to be resolved rather than be allowed to escalate to the point of breakdown of relations.[lv] Ermolov however moved in the opposite direction and started to escalate hostilities with Iran. By the time Sadeq Khan had arrived in Tiflis, Russian forces had moved to occupy Balagh lu using their position on Gokcha as a staging ground. By the time of the Council of Sultanieh, in June 1826, the Russians had attacked and occupied Bash Aparan (Aparan) north of Iravan, deep inside Iranian territory.

Besides the above provocations, two more events played a crucial role in escalating confrontation between the two sides. First, news of the treatment of Muslims in the Russian-occupied Caucasus created a highly charged atmosphere in Sultanieh, where the court had moved to in June 1826. The treatment of the Muslim population was directly related to General Ermolov's contempt for Muslims and his high-handed treatment of them. After removing from power some of the uncooperative khans who had sided with Russia during the first war (e.g., the khans of Shiravan and Qarabagh), the general moved to subdue the remaining populations in the region, often causing uprisings, especially in the mountainous regions. One observer has noted that while under his command, the general state of the economy of occupied territories improved, but "We cannot say as much for the system pursued towards the population in general, for nothing could be more tyrannical than the manner in which they were treated, whether Christian or Mohamedans."[lvi] Some reports indicated the raping of Muslim women by Russian soldiers.^lvii Even if some of these reports were exaggerated or inaccurate, they created much excitement and rage in Iran. More importantly, cultural complications related to the above developments played a role in the escalation of hostilities. In an interesting conversation with Mirza Abd al-Vahhab, Mo'tamed al-Dowleh, and while trying to explain British policy toward conflict with Russia, Willock made mention of the treatment of Muslims under Russian occupation and noted that this was no concern of Iran's in accordance with Treaty of Golestan.^lviii

Here, Russian mistreatment of the Muslim population in the occupied territories should be viewed within the cultural and religious context of the period. This is important in order to understand the type of pressure exerted on Fath Ali Shah by the Shi'i religious establishment. In this context, while it was true that by treaty and by law, the shah of Iran no longer had jurisdiction over a Muslim population which had now become subject to the Russian tsar, it was also true that moral obligation, precedent, and religious duty, obligated the shah to take action if that population was being mistreated. Fath Ali Shah Qajar was not a mere king of the guarded domain of Iran, but also a protector of Muslims—in this case protector of a region whose population was mostly Shi'a Muslim. If the Shi'a community was threatened with harm in any place, be it the Ottoman Empire or the Wahhabi movement in Arabia, the Iranian shah was expected to react accordingly. Hence, even at the best of times, mistreatment of Muslims under Russian occupation was not something the shah could easily ignore.

The second set of events that played a role in escalating hostilities between the two sides involved the developments in Russia in December 1825, as understood in Iran. The death of Tsar Alexander I, the accession of his younger brother Nicolas I, and the breakout of Decembrist rebellion in support of Constantine, the older brother of Nicolas, all occurred in rapid succession in December 1825. The rebellion was led by liberal-leaning elements in the Russian army against the conservative-leaning military establishment. The rebels supported Constantine, whom they viewed as having liberal leanings, but also demanded a constitution and had other liberal reforms in mind. The new tsar was also less popular than his older brother, which helped the rebels. Nevertheless, Nicolas put down the rebellion with relative ease by the end of December 1825. These developments were a surprise to many Russians and those who observed Russian society. However, in Iran, where the country had no permanent resident ambassador in St. Petersburg, and where repeatedly information on Russian society was in short supply, developments in Russia were misinterpreted and misunderstood.

For Qajar Iran, with its history of tribal warfare, rivalry between brothers for the throne was a familiar and acceptable process of succession. Centuries of tribal/dynastic rule had established their own unique set of cultural habits. In this context, the assumption was that open warfare between contending brothers for the throne in one empire opened opportunities for others, even foreign actors, to take advantage of the situation. Put simply, from the cultural perspective of Qajar Iran, many Iranian political leaders could have and did interpret the Russian events as a point of weakness. Hence, they spied an opportunity that could be used to Iran's advantage at a point when Iran was clearly being bullied by the general in Tiflis. One observer of the time has suggested that "Just at that period intelligence arrived of the military revolt at St Petersburg, after the death of the Emperor Alexander: this revolt was magnified in Persia into a civil war."[lix] News of Ermolov's military setbacks and other uprisings in the region only strengthened this view. Therefore, while clearly some Iranian statesmen had some knowledge of what had happened in Russia in 1825, as attested by Willock, news and details were sketchy and many inaccuracies existed.[lx] Hence, an exaggerated sense of events in St. Petersburg and the Decembrist rebellion existed in Tehran and Tabriz, which fueled the position of those who argued for the escalation of hostilities with Russia.

Council of Sultanieh

Under the above circumstances, the June/July 1826 Council of Sultanieh found a special meaning and turned the council into an historical gathering. Also of importance was the expected arrival of Prince Menshikov, the new tsar's envoy to the court of Tehran, who presumably was not associated with Tiflis policymakers. The expectation was that the prince would arrive with new orders from the new tsar that would show Russian flexibility and/or a solution to the crisis, which would then help avert all-out war. Already two factions had formed in the shah's court over developing policy toward Russia. Both factions were engaged intensely in lobbying the shah and his chief military commander, the prince regent. The first issue at stake was what to do if Russia did not evacuate the occupied Gokcha and Balagh lu territories. By this time, the names "Gokcha" and "Balagh lu" had gained such prominence in Iran that one observer suggested "these names had been introduced into too many discussions and had become too notorious in Persia."[lxi] In addition, as noted earlier, by this time Russian forces under

Ermolov's command had used their position in Gokcha to make deep incursions into the rest of Iravan. Other secondary issues were the condition of the Muslim community under Russian rule, and finally whether and how much Russia had been weakened as the result of its internal problems.

The two factions may be named the "war party" or the hawks and the "peace party" or the doves. The hawks had powerful personalities among them. These included a number of high-ranking ulama led by Aqa Sayyed Muhammad (Mojahed) Isfahani and Allahyar Khan Devellu-Qajar Asef al-Dowleh, the shah's recently appointed chief minister (*sadr-e 'azam*), and the exiled khans of the southeastern Caucasus. These were either khans who were displaced due to Treaty of Golestan (1813), or those who had fled to Iran in the post-Golestan period. The immigrant khans had been given new duties in Iran but had remained in contact with their former dominions. Among them were Hosein Qoli Khan Badkubeh, the former khan of Baku, and his cousin Ibrahim Khan Badkubeh; Sultan Ahmad Khan of Darband and Qobbeh; Mustafa Khan Shirvani of Shirvan; and Mehdi Qoli Khan Javanshir of Qarabagh.[lxii] The war party's basic position was that clear insult and aggression had been committed by the Russians. In a letter to the shah, Aqa Sayyed Muhammad, the chief mujtahid of Iraq who was on his way to meet the shah, pointed to the Russian occupation of Iranian territory and mistreatment of Muslims and made mention of the shah's responsibilities, "both as Sovereign of Persia, and as the head of the Mohamedian faith." He then went on to make clear that he expected the shah to act in defense of his reign and the faithful.[lxiii] In addition, the war party's assessment of Russian events was more optimistic than realistic, and it maintained that Russia was in a weak position both generally and in the Caucasus in particular because of the recent defeats suffered by Ermolov and because of the December 1825 events in St. Petersburg. Finally, the hawks advised that the shah's cause was just and his army ready, and that his reign would not witness such an advantageous state of affairs again.[lxiv] Mention should also be made of a reluctant Mirza Abol Qasem Farahani, Qa'em Maqam II. He had inherited his father's honorific title and had become a close advisor to the prince regent. However, he also had many enemies at the court who accused him, and even his master Abbas Mirza, of being soft on the Russians. He had been removed from the court of Tabriz by the shah but now was asked to join others in Sultanieh. It seems, in order to save his own position and to ward off criticism, he had cautiously joined the war party.

The doves also boasted a number of powerful figures. These included Mirza Abd al-Vahhab Neshat Isfahani, Mo'tamed al-Dowleh, the shah's chief scribe (*monshi al-mamalek*) and head of the royal office; Manuchehr Khan Gorji (the Georgian), the shah's chief of protocol (*ishik aqasi bashi*); Mirza Abu al-Hasan Khan Shirazi Ilchi, the shah's foreign minister; and Mirza Saleh Shirazi, an influential diplomat and court translator. The peace party generally dreaded Russian power and preferred military confrontation to be avoided at all cost. The doves were men who had more interaction with the outside world and were better acquainted with Russia. Two among them, Mirza Saleh and Ilchi, had visited Russia and had firsthand experience. This faction had high hopes for the Menshikov mission and believed that with a little flexibility on the part of the tsar, war could be avoided. As Ilchi put it to Willock on July 9, 1826, two days before Menshikov's arrival at Sultanieh, if the Russians acted justly "matters might be concluded to the satisfaction of all parties."[lxv]

Any evaluation of Iranian attitudes toward events in Russia and the Russian-controlled Caucasus should perhaps pay a good deal of attention to the role of Prince Regent Abbas Mirza and the court of Tabriz, as well as to Fath Ali Shah and the court of Tehran. Regarding Abbas Mirza's role, as noted since the early years of Fath Ali Shah's reign, the court of Tabriz had acted as a junior partner to the shah's court, which explains Abbas Mirza's two titles of crown prince and prince regent. Tabriz had had more contact with the outside world and its officials were more aware of international events, and more reform-minded compared to the court of Tehran. The prince regent was in charge of the defense of the Caucasus and Azarbaijan, and was the effective commander-in-chief of the army in the first war with Russia and would be so again in the upcoming conflict. In this context, the importance of his decision as to what course of action to take was only second to that of his royal father. Together with his chief minister Mirza Bozurg Qa'em Maqam I, the 24- year old Abbas Mirza had been against the peace treaty of 1813 and believed he could regroup and continue the war despite major defeats in 1812 and early 1813. During the interwar years, he was in charge of dealing with Ermolov and his provocative activities. On the other hand, both Abbas Mirza and Qa'em Maqam I were accused by the hawks of being indecisive against Russian aggression. The choice of Fath Ali Khan and the treaty he had signed in Tiflis in 1825 was used as a case in point. However, as noted before, Ermolov and other Russians accused Abbas Mirza and the court of Tabriz of being under British influence. Willock blamed the prince regent for the outbreak of the war and asserted that he had joined the hawks just before arriving at Sultanieh.[lxvi] Willock's own diary records as early as June 25, 1826 that the 37-year-old Abbas Mirza dreaded war with Russia and that the army of Azarbaijan, the core of the Iranian forces, was not in a state of readiness.[lxvii] One would expect someone who had gone from dreading war in June to advocating war in July to have at least put his forces on alert. Clearly, fighting the Russians for a second time and losing for a second time could not have been advantageous to Abbas Mirza's position in Iranian politics. The prince regent's behavior suggests that he was a reluctant worrier to the end and did not belong to either of the two factions. It seems clear that Abbas Mirza entered Sultanieh with much apprehension regarding the wisdom of war with Russia and at the time, the hawks accused him of being hesitant.

As noted, P. W. Avery rejected Willock's conclusion in this regard but suggested that Abbas Mirza and Qa'em Maqam I (d.1822) had devised a policy toward Russia often referred to as maintaining a state of "no war, no peace." The purpose of this policy, according to Avery, was to keep the Russian threat real so that the flow of money from Tehran would remain undisturbed, thus helping to secure Abbas Mirza's position against competition from his brothers. This analysis is similar to Ermolov's impression of Abbas Mirza, namely that his reforms were meant to strengthen his own claim to power. Avery's analysis undervalues two important historical facts. First, the "Ermolov factor" is underrated, and it is assumed that if Abbas Mirza wanted to resolve all border disputes with the general, it could have been done. From this perspective, the "Russian threat" is viewed as "made up" by the court of Tabriz rather than being a real strategic menace, which Russian imperialism undoubtedly was. Knowing what we know about General Ermolov, Abbas Mirza could not have possibly resolved the border disputes with Russia, and neither could he have predicted or prevented the Gokcha occupation. Even when he sent Fath Ali Khan to negotiate a solution to the Gokcha occupation, the situation got worse. Furthermore, Avery concluded that Abbas Mirza's policy eventually backfired, as he was largely responsible for creating an atmosphere of agitation against Russia, a situation that in the end he did not manage to control. In this case, he is presumably thinking about events after the occupation of Gokcha in early 1825 to the end of July 1826, when full-scale combat began. In this context, in a letter to his son, the shah spelled out the steps he had taken in accordance with the prince regent's council. These included moving with the army to Sultanieh, providing money to Abbas Mirza, and allowing the ulama to approach the royal encampment.[lxviii]

Abbas Mirza's courting of the ulama has been interpreted as his hawkish support for war with Russia. One historian has summed up his behavior as "[After failure of negotiations and refusal to ratify the Tiflis agreement,] he was no less eager than the ulama in taking the final steps to war and many of these steps he in fact coordinated with them."[lxix] As the effective commander-in-chief in the case of all-out war, Abbas Mirza had to prepare and posture for combat. All of the mentioned steps were in line for preparing for war should peace efforts fail, and they point to Abbas Mirza's attempt at preparing the ground, even though it seems he failed to prepare his army. This is particularly true on writing to the ulama and soliciting their support as part of a campaign of bringing public opinion behind the cause, should it become necessary. This was a common practice of the period and had been done before, as for example during the first war with Russia. That the commander of the armed forces and the crown prince of Iran had taken steps to prepare the shah's dominion for war in case it broke out, cannot equate to Abbas Mirza either wanting war or creating a situation that led to war. It made much sense to show to the Russians and the arriving Russian envoy that the Qajar army, the royal court, and public opinion were ready to defend what the Iranian side considered rightfully belonging to them. Such readiness could have acted as deterrence at a time when Iranians thought Russia was in a weak position due to its internal problems. It is also worth noting that all these steps could have probably been undone had there been a resolution to the Gokcha crisis. Willock, recording from the journal of Colonel McNeill, a member of the British mission in Iran, noted the following conversation between him and Prince Menshikov: "McNeill then told Menshikov that if the land of Gokcha and Balaku [Balagh lu] were returned, then peace had a good chance but if they were retained forcibly by Russia, then war was a strong possibility."[lxx]

The position and attitude of Fath Ali Shah also needs to be noted. The shah had a special relationship with the prince regent and seems to have listened to what he and his court at Tabriz had to say. The shah was the ultimate decision-maker even as he allowed all parties to voice their opinions. Similar to his predecessor, Fath Ali Shah seems to have had some religious conviction and much respect for the ulama, which made the latter a strong voice at his court and for the hawks. Unlike his uncle and predecessor, the shah was not a notable military commander, although in his younger years he was known to have led his uncle's army into battle. Yet, in all the years of war with Russia he rarely joined the front, and with one exception, never took direct command of troops in the field. Fath Ali Shah also dreaded war with Russia and would have taken the extra step to prevent it if he had the choice. He seemed to be aware of the lack of preparedness of his son's military for a major confrontation. In his conversations with the shah, Willock encouraged compromise with the Russians and expressed high hopes for the Menshikov mission.[lxxi]

The shah had attempted to reason with Ermolov by writing to him and offering various solutions. These included returning to pre-Gokcha-crisis borders and negotiating any exchange of territory based on good faith and good neighborly relations. If that did not work, then the shah proposed the mediation of a third neutral party, presumably Britain.[lxxii] Tiflis refused all such offers. By summer 1826, the shah's assessment of the situation was that the Russians were looking for a pretext to go to war and that Iran was in no condition to fight. In addition, the shah expressed that he wanted a settlement but that the Russians pushed beyond their limits on the frontier and that Russia was set to destroy him.[lxxiii] Hence, the shah too was hopeful that the Russian envoy would bring enough good news of flexibility to ward off any escalation of the conflict. Only two days before Menshikov's arrival, on July 9, 1826, the shah is on record suggesting he would work toward a settlement with Russia if the Gokcha dispute could be resolved.[lxxiv]

Thus began in Sultanieh, in June and July 1826, a grand game of chess by two court factions to try to neutralize one another by jockeying for a better position and trying to convince the shah and Abbas Mirza to follow their respective advice. The shah spent the month of June and early July listening to various parties and contemplating his decision. By July 11, the Russian envoy had arrived at Sultanieh. His mission had originated in St. Petersburg and not Tiflis; therefore, his message came from Nicolas I and not Ermolov, which raised hope for a peaceful resolution of the conflict. The Russian envoy was well received during his stop in Tabriz, and left a good impression to the extent that Willock's hope for a conciliatory message and attitude from the court of St. Petersburg was high. In Tabriz, the envoy delivered a letter from the new tsar to the prince regent. The letter was vague and general in content and talked about orders given to the governor of Georgia about maintaining the interest of Russia while not upsetting relations with the neighbors. The letter left details of the tsar's message to be delivered by Menshikov in person.[lxxv] However Menshikov, who held a number of audiences with the prince regent, refused to provide any details. His refusal prompted Abbas Mirza to tell Willock on July 8, 1826 that while he was similarly hopeful that something good would come out of Menshikov's mission, he also had his doubts. Abbas Mirza further elaborated that in his conversations with the Russian envoy, Menshikov had insisted on the ratification of the 1825 agreement with Ermolov concerning the Gokcha occupation.[lxxvi]

Prince Menshikov arrived in Sultanieh with expensive gifts and a presumed olive branch, which strengthened the cause of the peace party. He had a public audience with the shah on July 13 where he presented the monarch with a letter from Tsar Nicolas I. The prince's mission was to calm the atmosphere and provide information about the transition of power in Russia. However, he was not given authority to offer anything of substance, or anything that would remotely solve the crisis.[lxxvii] Hence, he had nothing to offer regarding the crisis of Gokcha. As negotiations were going on, in came the news that a large Russian force had moved against Bash Aparan (Aparan), in the northern part of the Khanate of Iravan, and had captured the town on July 8, 1826.[lxxviii] This development at a time when the Russian envoy was conducting negotiations with the shah, plus the fact that the envoy had nothing of substance to present, added fuel to the flames in the tense and highly explosive atmosphere of Camp Sultanieh. While even a semblance of a resolution to the Gokcha dispute would certainly have gone a long way in calming the mood, the Russian ambassador could only offer the shah the best friendly wishes of the new tsar and some expensive gifts, while Russian forces expanded their zone of occupation. Negotiations with the envoy stopped at this point and Menshikov was sent on his way. But since he was still on Iranian territory when large-scale combat broke out, he was treated rather undiplomatically near the Russian border by his hosts in Iravan, who apparently managed to confiscate some of the gifts meant for the shah (but which were not accepted), and by the sardar of Iravan who wanted to arrest him.

The second war between Iran and Russia had already begun in 1825 with the Gokcha occupation and then the expansion of the Russian zone of control to Balagh lu and Bash Aparan by the summer of 1826. The Council of Sultanieh convened to advise the shah and develop policy in this regard, and it ultimately decided to open full-scale hostilities. The anti-war party at the shah's court was outmaneuvered by events out of its control. Ermolov, it seems, had achieved his goal of triggering a confrontation. Ironically, perhaps because he thought so lowly of Iranians, he expected them to capitulate and not fight back. The unprepared state of Russian forces partially explains why, despite having 35,000 troops under his command, Ermolov was initially caught off guard and had to order a retreat on all fronts.

The shah personally ordered various military units to attack from different directions under the overall command of Abbas Mirza. Local rebellions against Russian garrisons in Talesh, Ganjeh, Shirvan, Shakki, and other locations helped the Iranian cause. Despite impressive initial victories in the summer of 1826, the second war with Russia was ultimately a catastrophe for Iran and resulted in the loss of Iravan and Nakhjavan.

The Battlefield[lxxix]

The beginning of major combat, in summer 1826, initially went well for Iran, even though it seems Abbas Mirza's military was not ready for a major confrontation. The reason for this was twofold. First, despite pushing for war, Ermelov was involved in a conflict in Chechnya, and because of this his forces were not prepared for the conflict and were unable to face the upcoming challenge. A lack of preparedness was one of the reasons he would lose his command in 1827. Second, the Muslim population had had it with Russian occupation and mistreatment, and with the encouragement of their former rulers, they rebelled. The rebellions were successful in Shakki, Shirvan, Qarabagh (with the exception of Shusha), Talesh, and Ganjeh, where Russian garrisons were either expelled, or retreated, or waited for the main Iranian army to arrive and expel them. Rebellions in Qobbeh, Badkubeh, and Darband, as well as Georgia, either did not happen or were unsuccessful. Shirvan fell to the Iranian army, under the Qajar commander Ibrahim Khan Sardar and former khan of Shirvan, Mustafa Khan, as the population rebelled against the Russian army.[lxxx]

The war had already started on July 8 in the Khanate of Iravan, when a Russian force attacked and occupied Bash Aparan forcing Sardar Iravani's units to retreat to Ashtarak, northwest of the fortress of Iravan. During July 25 and 26, a Russian force entered Talesh and settled at Garmi, south of Lankaran, as an Iranian force entered Talesh from the south and began to engage the Russian detachment. Between July 28 and 30, heated battle took place between the Sardar Iravani's forces and the Russian army. Sardar's force captured Pambak and Shuregol in northern Iravan while his brother, Hasan Khan Sari Aslan (Yellow Lion) conducted raids further to the north, making the Russians to retreat toward Tiflis.[lxxxi] On July 25, the Iranian army forced the Russians to retreat and laid siege to Lankaran, while between August 1 and 3, Sardar's force recaptured Bash Aparan and began engaging the Russians further north at Gyumri. On August 2, the Iranian army engaged and forced the Russians to retreat further north in Talesh, as the fortresses of Lankaran and Saliyan fell on August 12. In early August, Abbas Mirza began to cross the River Aras at the Khoda Afarin bridge into Qarabagh with an army of 35,000, while his vanguard intercepted a Russian battalion of 800 and defeated it in a pitched battle. Four hundred heads were sent to the shah's camp in Ardabil, and four hundred POWs (including the commander and seventeen officers, plus two cannons) were sent to Tabriz.[lxxxii] By August 6, Abbas Mirza had started the siege of Shusha, while his army was still engaging the Russians in Talesh. At this time, rebellions in Shirvan and Shakki brought these territories to the Iranian side. In Ganjeh, the rebellion of the population had forced the Russian garrison to retreat to the citadel, but with the arrival of Abbas Mirza's army, the Russian garrison retreated to Shamkor, leaving much of their guns and baggage behind.

At this point, a number of blunders spelled catastrophe and defeat. First, upon beginning the siege of Shusha, Abbas Mirza's maternal uncle and military commander, Amir Khan Devellu-Qajar, advocated storming the fortress, but Abbas Mirza overruled him as he had concluded the siege would be a long one. Instead, he ordered Amir Khan to take his firstborn, the young Muhammad Mirza (future Muhammad Shah) and his detachment and take charge of Ganjeh. Second, the Russian commander of Shusha, Colonel Iosif Reutt, disarmed the Muslim population inside Shusha, and with the help of the Armenians put up a good fight, and opened negotiations with the crown prince. Abbas Mirza's artillery was unable to open Shusha, and the siege became protracted. In order to buy time the Russian commander proposed negotiations, and Abbas Mirza inexplicably showed "generosity" and began engaging the Russian commander in fruitless back and forth, which gave Reutt time to wait for reinforcements.

Another blunder was the breakup of the chain of command. Amir Khan sent a letter to Abbas Mirza requesting five or six Nezam regiments and more cannons, so he could fight the incoming Russian reinforcements under Lieutenant General Valerian "Rostam" Madatov, adding, "If I defeat him, I will go to Tiflis, otherwise I will be murdered."[lxxxiii] Abbas Mirza gave him strict orders to take the confiscated Russian guns and baggage and stay within the fortress of Ganjeh, waiting for him to finish with Shusha. However, upon hearing of the approaching Russian army under General Madatov (10,000 men made up of Cossacks, twelve battalions of infantry, and twelve artillery pieces), Amir Khan took command of a 5,000-man cavalry force and with young Muhammad Mirza at his side, headed toward Shamkor. The Battle of Shamkor, on September 16, was a rout in favor of the Russian general. Amir Khan died in battle and Muhammad Mirza retreated to Ganjeh, and then the defenders of Ganjeh evacuated the fortress and retreated toward Shusha. Ganjeh fell to Madatov on September 17 without a fight. On September 22, General Ivan Paskevich arrived in the Caucasus with reinforcements and he took command on September 29. On the same day, Abbas Mirza began moving his army toward Ganjeh, leaving a small force to continue the siege of Shusha. The Battle of Ganjeh occurred on October 13–17, 1826, near the tomb of Nezami Ganjavi, the renowned twelfth-century Persian-speaking poet, just south of the city. As was the tradition, Abbas Mirza appointed three of his sons to accompany different segments of his army of around 30,000. Two of these sons, Jahangir Mirza and Khosrow Mirza, were underage and were accompanied by their teachers (*laleh*). The third was under Muhammad Mirza's command. However, in the heat of the battle, Abbas Mirza ordered the teachers to pull the two young princes back for fear of harm coming to them. This action triggered the collapse of his center and the rout of his army. This was the most decisive battle of the second war, and from this point on, defeat was looming. One observer made the following observation on the Battle of Ganjeh: "The action was at first well contested; and had Abbas Mirza possessed the talent of a commander, the Russian power in Georgia would have been at an end."[lxxxiv]

By 1827, the war was defensive and a losing one for Abbas Mirza. In January, Madatov conducted a fourteen-day raid south of the River Aras. In April, Etchmiadzin fell and in July, the fortresses of Abbasabad and Urdubad in Nakhjavan were put under siege. When Abbas Mirza arrived to relieve them, Paskevich defeated him on July 7 and both forts surrendered. In September, the fortress of Sardarabad fell under heavy bombardment, followed by the unthinkable: the impregnable fortress of Iravan fell after a siege and heavy bombardment. Paskevich pounded the walls of the fortress with eight 24-pounder heavy guns and four 4-inch mortars.[lxxxv] Sardar Iravani managed to slip out of the fortress before its fall, but his brother Hasan Khan Sari Aslan, and other commanders such as Hamzeh Khan Anzali and Mahmud Khan Maqsudllu, became POWs and were sent to Tiflis. They were released after the signing of the Treaty of Turkmanchay.

On October 24, 1827, Tabriz surrendered without a fight, even though Asef al-Dowleh, the hawkish chief minister, was in command of a 20,000-man army inside the citadel. A member of the ulama delivered the city to Paskevich. He was executed by the order of the shah after the Russian evacuation of Tabriz, and Asef would be flogged in public for his cowardice as the crown prince and the shah looked on. Ardabil fell on January 25, 1828, and its treasures, dating back to the Safavid period, were looted by the Russians. On February 2, 1828, Abbas Mirza signed the Treaty of Turkmanchay, named after a village, ceding Iravan and Nakhjavan, and agreeing to a heavy war reparation and other capitulations.[lxxxvi] Iran committed itself to pay Russia ten kurur in four instalments (each kurur was half a million tumans). The tsar reduced this payment by one kurur in 1829. As part of the treaty, the Russian tsar committed Russia to guaranteeing the continuation of the Qajar monarchy in the family line of Abbas Mirza, which clearly infringed upon and compromised Iranian sovereignty.

Causes of the Second Russo-Iranian War

There are many intertwined factors involved in the road to the second war with Russia, which began in 1825 and not 1826, as is popularly believed. Regarding Russian policy, differences between St. Petersburg and Tiflis seem to have been of tactical nature at most. Tsar Alexander's political arrangement with Ermolov had afforded the general a great degree of autonomy, which he used to pursue the very imperial ambition Russian statesmen had sought since the reign of Catherine II. In this context, blaming Iran for the outbreak of the Second Russo-Iranian War is similar to blaming the victim for fighting back. Russia became the aggressor by attacking the region and by occupying the Gokcha territory in 1825, and then attempting to dictate terms to Iran. The accord signed by Fath Ali Khan Fumeni in Tiflis and Ermolov's behavior after that was a blatant insult to Iran and an unprecedented attempt to strip the shah of his right to ratify the agreement. The reality was that in Russia, the Qajar ruling class faced an aggressive and persistent imperial power. The choices available to the Iranians were narrowing down to either war and resistance, capitulation, or a halfway solution between the two.[1] The war of 1825–8 would be the last time the Qajar state would confront Russia as an equal or be treated as an equal by European powers. Fath

---

1. Throughout the rest of the nineteenth century, the Qajar ruling class would try all three paths and would eventually settle for what it could hold on to by trying to play various world powers against each other.

Ali Shah had started the nineteenth century confident he could resist Russian incursions, thus engaging in a defensive nine-year war, while trying to find global allies and reform Iran's army. This phase ended with the Treaty of Golestan in 1813, after Iran suffered a number of military setbacks and the shah realized that the war was just too costly. From 1814 to the end of Ermolov's mission to Iran in 1817, the shah attempted without success to negotiate the return of some of the lost territories. Between 1817 and 1825, attempts at negotiating a final demarcation of the Caucasian border, between the arch imperialist Ermolov and Abbas Mirza's team in the court of Tabriz, failed to produce results. From 1825, Russian policy under Ermolov was on the offensive again. Ermolov was able to use his unique position as the commander and governor in Tiflis, and his special relationship with Tsar Alexander, to direct Russian policy to fulfill its own strategic vision of controlling the entire Caucasus.

In this context, had Iran accepted Willock's recommendation and settled the Gokcha dispute, it is highly doubtful that the settlement would have been the end of the story. In an audience and conversation with Tsar Nicolas I in St. Petersburg on October 28, 1827, Willock actually told the tsar that had Menshikov had the authority to order a temporary retreat from Gokcha, war could have been avoided. By the time Menshikov reached Sultanieh, almost a year and a half had passed since the Russian occupation of Gokcha and over seven months since Nicolas had come to power. The tsar surely should have had some idea about what was going on in the Caucasus, even if he was not fully aware of Ermolov's activities. Without answering Willock directly, the tsar responded that had the shah referred the dispute to his (the tsar's) adjudication, war would not have occurred.[lxxxvii] The Iranians actually tried to send an emissary to St. Petersburg, but Ermelov prevented it.[lxxxviii] While the tsar certainly had a historical opportunity in the form of Menshikov's mission to de-escalate the crisis, he chose not to. His statement on adjudication sounds disingenuous when one notes that Menshikov's only solution to the crisis was for the shah to ratify the Tiflis agreement on Gokcha and then take the issue up with the tsar.

However, the fact that Russia wanted the rest of the Caucasus as part of its imperial ambition did not necessarily mean that events had to lead to all-out war in the summer of 1826. Here the miscalculation of the Qajar statesmen and the factionalism at the court of Tehran played an important role. Certainly, compared to 1812–13, when Iran and Russia fought the last battles of the First Russo-Iranian War, Russia's internal situation was much stronger by 1825. In 1812, Russia had just ended a war with the Ottoman Empire and was engaging Napoleon's Grand Army in a war of survival, while at the same time fighting Iran. In 1825, Russia was engaged in minor conflicts, namely promoting Greek independence, but not a major war. Clearly, events in December 1925, i.e. Alexander's death, the Decembrist rebellion, and Nicolas's accession, created a sense of Russian vulnerability in the eyes of some statesmen in Iran. Hence, the Gokcha crisis could have been de-escalated had Iran, as the weaker party, accepted the diktat of Russia. After all, it seems that both the shah and his main commander, Abbas Mirza, dreaded war with Russia and believed their armed forces were not ready for combat. However, a number of events, including major miscalculations, led to the blunder on behalf of Iranian decision-makers. In this context, prior to and during Menshikov's visit to the royal encampment, news had arrived of further Russian incursions in the Iravan region, which only fueled the situation. Furthermore, the impasse of talks with Menshikov coincided with news of a successful revolt in Talesh and the expulsion of the Russian garrison. The misapprehension was that Russia was sufficiently weakened, and that its weakness would compensate for Iran's own shortcomings, thus providing a window of opportunity for victory. Hence, the hawks won the day due to a combination of circumstances and miscalculations. Nevertheless, in final analysis, Iranian statesmen may be blamed for miscalculating "the window of opportunity" to respond to Russian aggression, but not for starting the war.

Finally, even if Iran had been more successful in the battlefields of the Caucasus and even victorious against Russia during the second war, such victory would probably have been short-term. If Russian history is any witness, since the time of Peter I, Russia had shown stubborn persistence at pursuing the subjugation and annexation of peoples and territories belonging to its neighbors. The pattern of Russian wars with Sweden, Poland, and the Ottoman Empire suggests that tactical military setbacks would not stop Russia's imperial ambition. With regard to Qajar Iran, Russia's imperial ambition in the southeastern Caucasus did not come to an end with the Treaty of Golestan. The treaty was a convenient pause in a conflict that Imperial Russia envisioned would absorb all of the Caucasus up to the border of Iranian Azarbaijan.

The aftermath

The ratification of the Treaty of Turkmanchay by Russia initiated the Griboyedov mission of 1829 and the subsequent massacre of that mission in Tehran. Alexander Griboyedov entered Tehran at the head of a mission to deliver the ratified Treaty of Turkmanchay and to take care of other business including war reparations. However, upon insisting on the return of some former Christian female slaves who had become wives and mothers in Iran, he incited a riot in Tehran, which led to the death of almost all Russians in the Tehran embassy compound.[lxxxix] In this context, the nervous Iranian reaction was telling and shows how much attitudes toward Russia had changed in Iran. One Qajar historian sums up the reaction as follows: "When Crown Prince Abbas Mirza heard of the occurrence, he ordered all the soldiers and the nobles to put on black dress as a sign of mourning, all the bazaars to be closed for three days, and all the people to stop working."[xc]

The shah followed up by sending a diplomatic mission to Tsar Nicolas I, offering the monarch's deep regrets. The high-ranking mission was led by Abbas Mirza's son Prince Khosrow Mirza and arrived in St. Petersburg in 1829.

Prince Khosrow Mirza's mission was a proper and high-level delegation to the court of St. Petersburg in response to the death of Griboyedov and massacre of the Russian mission in Tehran. This was Fath Ali Shah's way of offering the tsar his deep regrets. The mission's important events and observations were written down by Mirza Mostafa Khan Afshar Baha' al-Molk, an official accompanying the prince. Similarly to his predecessors, Afshar made a number of interesting observations on Russian society and further demonstrated the change of attitude among the Iranians, and their loss of self-confidence in their encounters with Russia. While visiting a military training school in Moscow, he sadly noted the high level of education of Russian officers compared to the lack of education among Iranian ones. He was impressed by how Russian officers could lead a large number of soldiers in an orderly manner, while recognizing the weaknesses of the Iranian military and the enemy's points of strength and weakness too. Afshar wrote, "Truth be told, our military men have been training under the English for a while, but what have they learned except formal [useless] military drills?"[xci] He then quotes General Ivan F. Paskevich, the victor of the Second Russo-Iranian War, as telling him: "you cannot have better soldiers than you already have, for in the battle of Ganjeh they rushed up close to the mouth of our cannons, and stood their ground, they can walk five verses (*farsakh/farsanq*) ... but you do not have [competent military] leaders to lead them according to the needs of the time and location."[xcii]

Afshar too expressed his admiration for the "order" with which the Russians conducted themselves and organized their society. He seems to have been among the first Iranian officials to connect the dots and begin to understand that having modern weapons and drills was not enough for a modern military. He made the following observation and judgment with a sad tone: "It is regrettable that we clearly see the progress of our neighbor, which has been attained in as short time, but we are not thinking about doing the same so that we would not be always defeated by our neighbor ..."[xciii] Here Afshar alludes to reasons other than the military as key to the progress of Russia. Of course, for the rest of the century, Qajar Iran would toy around with the necessity of broader reform, accompanied by a further readjustment of attitudes toward Russia.

Crown Prince Abbas Mirza did not live long enough to become king. His last campaign was against rebellions in northern Khorasan in 1833. He used his Nezam force to quell the rebellion; however, his health deteriorated in that same year. He had been suffering from gout for some time and now the end was near. Hence, on one hand he made sure his royal father committed to his son Muhammad Mirza inheriting the throne, and on the other hand he began writing a number of letters to his 26-year-old son, preparing him for succession.[xciv] He passed away on October 25, 1833 and was buried in Mashhad at the Tomb of the eighth Shi'a Imam. He was forty-four years old. A document attributed to Abbas Mirza stands as his will, written in 1830. It portrays the man's sorrow for his defeats and mistakes, and gives instructions for his burial and the settlement of his debts.[xcv] Fath Ali Shah named Muhammad Mirza heir-apparent in June 1834, and passed away on October 24, 1934 in Isfahan; he was sixty-two years old.

CONCLUSION: SEVEN POINTS

What is the power that gives [Europe] so great a superiority over us? What is the cause of your progress and of our constant weakness? You know the art of governing, the art of conquering, and the art of putting into action all human faculties, whereas we seem condemned to vegetate in a shameful ignorance ...

Crown Prince Abbas Mirza[i]

Qajar history has gone through much revision and distortion during the post-Qajar period. Some of the revisions are valid observations; however, distortions remain which need to be addressed to set the record straight. As a study of early Qajar history, this book is an attempt to revisit the period, address the historical fallacies, and create a framework for better understanding this crucial period in the history of Iran. As such, the following seven points serve as a summary and analysis.

Point 1: Guarding the dominion

The Qajar ruling class had a clear understanding of its dominion's historical borders, which it referred to as *Iran*. Between the Islamic conquest of the seventh century and the establishment of the Safavid state in 1501, the name Iran was not used for any territorial state and remained a geographic and cultural term, referring to the Persianite world, where Persian-speaking peoples lived. The Safavid Empire (1501–1722), a Turkic Shi'a dynasty, began to refer to its dominion as Iran, which continued during the Qajar period (1796–1925). Iran during this period, however, was not a nation-state but one in the making. It would take the establishment of a strong national state, education system, national army, and other reforms to create a sense of national identity not just for the ruling class, but also for the general population. These would materialize during the twentieth century and after the constitutional revolution of 1906. However, it is hard to imagine the nation-state of Iran today, had the fragmented state of the pre-Qajar period continued.

Aqa Muhammad Shah aimed at establishing the borders of his empire as they were in the Safavid period. Indeed, he was preparing to attack Bukhara when in 1797 he had to rush back to the Caucasus to face the Russian invading army under Zubov, where he was assassinated. Hence, his project of reunification remained unfinished. However, both he and his successor, Fath Ali Shah, had some understanding of the upcoming challenge posed by European powers, namely Russia. What they both failed to understand was that the threat of European imperialism came not just from Russia, but also Britain out of India, France, and others. Otherwise, it is hard to understand why Fath Ali Shah signed the one-sided Anglo-Iranian Treaty with Malcolm in 1800. Nevertheless, the most important achievement of the period under study was the reunification of Iran and the creation of foundations and structures for its durability.

Point 2: Iran's war strategy

How realistic was Iran's strategy in defending against the Russian onslaught during the two wars? Aqa Muhammad Shah showed confidence in facing the Russian army, based on his understanding of Russian power and his own ability to withstand it. As noted, his strategy was to fight an asymmetrical war by avoiding a direct confrontation with Russian firepower, instead retreating and conducting a scorched-earth policy, and by employing traditional Iranian partisan warfare tactics. Could such a strategy have worked under the best of circumstances? As noted, the Russian Empire had clear advantages over Qajar Iran, in terms of population, military strength, wealth, and resources, and it could rely on the local Christian population and even unreliable local Muslim petty rulers to provide some support. In 1812, Russia threw these resources into the field and defeated the Qajar army and Napoleon's Grand Army simultaneously. On the other hand, for the shah's strategy to have worked, he needed to have reliable allies among the khans of the southeastern Caucasus, many of whom had repeatedly proven to be poor allies of the Qajar and more interested in preserving their own independence. Perhaps Aqa Muhammad Shah intended to exhaust the Russians, making them believe that the whole venture was not worth the cost. As we saw, this would not be the case as Russia showed much determination and persevered through difficulties. Once full battles between the two sides began in the summer of 1804, Iran attempted with limited success to use its traditional army, with numerical superiority, to break the siege of Iravan. However, the cost was high and Qajar rulers realized that without a modern military, facing off the Russian army was a losing proposition. Hence the Nezam-e Jadid reforms, first with the help of Russian renegades, then the French, and finally the British. The reforms did not work, partially because Qajar rulers were never able to shed their tribal culture of warfare. Furthermore, the Russians quickly and successfully addressed their disadvantages by building three north–south roads for faster movement of supplies, and establishing fortified positions as depots and for stationing forces in forward positions. Finally, the size, power, and resources of the Russian Empire far exceeded those of Iran, which could hardly engage in a protracted conflict.

Point 3: Global context

Iran's encounter with imperialism and the modern world must be viewed in a global context. Qajar Iran was not an exception when it came to military defeat and eventually sinking to the level of semi-colony in the nineteenth century. Aggressive Western imperialism overwhelmed older ruling dynasties/classes such as the Ottoman Empire, Egypt under Muhammad Ali Pasha, and the Qing Chinese Empire, to name a few. These were much more experienced and more powerful states and certainly much more prosperous empires than Qajar Iran. The Ottoman Empire was a European power with a long interaction with Europe as it progressed from the poor feudal period, or "dark age," to capitalism. The reforms implemented in Egypt and in the Ottoman Empire were far more extensive than the haphazard reforms initiated by Abbas Mirza, which were not followed up by his successors. Nevertheless, all the mentioned regions met the same fate as Iran. Hence, even if Iran's ruling class had fully understood the depth of challenges facing the new dynasty, and if it had actioned expansive reforms of the caliber implemented in the Ottoman Empire under Sultan Mahmud II and in Egypt under Muhammad Ali Pasha, it is doubtful it would have been able to avoid the turn of events.

Point 4: The role of the ulama

The Shi'i ulama establishment, both in Iran and in Iraq, generally supported the reforms and war efforts of the Qajar. There is ample evidence that the reforms of Abbas Mirza were not only unopposed by high-ranking ulama, but that the ulama were courted and issued edicts in support of war against Russia. There is evidence that Abbas Mirza's siblings tried to enlist the support of conservative elements (probably helped by some middle-ranking ulama) to undermine the Nezam-e Jadid reforms, but there is no evidence that it included high-ranking ulama of Iran and *'atebat*. In the run-up to the second war with Russia, Abbas Mirza provided the ulama with information on the Russian mistreatment of the Muslim population under its occupation, and solicited their support. This was done not to start a war with Russia but to prevent one. First, he needed to bring public opinion behind the cause should war break out, and the only way to do this was through the pulpit. Second, he wanted to project a united image to the Russians to deter Ermolov's aggressive behavior. Once high-ranking ulama reached Sultanieh in the summer of 1826, however, they became one factor among many who lobbied for war. Had the Gokcha crisis been resolved or had Menshikov offered a real solution, the royal court could have managed ulama pressure.

Point 5: Encounter with imperialism

Iran in the early nineteenth century was entangled in a web of European intrigue and diplomacy, which was difficult if not impossible to untangle. As the Ottoman Empire, native tribes of North America, and many other non-Western peoples had discovered, treaties, agreements, promises, etc., with imperialist powers were only worth the paper they were written on as long as they served the given power's interests. Once they did not, and the imperialist power was ready to resume hostilities, war broke out once again. During the period under study, the French promise of support was out the window once Napoleon made his peace with the tsar. The British promise of support, seemingly generous in 1809, created much hope in Iran—but this was when Britain was at war with Russia and France. In 1814, once France was defeated, the British revised the agreement to provide financial and military support on the condition that Iran did not ignite the war. When Russia began hostilities in 1825—and Willock, the British diplomat, attests to this—Britain blamed Iran and refused to help.

Point 6: Abbas Mirza

Abbas Mirza's role during this period of war and reform needs reevaluation. By all accounts, he was a selfless son of the shah, which set him apart from his siblings. He was also a brave warrior, a gallant rider, and an excellent expert shooter. He did not care for luxury, was much concerned with Iran's war effort, was eager to learn, and was one of the pioneers of promoting modernizing reforms. However, he could not have been so without the sober advice of his chief minister Mirza Isa Farahani Qa'em Maqam I, and his son and successor, Mirza Abu al-Qasem Qa'em Maqam II. Theirs was a partnership, with Qa'em Maqam I tutoring and guiding the young crown prince and together promoting policies that strengthened Iran's war efforts. This partnership at the court of Tabriz worked and had some positive results until 1822 when Qa'em Maqam I passed away. However, Abbas Mirza proved to be a poor military commander, and despite his yearning to learn the secrets of Western superiority, he failed to shed his nomadic cultural upbringing. Throughout this period, state security was lax both in Tabriz and in Tehran, providing an opportunity for spies to gain firsthand knowledge of state secrets in Iran. As a military commander, Abas Mirza failed to understand the meaning and significance of the chain of command. Furthermore, he failed to appreciate the need to protect his army by posting guard units. The above factors resulted in an avoidable military disaster. During the second war with Russia, the breakup of the chain of command resulted in the loss of Ganjeh and the death of his uncle, Amir Khan. During the Battle of Ganjeh against Paskevich, Abbas Mirza posting and then withdrawing his sons from the battlefield played a key role in the rout of his army. On the diplomatic side, during negotiations with Ermolov in 1825, he nominated a Russophile, Fatah Ali Khan Fumeni, whose father had been murdered by Aqa Muhammad Shah, to conduct negotiations. This was a time when the shah had ordered Qa'em Maqam II to leave Tabriz; therefore, Abbas Mirza was left without a prudent advisor. On his own, Abbas Mirza made a fatal mistake by nominating the wrong person to represent him in Tiflis. As such, Abbas Mirza's legacy must be viewed not only through what he achieved and wanted to achieve, but also his shortcomings.

Point 7: Deterrence

Throughout its interaction with Western powers during this period, Iran lacked deterrence. Nowhere was this more visible than in its two wars with Russia. Wars with Russia were costly in terms of both men and materials. While there are no reliable statistics, Iran's human loss must have been staggering. For example, at some points during the first war with Russia, local militia charged the Russian line with old weapons at high cost to their ranks. While medical science at this time was still primitive all over the world, it was even more so in Iran. Hence, many of those injured on the battlefield probably did not survive. Iran attempted to make the war with Russia costly enough for it to give up its aggression, thus creating a degree of deterrence. It did so by throwing its traditional army's numerical superiority into the field, and by trying to find a European ally to help it with both modern training and financial help; neither worked.

Iran has not invaded any other country since the fall of the Afshar Empire in 1747. However, a lack of deterrence would be a major problem for Iran for the rest of the nineteenth century and into the twentieth. Iran was attacked again by Russia in 1909, 1911, during World War I 1914–17, and by the USSR in 1920 and 1941–6. Britain attacked Iran in 1828, 1856, 1914–21, and 1941–5, and participated in the coup d'état against the nationalist government of Muhammad Musaddeq alongside the US in 1953. The US joined the occupation of neutral Iran during World War II, as well as leading the 1953 coup. During the Iran–Iraq War (1980–8), Iraq attacked Iranian cities with ground-to-ground missiles and attacked the Iranian military and civilians with chemical weapons, while Western powers provided it with technical and financial help. The US provided Iraq with diplomatic cover at the UN against war crimes and intelligence on Iranian troop movement, and attacked and sank Iranian naval vessels in the Persian Gulf. This historical background has prompted Iran today to develop a degree of deterrence by strengthening its indigenous military-industrial complex. The result has been the development of short- and medium-range ground-to-ground missile capability, its drone technology, and other aspects of its military. Ironically, the limited deterrence achieved after the end of war with Iraq is the subject of Western concerns, thus the demand that Iran dismantle it.

CHRONOLOGY

Date of events for this period can become confusing because of four different calendars used by various parties involved. The four are, Gregorian, Julian, Islamic Lunar and Iranian-Islamic Solar calendars. In order to avoid confusion, all dates had been converted to Gregorian calendar with as much accuracy as possible.

25 October 1722: Fall of Isfahan to Malik Mahmud Hotak

1722-1736: Civil war and foreign invasion.
12 September 1722: Treaty of St Petersburg, Tahmasp II ceded Iran's northern provinces to Russia.
26 April 1725: Murder of Malik Mahmud by his successor Ashraf.

1726
9 September 1726: Murder of deposed Shah Sultan Hosein and his family by the order of Malik Ashraf Hotak.
11 October 1726: Murder of Fath Ali Khan Qavanllu Qajar by the order of Safavid pretender Tahmasp II and with Nader's complicity.

1729
29 September 1729: Nader defeated Malik Ashraf at Mehmandust near Damghan.
11 November 1729: Nader defeated Afghan army at Murchehkhort, north of Isfahan and fall of that city.
29 December 1729: Accession of figure head pretender Tahmasp II to Safavid throne in Isfahan.

1730
15 January 1730: Final defeat of Ashraf Hotak by Nader and end of Afghan domination of former Safavid dominion.
3 May: Murder of Malik Ashraf Hotak.
11 June 1730: Nader defeated an Ottoman army and recapturer Hamadan.
6 September 1731: Ottoman army defeated Tahmasp II.

September 1722: Russian army occupied Darband
2
3 June 1724: Treaty of Istanbul dividing western and northern Iran between Ottoman Empire and Russia.

28 January 1725: Death of tsar Peter I.

1732
10 January: Treaty of Baghdad, after defeat, Tahmasp II ceded western provinces to the Ottoman Empire.
2 February: Fall of Herat to Nader's army.
25 August: Nader removed Tahmasp II from throne and replaced him with his infant son Abbas III.
19 December 1733: Nader's treaty with Ottoman Empire ending Ottoman occupation and, temporarily, hostilities.
29 August 1734: Fall of Shamakhi in Shirvan to Nader's army.

1735
9 July: Fall of Ganjeh to Nader's army.
11 September: Fall of Tiflis to Nader's army.
3 October: Fall of Iravan to Nader's army.

1736
7 March: Nader Shah Afshar's coronation.
14 July 1736: Nader Shah defeated an Ottoman army at the battle of Aparchay in Iravan followed by Treaty of Istanbul where the Porte ceded all the previously occupied territories.

1737
27 April: Fall of Bahrain to Nader's army.
2 August: Fall of Balkh to Reza Qoli Mirza, Nader's son.

1738
24 March: Fall of Qandahar to Nader Shah.
11 July: Fall of Ghazni followed by fall of Kabul to Nader Shah.
18 September: Fall of Jalalabad to Nader.
27 December: Fall of Lahore to Nader Shah.

1739
24 February: Nader Shah decisively defeated the army of Mughal emperor of India, Muhammad Shah Gorkani, in the battle of Karnal.
20 March: Noruz, Nader Shah's triumphant entry in Delhi.
27 March: Nader Shah's royal decree relieving his subject of tax obligation for the next three years.
15 May: Murder of Tahmasp II and his children by the order of Reza Qoli Mirza.

1740–48: Austrian War of Succession

1741
15 May: Failed assassination attempt on Nader Shah in Mazandaran.
14 September: Fall of Bukhara to Nader Shah.
26 November: Fall of Khiva to Nader Shah.
14 March 1742 Birth of Aqa Muhammad Khan Qavanllu-Qajar.
20 June 1747: Assassination of Nader Shah in Fathabad of Quchan.
5 July 1747: Adel Shah, Nader's nephew, claimed the Afshar throne in Mashhad.

1747–1759: Civil War
2 April 1748: Aqa Muhammad Khan, the six year old son of Muhammad Hasan Khan Qajar, was captured and ordered castrated by the order of Adel Shah.
7 June 1748: Adel Shah defeated and blinded by his brother Ibrahim Mirza who claimed the throne in western Iran while Nader's grandson, Shahrokh claimed the throne in Khorasan.
8 December 1749: Murder of Ibrahim Mirza.

1751
Birth of Hosein Qoli Khan Qavanllu Qajar (Jahansuz-world burner), Aqa Muhammad Khan's full brother.
February 1751: By this month, Irakli, ruler of eastern Georgia, had managed to dominate all the khanates of eastern Caucasus.
9-27 August 1758: Failure of a 50,000 strong Qajar army under Muhammad Hasan Khan at siege of Shiraz.
26 December 1758: Defeat of Qajar army by Karin Khan Zand at battle of Gonabad.
12 February 1759: Death of Muhammad Hasan Khan Qavanllu Qajar
7 July 1772: Birth of Fath Ali Shah Qajar (Baba Khan Jahanbani-world guardian)
30 March 1777: Death of Hosein Qoli Mirza Jahansuz.

1779
2 March: Death of Karim Khan Zand; his brother Zaki Khan claimed power on behalf of Karim's sons, Abu al-Fath Khan and Muhammad Ali Khan.

1762-96: Reign of Catherine II

1768-74: First Russo-Ottoman War

5 August 1772: First partition of Poland

1773- Saudi-Wahhabi capture of Riyadh

21 July 1774: Treaty of Kuchuk Kainarji

4 July 1776: American Declaration of Independence

1779-1796: Civil war and unification.
2 April: Aqa Muhammad Khan defeated his two half-brothers, Reza Qoli and Morteza Qoli, for control over the Qavanllu branch of the Qajar tribe of Astarabad.
14 June: Murder of Zaki Khan Zand by his own guards while attempting to capture Isfahan.
29 June: Abu al-Fath Khan Zand (son of Karim Khan) ascended to throne.
22 August: Abul al-Fath Khan overthrown by Sadeq Khan (brother of Karim Khan).

1780
1 June: Sadeq Khan defeated and blinded by Ali Murad Khan Zand whe moved the capital to Isfahan.

1781:
Aqa Muhammad Khan's first encounter with the Russians under Count Voinovich

1782:
Aqa Muhammad Khan invaded Gilan and defeated Hedayatallah Khan Rashti (Fumeni).

1784:
A Zand army dispatched by Ali Murad Khan captured Mazandaran but was defeated and withdrew in November

1785:
11 February: Death of Ali Murad Khan Zand.
6 April: Ja'far Khan Zand (son of Sadeq Khan) ascended to throne and returned the capital to Shiraz.
Summer: Aaq Muhammad Khan defeated Ja'far Khan Zand and captured Isfahan

1786
12 March: Conquest of Tehran by Aqa Muhammad Khan-Tehran became Qajar capital;
October: Second invasion of Gilan and defeat and death of Hedayatollah Khan Fumeni (Rashti).

24 July 1783: Treaty of Georgievsk

1784: Death of Solomon king of Imereti in Western Georgia

1786: Shamkhals of Tarki treaty of submission with Russia.

1789 4 January: Birth of Muhamad Ali Mirza (Dowlatshah), Baba Khan's first born son, followed by birth of Muhammad Qoli Mirza (Mulk Ara), Muhammad Vali Mirza, Abbas Mirza (12 August-Prince Regent and Crown Prince), and Hosein Ali Mirza (2 September-Farman Farma). 23 January: Assassination of Ja'far Khan Zand followed by internal war among Zand pretenders 8 May: Lutf Ali Khan Zand, the victor of Zand internal conflict entered Shiraz. 25 June: Inconclusive battle between Zand and Qajar armies eight miles North-West of Shiraz 25 June-7 September: Unsuccessful siege of Shiraz by Aqa Muhammad Khan	**1787-91**: Second Russo-Ottoman War **1789** 5 May: The Estates-General convened in the Versailles. 17 June: The Third Estate declared itself the French National Assembly. 14 July: The storming of the Bastille in Paris. 27 August: French declaration of the Rights of Man.
1790: Aqa Muhammad Khan ordered execution of his brother, Ja'far Qoli Khan, in order to secure the throne for his nephew Fath Ali Khan (Baba Khan); defeat of Sadeq Khan Shaqaqi and Qajar conquest of Azarebaijan.	
1791 Haj Ibrahim Kalantar switched sides and delivered Shiraz to Aqa Muhammad Khan Qajar.	
1792 5 June: Aqa Muhammad Khan marched on Fars to relieve Shiraz from a Zand siege. 21 July: Aqa Mhuammad Khan Qajar entered Shiraz	
1794 11 June: Start of siege of Kerman by Aqa Muhammad Khan's army. 23 October: Fall of Kerman. 29 October: Arrest of Lutf Ali Khan Zand in Bam and his delivery to Aqa Muhammad Khan. 3 November: Lutf Ali Khan blinded and sent to Tehran and the remaining royal jewelry in his possession confiscated. 26 December: Murder of Lutf Ali Khan Zand in Tehran.	 **23 January 1793**: Execution of Louis XVI; Second partition of Poland.

1795

20 January: Aqa Muhammad Khan appointed Fath Ali Khan (Baba Khan) governor (*beglerbaigi*) of Fars, Kerman, and Yazd, and appointed Ibrahim Khan Kalantar his chief adviser.
18 Feb: Aqa Muhammad Khan appointed Ibrahim Khan Kalantar chief minister with the title *I'timad al-Dowleh*.
4 May: Aqa Muhammad Khan left Tehran for the Caucasus.
15 May: Aqa Muhammad Khan's army arrived at Sultaniyyeh
20 May: Qajar army moved from Sultaniyyeh to Zanjan
7 July-9 August: Siege of Shusha by Aqa Muhamma.
11 July: Khan of Qarabagh attempt at raiding the Qajar army failed
9 August: Khan of Qarabagh offered to submit
10 September: Aqa Muhammad Khan's force of 40,000 defeated Irakli's army at Rustavi (or Rosht—2.5 kilometers southeast of Tiflis).
September: 11-13: Siege and sack of Tiflis
24 Sep: After 9 days in Tiflis, Aqa Muhammad Khan left for Ganjeh
28 September: Aqa Muhammad Khan arrive at Ganjeh and met Javad Khan and summoned the khan of Iravan
Sep.-March: Aqa Muhammad Khan spent in Qarabagh near Shusha.
27 October: Aqa Muhammad Khan arrived at Javad near River Kur.
28 November: Fall of Shirvan to Qajar army.

1796

January-February: Aqa Muhammad Khan spent winter in Khalakhal and then moved to Mughan where he accepted kingship before Noruz.
26 April: Aqa Muhammad Shah arrived in Tehran; also beginning of Russian punitive attack on the Caucasus under Gen. Valerian Zubov (*Qizil Iyagh*)
4 May: Russian occupation of Darband and arrest of Shaykh Ali Khan.

1795

2 August: Gen. Gudovich asked Gen. Zubov for instructions regarding Aqa Muhammad Khan's military movements.
28 May: Russian Council of State recommended that Gudovich be authorized to send reinforcements to Tiflis but this was not acted upon
Early October: Gen. Gudovich sent two battalions to Tiflis which reached the city only in December.
24 October: Third partition of Poland

9 July 1762: Tsarina Catherine II ascended the Russian throne.

6 May: Aqa Muhammad Shah's coronation in Tehran. Appointment of Fatah Ali as his heir apparent with the title of *Jahanbani* (world protector)
9 May: Escape of Shaykh Ali Khan from Russian captivity
14 May: Aqa Muhammad Khan left Tehran for Khorasan.
24 May: After supporting a failed uprising by Shaykh Ali Khan, Hasan Qoli Khan of Qobbeh submitted to the Russians; by the end of this month the khans of Shirvan and Baku also submitted
13 June: Aqa Muhammad Shah left Tehran for Khorasan
2 July: Khan of Qarabagh submitted to the Russians; French mission under Oliver entered Tehran
26 August: News of Russian invasion reached the shah in Mashhad.
20 September: Aqa Muhammad Shah arrived in Tehran
26 December: News of Russian withdrawal reached Tehran.

1797
16 March: Aqa Muhammad Shah named Fath Ali Khan (Baba Khan Jahanbani) heir to the throne (*vali ahd*).
25 April: Shaykh Ali Khan re-captured Darband
28 May: Aqa Muhammad Shah arrived in Ardebil on his way toward the Caucasus.
3 June: The shah sent a 10,000 man force to subdue Talesh
4 June: Leaving the bulk of his army at Ardebil, the shah moved with 8000 troops toward Shusha
8 June: Aqa Muhammad Shah received the submission of Shusha after Ibrahim Khan Javanshir fled the city.
16 June: Aqa Muhammad Shah was assassinated in Shusha
17 July: Fath Ali Khan (Baba Khan Jahanbani) entered Tehran.
29 July: Fath Ali Shah ascended the throne
August: The shah's army defeated Kurdish chieftain, Sadeq Khan Shaqaqi, at the Battle of Khak-e Ali near Qazvin.

1796
17 November: Death of Catherine II

1796-1801: Tsar Paul I

3 December: News of Catherine's death reached Zubov who commenced Russian withdrawal.

22 August: Defeat of Fath Ali Shah's half-brother Hosein Qoli Khan.	
1798	**1798**
21 March: Fath Ali Shah's coronation in Tehran. June: Qajar army defeated Muhammad Khan Zand 18 September: A Qajar army defeated Ja'far Qoli Khan Donboli near Khoy	12 January: Death of Irakli the Vali of Gorjestan 20 July: Battle of the Pyramid and French conquest of Egypt. 1-3 August: Sinking of French Navy in the Mediterranean Sea at the Battle of Abu Qayr Bay (Abu Kheyr) or the Battle of the Nile
1799	
20 March 1799: Abbas Mirza appointed price regent (*na'ib saltaneh*) May: Fath Ali Shah's first Khorasan campaign 29 November: Maj. Gen Lazarov and 5000 Russian troops arrive in Tiflis 7 Sep: Giorgi XII (Gorgin) gave instructions to his representatives to ask Russia to annex Georgia 7 November.: A Russian force under Gen. Lazarov defeated a Lezgian force under Umm Khan near the village of Suhrajo by the River Kibir (Lori) in Daghestan 8 November: Arrival in Tiflis of P.I. Kovalenskii, Russian Resident to Georgia. 28 Dec: Death of Giorgi XII (Gorgin) the last Bagration ruler of Georgia	**1799** 4 April: Death of Tipu (Sahib) Sultan in Mysore.
1800	
1 Feb: Malcolm entered Bushehr 10 Ma1rch: Death of Umm Khan of Lezgi June: Fath Ali Shah's second Khorasan campaign 14 Nov: Malcolm entered Tehran 17 Nov: Malcolm had an audience with Fath Ali Shah 29 Dec.: Anglo-Iranian Treaty.	
1801	**1801**
29 Jan.: Malcolm left Tehran for India August: Fath Ali Shah defeated his brother and challenger to the throne, Hosein Qoli Khan 15 April: Murder of Ibrahim Khan I'timad al-Dowleh (Kalantar) 25 April: Fath Ali Shah's third Khorsan campaign	18 January: Imperial edict annexing Georgia 23 January: Lt. Gen. Karl Fedorovich Knorring appointed commander of the Caucasian Line (removed in 1802) 11 March: Assassination of Tsar Paul I May: Arrival of Lt. Gen. Knorring in Tiflis 12 September: Alexander I ordered annexation of Georgia

1802
21 April: Wahhabi-Saudi sack of Karbala.
May: Fath Ali Shah's forth Khorasan campaign
September: Marriage of Abbas Mirza

1803
30 May: Defeat of Trukmen rebellion in Qara Tapeh and Astarabad and capture of Mashhad by Muhammad Vali Mirza and arrest of Nader Mirza Afshar.
15 December: Beginning of Russian siege of Ganjeh

1804
15 January: Storming and fall of Ganjeh under heavy Russian bombardment.
March: Russian army entered Khanate of Iravan from the north west (River Arpachay) and encamped east of the river opening negotiations with Muhammad Khan Qavanllu Qajar the khan of Iravan.
7 June: Abbas Mirza moved the army's headquarter to Nakhjavan
19-20 June: First major encounter with Russian force north west of Iravan at Pambak was inconclusive. The two forces lined up further to the south at Uch Kelisa (Echmiadzen)
28 June: Russian forces open hostilities by attacking Iranian positions.
30 June: Hostilities ended inconclusively.
1 July: The badly bruised Iranian army began an orderly pull back to Sadrak. Russian army moved east to lay siege on Iravan.
7 July: Arrival of Fath Ali Shah with fresh re-enforcements
8 July: a 50,000 Man Iranian force began surrounding the Russian army laying siege on Iravan.
10 July: End of siege of Iravan and retreat of Russian army toward Tiflis.

1802
21 April Saudi-Wahhabi sack nas massacre of Karbala
September: Alexander I appointed Gen. Paul Tsitsianov governor of the Georgia and Commander of the Caucasian Line.

1803
Saudi-Wahhabi temporary conquest of Mecca
6 February : Tsitsianov entered Tiflis
April: Russian defeat of Lezgis and capture of Jar and Balakau in Daghestan.
16 April: Russian annexation of Imeritia in western Georgia.
21 April: Death of Gen. Lazarov by Queen Daria Bagration of Georgia
25 October: Exile of Queen Daria and the rest of the Georgian royal family to Russia

1805	1805
29 March: A 25,000 man Iranian force under Abbas Mirza entered Qarabagh at Khoda Afarin. 30 March: Skirmishes with Russian forces south of Shusha. 2 April: The two armies lined up at two kilometer distance south of Shusha. 3 April: Major encounter between the two armies but inconclusive—high casualties for Iran. 5 April: Scattered skirmishes between the two armies. 6 April: A battalion of Russian forces led by Col. Pyoter Kotlyarevsky was unsuccessful in its attack on the Iranian line. 7 April: With the arrival of re-enforcements Col Koltyarevsky attempted and succeeded in capturing two lost hills on the eastern side of the battle field. 8 April: Five Iranian regiments attacked the hills and captured one before losing it again. 9 April: With arrival of re-enforcements for the Iranian army, the Russian army began an orderly retreat to Shusha and then to the fort of Askaran to the north east. 10 April: Iranian army reached Shusha before noon and laid siege while the rest of the force moved to Askaran.. 11 April: Unsuccessful attack by Iranian forces on Shusha 12 April: An unsuccessful cavalry attack on Shusha by Iranian forces. Iranian army's pursuit of remnants of the Russian force and siege of Askaran proved ineffective. 13 April: the remnants of the Russian forces managed to use a northern route to make a daring escape to Shah Bulaghi in the Khanate of Ganjeh. 14 April: Iranian army rested at Shusha. 26 May: Ibrahim Khalil Khan of Qarabagh signed articles of submission with Russia. 1 June: Selim Khan of Shakki, signed articles of submission with Russia. 25 June: The shah and imperial army arrive at Takht-e Tavous in Qarabagh 3 July: Iranian army began to march north.	Saudi-Wahhabi conquest of Medina. 14 October: French route of Prussian army at Jena. 21 October: Battle of Trafalgar 2 December : Route of Russian army by the French at the Battle of Austerlitz

6 July: Iranian army reached Tartar River and began to engage Russian forces pushing them toward Ganjeh.
August: Early this month Iranian forces reached Ganjeh and began to engage the Russian army and lay siege on Ganjeh.
9 August: Russian army attacked with full force and heavy bombardment in an attempt to encircle the besieging Iranian army.
10 August: Iranian army began to retreat in two columns, one to the east and south and the second to the south of Ganjeh.
11 August: Russian forces attacked the two columns attempting and succeeding in splitting the Iranian army into two.
12 August: The eastern column of the Iranian force began a disorderly retreat toward south while the south eastern column retreated toward Iravan.
13 August: Iran's south bond column reached Iravan.
14 August: Fall of Shusha to the Russians
15 August: The remnant of the eastern column crossed the Aras at Khoda Afarin.
30 September: French envoy Romieu's audience with Fath Ali Shah.
5 October: Russian army under Gen Zavalishin landed at Enzali.
12 October: Rumieu's death in Tehran.
18 October: Gen Zavalishin's force retreated from Enzali.
18 November 1805: Gen Zavalishin's reinforced army landed south of Badkubeh and laid siege from land and sea
25 November: A 10,000 man Russian army under Gen Tsitsianov entered Shamakhi (Shirvan).

1806
6 January: End of Russian siege of Baku. Mustafa Khan of Shirvan signed articles of submission with Russia.
20 Feb: Tsitsianov assassinated outside Baku.
March: Fath Ali Shah's administrative reforms (*eslahat-e arba'a*)
17 May: Arrival of Jaubert mission in Ardabil and audience with Abbas Mirza

1806
Saudi-Wahhabi second conquest of Mecca.
December 1806-1812: Russo-Ottoman war
Feb 1808-May 1809: Finish War (Russo-Swedish War)

24 May: Abbas Mirza's army headquarter moved to south of Khoda Afarin
June-August: War with Ottoman governor of Baghdad over who should appoint the ruler of Shahr-e Zur (Irbil region)
2 June: Assassination of Ibrahim Khalil Khan Javanshir by the Russians.
5 June: Arrival of the Jaubert mission in Tehran
8 June: Iranian army crossed Khoda Afarin heading to Aq Bulagh
13 June: news of an anti-Russian coalition by the khans of Daghestan, Shakki, and Talesh.
19 June: Jaubert's audience with Fath Ali Shah
21 June: Fall of Darband to Russian Gen. Bulgakov.
30 June: Battle of Khanishin south of Shusha
31 June: Retreat of Iranian army to Aq Bulagh
2 July: Russian attack on Iranian guards at Saliyan bridge,
3 July: Iranian counter attack and recapture of the Saliyan bridge.
6 July: Arrival of Iranian reinforcement and resumption of hostilities in Qarabagh.
7 July: Retreat of Russian army to north of Tartar River.
26 July: The shah appointed Muhammad Ali Mirza Dowlatshah governor of Kermanshah, Iraq-e Ajam (Hamadan) and Iraq-e Arab up to gates of Baghdad
Late July: Fall of Baku and Shakki to Russian army
9 October: An 11000 man Iranian cavalry force moved to attacked Russian positions north of Kur River but retreated after sea landing of a Russian force behind it, north of Lankaran.
November: Fath Ali Shah's administrative reforms. Mirza Shafi' received the title of *Sadr-e 'Azam* and Mirza Bozorg the title of *Qa'em Maqam*.

1807	1807
16 February: Arrival of Russian mission under Istifanov with news of Gen. Gudovich assuming command of Russian forces 16 April: Departure of Istifanov mission from Tehran May-July: Skirmishes with Russian army at Qarabagh-Shakki border 17 May: Arrival of Fath Ali Shah at the Pasture of Sultanieh 5 June: Arrival of Bontems mission in Iran 11 June: Bontems audience with Abbas Mirza 19 June: Bontems audience with Fath Ali Shah 4 Dec : Gardane mission arrived in Tehran 7 Dec: Gardane's audience with Fath Ali Shah 20 December: Franco-Iranian agreement signed	4 May: Treaty of Finkenstein 2 June: Russian army checked the advance of Ottoman army at Obilesti in Wallachia. 14 June: French defeat of Russia at Friedland 18 June: Russian general Gudovich defeated an Ottoman army at the battle of Arpachai in Iravan. 29 May: Overthrow of Ottoman Sultan Selim III 7 July: Treaty of Tilsit
1808	**1808**
By the order of FAS the training of *Nezam Jadid* military started. 5 January: Birth of Abbas Mirza's son Muhammad Mirza (future shah) 17 April: Malcolm left Bombay for Bushehr June: Malcolm returned to India. 11 Oct: Gen Gudovich's letters to Abbas Mirza and Mirza Bozorg, demanding Iran accept Russian terms and offer of peace. October: 8000 man Russian force under Gen. Gudovich moved toward Khanate of Iravan 13 October: Skirmishes between the Russian army and forces of Sardar of Iravan on the north west of the khanate. 14 October: Hartford Jones mission to Iran arrived in Bushehr 26 October: Inconclusive battles between the two armies near the fort of Iravan 31 October: Russian army began the second siege of Iravan. 10 December: Russian army breached the wall of Iravan but was repulsed. 11 December: Abbas Mirza defeated Gen. Gudovich at Battle of Nakhjavan 17 December: Fall of Qobbeh to Russain army; Jones left Bushehr for Tehran	8 February: Anglo-Swedish Alliance 21 February: Start of Finish War between Sweden and Russia. 29 July: Assassination of deposed Ottoman Sultan Selim III

18 December: Abbas Mirza defeated Gen. Nebelsin in Nakhjavan and ended the second siege of Iravan.

1809
12 February: Gen Gardane left Tehran
14 February: Jones arrive in Tehran
17 February: Jones received by FAS
19 March: Anglo-Iranian Treaty signed by Jones and Mirza Shafi' and Sadr.
July-August: Skirmishes with Russian army continued followed by peace negotiations by the end of the year.
April: Gen. Alexander Tormozov replaced Gen Gudovich
22 July: Fath Ali Shah arrived at the pasture of Ujan and ordered Muhammad Ali Mirza Dowlatshah to attack Georgia and Abbas Mirza to attack Ganjeh.
Dowlatshah captures Imamli and Vartanav then retreated.
September: Rebellion of Mir Mustafa Khan Talesh was defeated by the shah's army and he submitted.

1810
Abbas Mirza attempted to bring the Ottomans into the war.
8 February: Malcolm arrive in Bushehr for the third time.
April 19: Gen. Tormazov-Mirza Bozorg negotiations for 18 days at Askaran; Iran's stand toughened after the arrival of Jones.
23 June: Fath Ali Shah arrive at Pasture of Sultanieh.
August: Ottoman-Iranian treaty of alliance against Russia.
5 September: An Iranian force under Hosein Khan Sardar Iravani was defeated near the fort of Akhalsikh, 8000 killed.
5-12 Sep: Defeat of Ali Mirza (Zill al-Sultan) son of Fath Ali Shah in attempting to capture Ganjeh
23-28 September: Successful raids on Russian positions in Qara Kelisa (Vanadzor of Lori) but failure to capture Hammamlu (Spitak)

1809
17 September: Russian victory in the Finish War and Treaty of Fredrikshamn.

1810
22-30 May: Russian army defeated the Ottoman army at Silistria in northern Bulgaria.
26 August: Russian army defeated and Ottoman army at Batyn in northern Bulgaria.
9 September: Fall of Ottoman fortress of Rousse (northern Bulgaria) to Russian army.
26 October: Russian army defeated an Ottoman army at Vidin in northern Bulgaria.

1811

24 March: Ouseley entered Bushehr
June: Jones and Malcolm left Iran
April: Arrival in Tehran of an Ottoman delegation under Abd al-Vahhab Effendi to further coordinate joint efforts against Russia.
June: Failure of a joint Ottoman-Iranian attack on Russian forces.
September: Inconclusive military skirmishes.
14 Nov: Ouseley received by Fath Ali Shah.

1812

10-15 February: Iranian army routed a Russian force at Battle of Sultanabad (Sultanbout) near Shushi.
February-April: Anti-Russian rebellion in Georgia led by Alexander Bagration; skirmished between Iranian and Russian forces in Shuregul and Pambak; rebellion of Mir Mustafa Khan Talesh backed by Russia.
15 March: Defeat of Russian forces at Khoda Afarin.
12 June: Anglo-Iranian agreement signed by Ouseley
28 July: Start of new round of fighting between Russia and Iran.
August: A forty day truce between Iran and Russia mediated by the British ambassador to Tehran.
5 September: Abbas Mirza moved with a 10,000 man force and captured Lankaran and the rest of Talesh and moved his army toward Qarabagh..
30 October: Russian forces attacked Iranian army at Aslanduz
31 October: Russians attacked Iranian army for a second time and defeated it.
25 December: Fall of fortress of Arghavan (Talesh) to Russian army.
31 December: Beginning of Russian siege of Lankaran.

1811

1811-1818: Ottoman Saudi-Wahhabi War.
An Egyptian force landed at the port of Yanbu on behalf of Ottoman Sultan.
22 June: Russian army under Gen. Kutuzov defeated an Ottoman army near Rousse in Bulgaria.
10 December: A Russian force under Gen Pyotr Kotlyarevsky captured Ottoman fortress of Akhalkalaki in the Caucasus.

1812

24 May: Treaty of Bucharest ending Russo-Ottoman war.
18 June: The US declared war on Britain.
24 June: The French Grand Army crossed the River Neman in Poland
28 June: Napoleon entered Vilna
16-19 August: Inconclusive clashes between French and Russian forces at Smolensk
7 September: Russian forces routed at the Battle of Borodino
1 September: French Occupation of Moscow
19 October: Start of French retreat
December: Recapture of Medina by Ottoman forces
14 December: French army out of Russia

1813 1 January: Fall of Lankaran February: Rebellion of Yusuf Kashghari in northern Khorasan followed by other rebellions in the region. 12 October: Treaty of Golestan **1814** 25 November: The second agreement between Iran and Britain signed by Morrier and Henry Ellis in Tehran; the Ilchi mission to Russia **1817** 29 April: Yermonl left Tiflis for Iravan 3 May: Gen Yermolov entered Iravan 10 September: Yermolov received by Fath Ali Shah at Sultanieh **1819** 12 July: Death of Mirza Shafi' Mazandarani, the shah's chief minister and appointment of Sadr-Isfahani as his successor. **1821** 1821-1823: Iran-Ottoman War 14 November: Death of Muhammad Ali Mirza Dowlatshah. **1822** 14 August: Death of Mirza Bozorg the first Qa'em Maqam. **1823** July: Treaty of Erzerum ending Ira-Ottoman war. 19 October: Death of Sadr-e Isfahani the shah's chief minister 23 October: Abdallah Khan Sadr-e Isfahani (Amin al-Doeleh) appointed chief minister.	**1813** March: Recapture of Mecca by Ottoman forces. **1814** July: British victory at the Battle of Lundy's Lane August: British victory at the battle of Bladensburg and burning of Washington D.C. September: American victory at the Battle of Plattsburg. **1815** June: Major British defeat at New Orleans. **1816** Gen. Yermolov appointed governor of Georgia 22 Oct: Gen. Yermolov arrive in Tiflis **1819** Fall of Dir'ya to Ottoman army. 19 August: Mustafa Khan fled to Iran and Russia annexed Shirvan **1820** Gen. Yermolov removed the khans of Ghazi Qumuq and Shirvan whose khans fled to Iran. **1822** 21 November: Mehdi Qoli Khan Javanshir fled to Iran and Qarabagh was annexed by Russia.

1825

31 January: Arrival of Fath Ali Khan Biglerbeigi, the shah's envoy, in Tiflius.
February: Temporary Russian occupation of Lake Gokcha territory
28 March: Fath Ali Khan signed the Tiflis Accord with Gen. Yermolov over Gokcha dispute.
19 May: Removal of Amin Dowleh and appointment of Allahyar Khan Devellu Qajar, the Asef al-Dowlwh as sadr-e 'azam.
25 May: Arrival of Aqa Sayyed Hashem Mujtahed in Tehran to encourage the shah to go to war.
June: An 1800 man Russian infantry force with four canons reentered Gokcha territory.
5 September: Mirza Abu al-Hasan Khan Shirazi (Ilchi) appointed foreign minister.
19 October: Occupation of village of Balagh lu by a Russian unit with two canons and its withdrawal after arrival of Iranian military units in the area.
23 Oct: Mirza Sadeq Marvazi, the shah's envoy to Tiflis, left Tabriz for Tiflis
23-29 November: Negotiations between Mirza Sadeq and Gen. Valiaminov in Tiflis

1826

March: Arrival of Mirza Sadeq in Tehran
12 June: Fath Ali Shah arrived at Sultanieh
8 July: Abbas Mirza arrived at Sultanieh
10 July: Prince Menshikov arrived at Sultanieh
11 July: Arrival of a group of mujahids led by Aqa Sayyed Muhammad Isfahani from Kazemein
13 July: Menshikov had an audience with the shah
14 July: Second group of mujtahids led by Mullad Ahmad Naraqi arrived at Sultanieh
16 July: Abbas Mirza left Sultanieh
24 July: Menshikov left Sultanieh
24 July: The shah left Sultanieh for Ardabil

1825

Dec 1: Death of Alexander I and Nicholas I Tsar of Russia.
Dec 26: Decemberist Revolt.

1826

April 6: Anglo-Russian Protocol of St. Petersburg.

Second War: Phase I

8 July: Russian attack on Bash Aparan
25-26 July: Russian army reinforcement crossed into Talesh from the north and occupied Garmi, south of Lankaran while Iranian army entered Talesh from south and lined up against the Russian force.
28-30 July: Battle of Bash Aparan, Sardar Iravani opened hostilities by attacking Russian forces at Bash Aparan; Abbas Mirza crossed into Qarabagh
25 July: Fall of Lankaran to Iranian army.
1-3 August: Battle of Gyumri, north-Iravan.
2 August: Iranian army in Talesh engaged and pushed the Russian force toward north.
6 August: A force of 35000 under Abbas Mirza laid siege on Shusha while Talesh was captured followed by switching sides of Shakki, Shirvan.
19 August: Fall of Ganjeh to Iranian army.
9-12 August: Siege and fall of Lankaran by Iranian forces.
2 September: British envoy, Kinser MacDonald, had an audience with Fath Ali Shah.
5 September: Fath Ali Shah arrived in Ardebil
14 September: Fath Ali Shah arrived in Shusha.
16 September: Battle of Shamkor, defeat of Amir Khan Qajar and Muhammad Ali Mirza by Gen. Madatov outside Ganjeh.
17 September: Fall of Ganjeh to Russian army
22 September: Paskevich arrived in Caucasus
29 September: Abbas Mirza moved toward Ganjeh; Paskevich took command of the front line
13-17 October: Battle of Ganjeh: defeat of Abbas Mirza by Paskovich and Madatov.
27 October: Paskevich arrive in Shusha

Phase II

1827
9 January: Gen Madatov's 14 day raid north and south of Aras.
28 April: Fall of Uch Kelisa (Etchmiadzin) to Gen. Diebitch.
5 July: Battle of Khan Bulagh in Nakhjavan; Abbas Mirza's army arrived before fort of Abbas Abad which was under siege.
7 July: Abbas Mirza defeated by Paskevich and forts of Abbas Abad and Urdubad captured by Russian army.
17 August: Battle of Ashtarak near Iravan led by Abbas Mirza with limited defensive success.
19 September: Fall of Sardar Abad
1 October: Fall of Iravan
3 October: Fall of Marand
24 October: Fall of Tabriz

1828
25 January: Fall of Ardabil
2 February: Treaty of Turkmanchay
18 October: Griboydov arrived in Tabriz
22 December: Griboydov arrive in Tehran

1829
11 February: Massacre of the Russian mission in Tehran.
29 July: Khosrow Mirza's mission of apology arrived in Moscow
11 August: Khosrow Mirza's mission of apology arrived in St Petersburg.
22 August: Khosrow Mirza's audience with Tsar Nicolas I at Winter Palace in St Petersburg.

1833
25 October: Death of Abbas Mirza in Mashhad.

1834
June: Muhammad Mirza name heir to the throne.
24 October: Death of Fath Ali Shah in Isfahan.

1827
28 March: Yermolove replaced by Paskevich and Madatov was relieved of his command.

1828-1829
April 1828-Septemebr 1829: Russo-Ottoman War.
19June: Ottoman Qars (Kars) put under siege by Russian army.
23 June: Fall of Qars.
2 July: Fall of Ottoman Akhalkalaki to the Russian army.
15 August: Fall of Ottoman Akhaltsikhe to Russian army.
28 August: Fall of Ottoman Bayazid to Russian army.
June: Fall of ottoman Erzurum to Russian army.
29 September: Fall of Ottoman Varna (Bulgaria) to Russian army.

1829
19 June: Fall of Ottoman Sillistra to Russian army.
22 August: Fall of Ottoman Edrine (Adrianople) to Russian army.

BRIEF BIOGRAPHIES OF NOTABLE IRANIAN ACTORS:

Abd al-Vahhab, Neshat-e Isfahani (Mo'tamed al-Dowleh)- A famous literary figure and calligrapher in the court of Fath Ali Shah (d.1834). He was very much trusted and respected by the shah who, following his administrative reforms of 1809, appointed him his chief of staff (*monshi al-mamalek*) with the new title *mo'tamed al-mamalek* (the trusted of the state replacing Mirza Reza Qoli Nava'i.). The office of *monshi al-mamalek* up to 1809 included responsibility for foreign affairs and the shah's chief of staff, but after this date the responsibility of foreign affairs was given to another ministry. He was a staunch opponent of the second war with Russia arguing that the Qajar state did not have the capability and was not ready for such a conflict. [Mehdi Bamdad, *Tarikh-e rejal-e Iran*, vol.2, (Tehran, 147/1968), 318-320].

Ali Khan Saliyani- Son of Ibrahim Khan originally from Rudbar, ruler of Saliyan (in southern Shervan) during early years of Fath Ali Shah's reign. He fought on the Iranian side against the Russians and with the occupation of Saliyan, fled to Iran and his hereditary rule was abolished. [Ali Pur-safar, *Hokumatha-ye mahali-ye Qafqaz dar asr-e Qajar* (Tehran, 1377/1998), 103,104].

Ali Qoli Khan Shahsavan- One of the main commanders of Aqa Muhammad Shah's army who participated in the conquest of Tiflis in 1795. He was considered one of the best commanders in Abbas Mirza'a army who played a crucial role in encircling the Russian army in 1804 and during the first siege of Iravan. [Bamded, vol.1, 306; Jamil Qozanlu, *Tarikh nezami Iran*, vol.2 (Tehran, 1315/1935), 89; Jamal Javanshir, *Tarikh Karabagh* in *Two Chronicles on the History of Karabagh*, (Costa Mesa, 2004), 89].

Allahyar Khan Devellu-Qajar (Asef al-Dowleh)-Eldest son of Muhammad Khan Devellu -Qajar (Rokn al-Dowleh, also known as *tajbakhsh* or crown giver/king maker). He was Fath Ali Shah's chief minster 1824-1828, which was an exceptional appointment for a Qajar to become chief administrator. He was the shah's son-in-law and his sister was married to Abbas Mirza. His father played a key role in keeping the capital safe for Fath Ali Shah's arrival following Aqa Muhammad Shah's assassination in 1797. Asef was a hawkish supporter of escalating the second war with Russia and performed poorly in the battlefield and one of the first to flee to Tabriz. He was in command of troops in the citadel of Tabriz when the city was delivered to the Russians without a fight. He was put under house arrest and after release, he was ordered flogged in public by the shah for his cowardly performance. He was instrumental in fomenting public opinion against Russian ambassador Geriboydev, which resulted in massacre of Russian mission in Tehran in 1829. [Afshari, 59-67].

Amanallh Khan Afshar-Khamseh- Son of Farajallah Khan Afshar (*Nasaqshibashi*), from the prominent clan of Afshar of Khamseh and briefly governor of Khamseh (Zanjan). He was one of the leading commanders in Fath Ali Shah's army and one of the commanders sent to help Ibrahim Khalil Khan Javanshir in 1806 but arrived after his assassination by the Russians. [Bamdad, vol.1, 133; Muhammad Taqi Sepehr, *Nasekh al-tavarikh*, vol.1, (Tehran, 1377/1998), 171].

Amir Khan Devellu-Qajar (Sardar)- (d.1826) Son of Fath Ali Khan Devellu-Qajar, maternal uncle of Abbas Mirza and one of his main commanders. Killed at the battle of Shamkor during the second war with Russia. [Bamdad, 170-171].

Askar Khan Afshar-Orumi- A commander of Abbas Mirza's army who in 1805 was send to help against the Russian siege of Baku, which was successfully broken. In 1809, the shah sent him as ambassador to France, which did not produce positive results. He became a freemason while in Paris, perhaps the first Iranian to join a lodge. [Bamdad, vol.1, 446-447 and vol.2, 336-37].

Farajallah Khan Shahsavan-A commander of Abbas Mirza's army and one of the prominent chiefs of Shahsavan tribe of Ardadil and Mughan. He participated in wars against Tsitsianov over Baku in 1805. He was one of the commanders sent to help Ibrhim Khalil Khan Javanshir in Qarabagh but was late and arrived after his assassination. Later in 1806, the shah sent him to aid Sheikh Ali Khan of Qobbeh, but the people of Nukha rebelled against both and expelled them from the town before arrival of Russian army. [Bamdad, vol.2, 112, and vol.3, 78].

Hamzeh Khan Anzali- One of Abbas Mirza's commanders on the Iravan front during the second war with Russia. He was one of the defenders of Iravan, which fell to Gen parkevich after a twelve day siege.

He became a prisoner of war alongside Hasan Khan Sari Aslan, and Mirza Mahmud Khan Maqsudllu-astarabadi. They were taken to Tiflis and released after Turkmanchay. [Bamdad, 461].

Hosein Qoli Khan Badkubeh- The khan of Badkubeh (Baku), who sided with Iran during the Russo-Iranian Wars. In 1805 when the Russian army landed on the shores of Baku, with the help of the shah and the khans of Qobbeh-Darband and Lezgi, he repulse the Russian siege. In early 1806 he tricked the Russian commander Tsitsianov to meet him outside the city walls where he and his entourage were assassinated by the khan's cousin, Ibrahim Khan Badkubeh. When the Russian army approached Baku once again in late 1806, the people of the town rebelled against the khan rather than go through another Russian siege. Subsequently, Hosein Khan and his immediate family fled to Iran. He participated in the second war with Russia and laid siege on Baku in the summer of 1826 but had to withdraw after Abbas Mirza's defeat at Ganjeh. After settling in Iran's Arak rejoin, the family came to be called Badkubeh, while another branch of the family that remained and collaborated with the Russians came to be called Bakikhanov. [Bamdad, vol.1, 446-447. Pur-safar, 101].

Hosein Qoli Khan Qavanllu-Qajar Qazvini (Sardar Iravani-1742-1830)-Son of Muhammad Khan Qajar, governor of Iravan during the reign of Fath Ali Shah. He was the older brother of Hasan Khan Sari Aslan (yellow lion). The two brothers started their career as royal guards in the court of Aqa Muhammad Shah. He became commander of the royal guards (*qoleler aqassi*) early in Fath Ali Shah's reign and played a major role in defeating Sadeq Khan Shahqaqi at the battle of Khak-e Ali in August 1797. Next, he participated in the shah's campaigns in Khorasan between during 1799-1803 and became a military commander to Muhammad Vali Mirza, the shah's son and ruler of Khorasan. In 1806 he was recalled to Tehran and made general in the imperial army by the shah and was sent to Qarabagh to the aid of Ibrahim Khalil Khan Javanshir but reached Shushi after the Russians had murdered the khan. He became governor of Iravan in 1806 and ruled over it until 1827 with the title *Sardar Iravani* (Commander of Iravan). He commissioned building of the fort of Sardar Abad, west of Uch Kelisa (Echmiadzen). His younger brother, Hasan Khan Sari Aslan, was one of his main commanders. The Sardar was one of the most capable commanders in the Qajar army and defended Iravan against the Russians a number of times. Finally, defeated in October 1927 by Gen. Paskevich, he managed to escape before the fall of Iravan. His brother and other commanders became prisoners of war and transferred to Tiflis. [Bamdad. vol.1, 401-404; George Bournoutian, "Husayn Qoli Khan Qazvini Sardar of Erevan: a Portrait of a Qajar Administrator," in *Iranian* Studies 9:2/3 (1969), 63-79].

Ibrahim Khalil Khan Javanshir of Qarabagh (d.1806)-Son of Panah Ali Khan, the ruler of Qarabagh until he was murdered by the Russians near Shushi. He changed sides several times in the conflict between Iran and Russia. His son and successor, Mehdi Qoli Khan collaborated with the Russians until he fled to Iran in 1822. His grandson, Ja'far Qoli Khan also collaborated with the Russians and played a role in Ibrahim Khalil's murder and was rewarded the Khanate of Shakki until he was removed and fled to Iran. [Muriel Atkin, "Strange Death of Ibrahim Khalil Khan of Qarabagh," in *Iranian Studies*, 12:1/2 (979), 79–107; Bamdad, vol.1, 10-13].

Ibrahim Khan Shirazi (Kalantar-I'timad al-Dowleh)- Also known with the title *tajbakhsh* (He who bestows the crown or king-maker), son of Haj Hashem Shirazi, from a prominent Jewish family originally from Qazvin which had converted to Islam. This family later took the last name of Qavam-shirazi. Ibrahim Khan served the Zand rulers and was chief minister to Lutf Ali Khan but betrayed him in favor of Aqa Muhammad Khan. Next he became the chief minister to Aqa Muhammad's heir-apparent Baba Khan Jahanbani (future Fath Ali Shah) when he was governor of Fars, then he became the shah's chief minister with the title *I'timad al-Dowleh* (The trusted of realm), replacing Mirza Shafi' Mazandarani in 1796. After the assassination of Aqa Muhammad Shah in 1797, he continued to be chief minister to Fath Ali Shah until his execution by the order of the shah in 1801. He played a crucial role in the victory of Aqa Muhammad over Lutf Ali and again after the assassination of the shah in collecting forces and organizing stste finances for Fath Ali Shah to defeat his completion. He negotiated and signed the Anglo-Iranian Treaty of 1800 on behalf of Iran. [Parviz Afshari, *Sard 'azamha-ye selseleh-ye Qajar*, (Tehran, 1373/1994), 49/1970), 14–20; Bamdad, vol.1, 21-28].

Isma'il Khan Sardar Damghani- Also known as Isma'il Beg Gholam and Isma'il *Qezel* (red Isma'il), was from Sangesar (Semnan) but came to be known as "Damghani." He was commander of Fath Ali Shah's royal guards (*gholaman khaseh*) and his most trusted officer who had the privilege to enter the imperial harem and visit the shah. He and his brothers (Zolfaqar Khan, Mottaleb Khan and Muhammad Ali Khan) started their careers as royal guards in the court of Fath Ali Shah. They earned the shah's trust and moved up the ladder of power and became respected commanders in the shah's army. During the first siege of Iravan in 1804, Isma'il Khan led the vanguard units of Abbas Mirza's army and again during the battle of Qarabagh in 1805 he spearheaded the army. In 1806, the shah sent him, Sardar Iravani, and Amanallah Khan Khamseh-Afshar to help Ibrahim Khalil Khan Javanshir of Qarabagh, but they were late, as the Russians had already murdered the khan. . He died in 1812 during the battle of Aslanduz. [sbd al-Razzaq Donboli, *Ma'aser-e Sultaniyyeh* (Tehran, 183/2004), 227, G. Drouville, *Safarnameh-ye Drouville* (Tehran, 1337/1958), 159-161; Mirza Muhammad Sadeq Marvazi, *Ahang-e sorush ya tarikh jangha-ye Iran-Rus* (Tehran, 169/1990), 95; Bamdad, vol.1, 132-134].

Javad Khan Ziyadllu (Ziyadughllu) Qajar-Hereditary ruler of Ganjeh whose clan name is pronounced both Ziyadllu and Ziyad Ughllu. Similar to other khans of the Caucasus, he vacillated between Russia and Iran a number of times before coming down on the side of Iran. In 1804, Russian army invaded Ganjeh and Javad Khan put up stiff resistance but was defeated after heavy Russian bombardment. The Russians killed him, along with his son and many members of his family and massacred many civilians of Ganjeh. His other son, Ughuzlu Khan fled to Iran and returned to Ganjeh in summer of 1826 and retreated with Iranian army and was captured by the Russians shortly after. The prominent Ziyadkhanov family of Ganjeh is his descendant, [Bamdad, vol.1, 287-288; George Bournoutian, "Prelude to War: the Russian siege and Storming of Ganjeh, 1803–1804," in *Iranian Studies*, 50:1 (2017), 107-125].

Kalb Ali Khan Kangarllu-Qajar- From prominent Kargarllu clan of Nakhjavan, he was the khan of Nakhjavan and related to Muhammad Khan Qavanllu-Qajar, khan of Iravan until 1805. He resisted Aqa Muhmmad Khan initially but submitted to him 1796. In 1797, he joined the Russians during the Zubov campaign and was caught and blinded by the shah and removed from his position. Fath Ali Shah reinstated him and his family to Nakhjavan but removed him again in 1807. One of his sons, Sheikh Ali Khan, was the commandant of the fort of Urdubad and the other, Ehsan Khan, commandant of the fortress of Abbas Abad, both in Nakhjavan. During the second Russian war, in

1827, both brothers betrayed Iran and delivered the strongholds to the Russians without fight and received appointments and other rewards. [Bamdad, vol.5, 121, George Bournoutian, *the Khanate of Eravanunder Qajar Rule 1795-1828* (Costa Mesa, 1992), 8-9; Donboli, 192, Pur-safar, 167-169].

Manuchehr Khan Gorji (Mo'tamed al-Dowleh) – (d.1847) A capable administrator who served both Aqa Muhammad Shah and Fath Ali Shah. Known as the Georgian (Gorji-d.1847), he was actually an Armenian captured by Aqa Muhamad Khan in his Georgian campaign of 1795. He was castrated and became one of the most powerful state functionaries. He became chief of court eunuchs (*ich aghassi*) and later chief Chamberlain of the court (*ishik aghassi bashi*) in Tehran. Later be became governor of Isfahan until his death. He was in opposition to the second war with Russia. [Bamdad, vol.4, 159-163].

Mehdi Qoli Khan Devellu-Qajar- One of the most competent commanders of Abbas Mirza in the Russian wars over Iravan (1804) and Qarabagh (1805). Son of Muhammad Zaman Khan and nephew of Mustafa Khan Qavanllu-Qajar, a commander of Aqa Muhammad Shah. In 1804, he commanded a cavalry force and made the first contact with the invading Russian army under Gen. Tsitsianov. In 1806 after the failure and retreat of Abbas Mirza from Ganjeh, he commanded the regrouped and resupplied branch of the army in Iravan and subsequently became the governor of Iravan until 1806. [Bamdad, vol.4, 176; Qozanlu, *Tarikh nezami Iran*, vol.2, 736 and 748.)

Mir Mustafa Khan of Talesh- (d.1814) Son of Qara Khan and hereditary khan of northern part of Talesh until his death. He cooperated with Russians and considered Russia the lesser danger to his dominion. He helped Aqa Muhammad Khan's brother who was backed by Russia but was defeated by Aqa Muhammad twice in 1790s. In 1795, a Qajar force under Mustafa Khan Devellu-Qajar defeated him and captured Lankaran. He cooperated with Gen. Zubov's invading army in 1796 and received the rank of colonel in the Russian army. In May 1797, Aqa Muhammad Shah recaptured Lankaran for the second time. His dominion fell under Russian control after Golestan Treaty (1813). His son and successor, Hasan Khan, sided with Iran during the second war. [Hosein Ahmadi, *Talesh az dowran- Safavieh ta payan jang dovvom Iran va Rus* (Tehran, 1380/2001), 111-112; Bamdad. vol.4, 106-107, Pur-safar, 158-163].

Mirza Asadollha Nuri, son of Khawjeh Aqa Baba Beg and father of Mirza Aqa Khan Nuri, a future chief minister under Nasser al-Din Shah Qajar. In 1780, he joined Aqa Muhammad Khan in his conquest of Mazandaran, and entered his service and was named revenue officer, a position he kept under Fath Ali Shah and later became his minister of the army. [Bamdad, vol.1, 118-119].

Mirza Abu al-Qasem (Qa'em Maqam II, 1779-1835)-Son of Mirza Isa (Bozorg) Farahani (Qa'em Maqam I) who inherited his father's title and position after his death in 1822 and became Abbas Mirza's chief advisor. The shah removed him from that position because of opposition in the court of Tehran regarding political decisions in the court of Tabriz. He was reinstated in 1826 and was apparently against the second war with Russia but unable to voice his strong opposition because of his vulnerable position at the court. He was instrumental in putting Muhammad Shah on the throne after Fath Ali Shah's death in 1834 but was ordered murdered by the new shah. He was also a noted literary figure, credited with reforming Persian language. [Afshari, 93-95, Abbas Amanat, "Russian Intrusion into the Guarded Domaain: Reflections of a Qajar Stateman on European Expansion," in *Journal of American Oriental Society*, 113:1 (1993), 35-56, Bamdad, vol.1, 60-64].

Mirza Isa (Bozorg) Farahani (Qa'em Maqam I- d. 1822)-From Farahan in Araq-e Ajam (Arak), belonged to the Persian speaking scribal class providing crucial bureaucratic service to ruling dynasties of Iran. He began his service at the court of Karim Khan Zand in Shiraz and then entered the service of the Qajar shahs. He was appointed chief minister to Abbas Mirza after the latter's was appointment governor of Azarbaijan, in Tabriz. In 1805, he accompanied the prince to Tabriz where Abbas Mirza took charge of war with Russia. As his teacher and chief advisor, Mirza Bozorg was instrumental in guiding Abbas Mirza to initiate modern military reforms and later sending students abroad and establishing the first printing press in Tabriz. During the first war with Russia he was commissioned to solicit support of the ulama, which he did and which was published in a collection titled *Resale-ye jahadiyyeh*. He received the title of Deputy to the Chief Minister of the Shah (*qa'em maqam*) in 1806 and groomed his elder son, Mirza Hasan, to succeed him but upon his death in 1812, he made his other son, Abu al-Qasem, his successor who inherited his father's title and became Qa'em Maqam II. Mirza Bozorg died in the plague of 1821-22. [Afshari, 90-93].

Muhammad Hosein Khan Qavanllu-Qajar- The Khan of Iravan until 1805 who during the Russian advances in the region, and similar to other local khans, attempted unsuccessfully to play Russia and Iran against each other in order to save his own position. Aqa Muhammad Khan forced his submission in his campaign of 1795, but the khan returned to his old habits after the assassination of the shah. When open war broke out in summer 1804, the khan initially sided with Russians, but later asked for pardon from the shah. Finally, Fath Ali Shah removed him and his family from Iravan and sent them to internal exile in 1805. [Bamdad, vol.3, 272-273].

Muhammad Hosein Khan Sadr-e Isfahani (d.1823) - Son of Muhammad Ali from a prominent family of Isfahan. He hosted Aqa Muhammad Khan in Isfahan and financially supported his campaign against the Zand in Shiraz and was rewarded by the shah who appointed him governor of Isfahan. He continued in this post during early years of Fath Ali Shah's reign. In 1806, he was appointed mint-master of the dominion (*musto'fi al-mamalek*) and received the title *amin al-dowleh* (trusted of the state). In 1813, he received the title of *amir nezam* (commander of the army) and became governor of Fars and Araq-e Ajam (Arak), and passed on his previous title to his son Abdollah. He became the shah's Sadr-e 'Azam (chief minister) 1818-1823 and was involved in peace negotiations with Ottoman Empire, which led to the Peace Treaty of Erzurum in 1823. He immigrated to Baghdad where he died. [Afshari, 45–55].

Muhammad Shafi' Qadimi-Mazandarani (Sadr-e 'Azam) - Son of Mirza Haji Ahmad, from an Isfahani family which had resettled in Mazandaran after the fall of Nader's empire in 1747. He was a religious and literary scholar who joined Aqa Muhammad Shah and later Fath Ali Shah. He was Aqa Muhammad's Chief Minister until 1796 when he was replaced by Ibrahim Khan Kalantar. He was a chief enemy of Ibrahim Khan and played a part in his demise in 1801. Following the murder of Ibrahim Khan, he became Fath Ali Shah's chief minister until his death in 1818. He singed the Anglo-Iranian treaty (1809) with Hartford Jones on behalf of the shah. [Afshari, 32-38].

Mustafa Khan Devellu-Qajar- Son of Muhammad Hosein Khan one of Aqa Muhammad Khan's military commanders. He aided Aqa Muhammad in his wars of unification and was killed during his Caucasian campaign of 1795. [Bamdad, vol.4, 108-112, Sepehr, vol.2, 78).

Mustafa Khan of Shirvan- Ruler of Shirvan, he cooperated with Russia and was defeated and removed by Aqa Muhammad Khan in 1795 until he agreed to pay him taxes. He once again rebelled and joined the Russians in 1805 prompting Fath Ali Shah to send an army to force his submission. In 1806, he went to the Russian side once again. Shirvan was ceded to Russia in 1813 and Mustafa Khan was removed and fled to Iran in 1820. He returned briefly with the Iranian army in 1826, but after Abbas Mirza's defeat, fled to Iran once again. [Bamdad, vol.4, 105-106].

Pir Qoli Khan Shambayati-Qajar- He was a mid-level commander in Aqa Muhammad Khan's army during his conquest of the Caucasus in 1795. He became governor of Khoy and Slamas in Azarbaijan and commanded other campaigns, including in 1800 in Khorasan and throughout the first Russo-Iranian War. Durin war with Russia, was a major commander in Abbas Mirza's army and commanded the northern sector of the battlefield during the first siege of Iravan in 1804. He played a major role in encircling Gen. Tsitsianov's army and preventing resupplies reaching it. [Bamdad, vol.1, 201–202, Donboli, 190].

Reza Qoli Nava'i (Monshi al-Mamalek)- Son of Abd al-Majid from the village of Nava in Larijan district. He was a trusted functionary in the courts of Aqa Muhammad Shah and Fath Ali Shah. Aqa Muhammad put him in charge of taking delivery of Zand family and jewelry and bringing them to Tehran in 1791. As *monshi al-mamlek* he was in charge of both foreign affairs and acted as the shah's chief of staff until 1809 when Fath Ali Shah appointed him the chief minister of his fourth son, Muhammad Vali Mirza the ruler of Khorasan. [Bamdad, vol.2, 37-38]

Sadeq Khan Az al-Dinllu: A capable military commander in Abbas Mirza's army. During the spring and summer of 1805 participated in the Battle of Qarabagh with the rank of colonel (*sarhang*). During 1805 battle of Shushi, he was a commander of cavalry and showed much courage and was wounded. He became a commander in *Nezam Jadid* and killed defending Lankaran in 1813. [Donboli, 228; Jones, *Dynasty of the Qajars*, (London, 1833), 229; Qozanlu, *Tarikh nezami Iran*, vol.2, 735].

Sadeq Khan Shaqaqi- A Kurdish chieftain who fought against Aqa Muhammad Shah but later submitted and joined him. He was present in Shushi when the shah was assassinated in May 1797. Subsequently he took the royal jewelry and gave refuge to the assassins, and rebelled against Fath Ali Shah. He was defeated and surrendered and gave back the jewelry and was given a minor governorship position. He rebelled again in 1799 and was defeated, and killed by the order of the shah. [Reza Qoli Hedayat, *Fehrest al-tavarikh* (Tehran, 171/1994). 334].

Salim Khan Shakki- Son of Hosein Khan and grandson of Haji Chalabi, hereditary rulers of Shakki. He was a son-in-law of Ibrahim Khalil Khan Javanshir of Qarabagh and joined him in submitting to Russian in 1805. In 1806, Fath Ali Shah sent Farajallah Khan Shahsavan to his aid after the Russians defeated him. Selim fought the Russians twice in 1806 and lost when the Lezgis in his army defected to the Russians and the people of Nokha did not allow him into the city. He fled to Iran and settled in Ardabil. The Russians made Ja'far Qoli Khan Javanshir (grandson of Ibrahim Khalil) the new khan of Shakki but removed him in 1811 thus ending local rule of the khanate. [Bamdad, vol.2, 112, Pursafar, 118-123].

Sheikh Ali Khan of Qobbeh and Darband- Son of Fath Ali Khan hereditary ruler of Qobbeh, Darband and (at one point) Shirvan and Baku. Fath Ali Khan was an adversary of Javanshir and intended to capture Azarbaijan but was stopped by Javanshir. Sheikh Ali Khan was related to the Lezgi tribe of Akhusha and the Shamkhal of Tarkov north of Darband. He opposed Aqa Muhammad in his campaign of 1795 and sought Russian help, but when the Russians arrived not to help but to rule, he turned against them. Gen. Zobov's siege of Darband resulted in the local population rebelling against Sheikh Ali and delivering the fort to the enemy. Sheikh Ali was subsequently arrested by the Russians but fled and returned to Darband after Russian withdrawal in late 1796. He lost Darband to Muhammad Khan Ghazi of Qomuq in 1800 but retook it upon his death in 1803. During the first Rosso-Iranian War, he generally sided with Iran and received aid from Abbas Mirza. In 1805, he joined Surkhay Khan in helping the khan of Baku, with help from Abbas Mira, to break Russian siege of that city. In 1806, he lost Darband to the Russians, after the local population again refused to fight. However, with aid from Iran he held on to Qobbeh and opened dialogue with the Russians with the hope of maintaining his position in Qobbeh. In 1808, a combined Russian-Shirvan force defeated him and captured Qobbeh and Shaykh Ali fled to Daghestan. In 1810 and again in 1811, he attempted to recapture Qobbeh with help from his allies in Daghistan but despite some tactical successes, he ultimately failed. He continued to fight the Russian occupation army after Treaty of Golestan until his death sometime before 1820. Sheikh Ali Khan was one of the more daring and persistent local rulers fighting Russia. [Abbas Qoli Aqa Bakikhanov, *the Heavenly Rose-Garden* (Washington D.C., 2009), 200-201, Javanshir, 83-84, Pur-safar, 65-69].

Suleiman Khan Qavanllu-Qajar (E'tezad al-Dowleh--1769-1806)- Son of Iskandar Khan, maternal cousin of Aqa Muhammad Shah, one of his military commanders who conquered Talesh and Azarbaijan in 1790s. He was close to Aqa Muhammad who affectionately called him *khal oghli* (maternal cousin). Suleiman Khan had remained behind in Adineh Bazar-Mughan guarding five of the shah's nephews while he went out to capture Shushi in May 1797. After the shah's assassination few days later, he rebelled against Fath Ali Shah but later submitted and pardoned. In the summer of 1804, when the fifteen-year-old Abbas Mirza was sent to confront the Russian army, Suleiman Khan acted as one of his main military commanders. In 1805, when the new shah dispatched Abbas Mirza to Azarbaijan to take permanent command of the Russian war and governorship of the region, Suleiman Khan accompanied him as one of his tutors and stayed with him until his death. [Bamdad, vol.2, 118-119].

Surkhay Khan II (سورخای) of Daghestan (d. 1827)-Son of Muhammad Khan and ruler of Ghazi Qomaq in southern Daghestan. He was a rival of the khan of Qobbeh and Darband until arrival of Russian army when he allied himself with Sheikh Ali Khan of Qobbeh. In 1805, he sent his son, Nuh Khan, to join him in order to aid the khan of Badkubeh (Baku) against a Russian siege. In 1811, he again sent Nuh to aid Sheikh Ali retake Qobbeh from the Russians but, after initial success, they were defeated and Sheikh Ali fled to Daghestan. Next, the Russian army came after Surkhay Khan who fled to Iran and returned to his dominion in 1814. He was once again forced to flee to Iran in 1820 after Gen. Eermolov removed him and the khans of Shirvan and Qarabagh and put their dominions under direct Russian rule. (Pur-safar, 52-54).

Umm Khan (عم) of Avar- Son of Nousal or Nursal Khan, Lezgi chieftain and ruler of Avar in northern Caucasus. He was related by marriage to Ibrahim Khalil Khan Javanshir and similar to him, he at times allied with the Russians and at other time fought against them while he competed with other khans of the region for domination. The Russian army defeated him decisively in November 1799, he died in March 1800. (Pursafar, 16, Javanshir, *Two Chronicles*, 84).

BRIEF BIOGRAPHIES OF NOTABLE RUSSIAN ACTORS:

Ermolov (Yermolov), Aleksey P- (1772-1861) was born a Russian noble family. He participated in the Napoleonic wars with distinction and appointed Governor of Georgia and commander of Independent Georgian Corps in 1816, which lasted nine years. He headed a diplomatic mission to Iran in 1817. He treated the Muslim population of Russian occupied southeaster Caucasus with a heavy hand and was instrumental in igniting the second Russo-Iranian war. [Alexander Mikaberidze, *the Russian Officer Corps in the Revolutionary and Napoleonic Wars* (New York, 2005), 95-97].

Gudovich Count Ivan Vasilyevich- (1741-1820) was born into a prominent Russian nobel family. and was a military leader of Ukrainian descent. He participated in the Russo-Ottoman was 1188-1791 an was appointed Russian military commander of the Caucasus line. He resigned after the fall of Tiflis in 1795, when overall command was given to Gen. Valerian Zobov. Reinstated as commander and governor of Russian Caucasus in 1808 when he unsuccessfully laid siege on Iravan for a second time, after which he was removed from his post. (Mikaberidze, 142-143]

Knorring Karl. F. –Ltd. Gen. in Russian army, appointed commander of Russian forces in the Caucasus in 1799. Appointed administrator in chief of the Caucasian Line and a key player in the annexation of eastern Georgia. Removed from his post because of his mistreatment of the Georgian royal house and charges of corruption.

Kotlyarevskii Pyotr S- (1782 –1852) A Russian military hero of the early 19th century. He was known an *Qezil Mayor* (red major) to the Iranian in local Turkic dialect. When a major in Russian army, he along with Col. Kariagin fought Abbas Mirza larger force with 600 men and 2 guns- of the 17th Jagers in 1805 in Qarabagh. Successfully retreated from Shushi to the fort of Askaran and then to the fort of Shah Bulaghi. He lost one third of his force before he rescued by Tsitsianov. He Defeated Abbas Mirza at Aslanduz (1812) and captured Lankaran (1813). (Mikaberidze 203-204).

Lazarev Ivan P (Lazarian)-(d.1803) Maj. Gen in Russian army, he was a member of wealthy Armenian family. Appointed in 1799 commander of a Russian Jager regiment in Tiflis, trained to fight in mountainous terrain. Dowager Queen Daria of Georgia killed him when he forced his way into her private quarters. [George Bournoutian, *Russians and Armenians in Transcaucasia*, (Costa Mesa, 1992), 46].

Lisanevich Dimitri T- (1780-1825) Colonel in Russian army stationed in Shushi. He was responsible for the murder of Ibrahim Khalil Khan Javanshir, the khan of Qarabagh, and his entourage in 1806. He spoke local Turkish, and was infamous for his bad temper and cursing, thus the title "crazy major" (*dali mayor*) by the locals. Killed in a bout in 1825.

Madatov Valerian "Rostam" G- (1782-1829) He was born in an Armenian noble family (*melik*) called Madadiyan. He was Ltd. Gen. in Russian army Empire. He was second in command to Gen. Paskevich during the second Russo-Iranian War. [Mikaberidze, 239-240].

Nebolsin Peter F-(d.1810) Maj. General in Russian army (1804) participated in a number of battles in 1806-1810 in Caucasus. (Mikaberidzs, 271).

Paulucci Filippo-(1779 – 1849) An Italian marquis and an adjutant general in Russian army. He took part in the war against the Ottoman Empire in 1810. Appointed quartermaster of the Caucasian Army in 1811 and later Governor of Georgia, where he simultaneously had to wage war against the Ottoman Empire at Qars (Kars), and Iran in Qarabagh and other insurgents in eastern Caucasus. [Mikaberidze, 299-300].

Paskevich Ivan F- (1782-1856) A Ukrainian-born General in Russian army. For his victories, he was made Count of Erivan in 1828 with the title *Irvanskii*. He attained the rank of field marshal in the Russian army, and later in the Prussian and Austrian armies. [Mikaberidze, 296-298].

Rtischev Nicolas E-(1754-1835)—A Maj. Gen. in Russian army. Appointed commander of Russian army in Georgia in 1811 and governor of Russian occupied Caucasus in 1812. He took vigorous measures in defeating anti-Russian uprisings in Daghestan, eastern Georgia, and mountainous regions of north Caucasus. He was the heist ranking Russian official at the time of signing of Treaty of Golestan. [Mikaberidze, 341].

Reutt Iosif A-(b.1786) Polish born Ltd. Gen. in Russian army, participated in the first battle of Iravan (1804), fought in campaign against Shirvan (1805), and siege of Baku (1806), commanded defense of Shusha in summer 1826. (Bornoutian, *Russians and the Armenians*, 261).

Suvorov Alexander Vasilyevich (1730-1800), one of the most influential generals of Russian army, born into a Russian noble family of Swedish descent. He fought in the Seven Years war and during 1787-1791 was mostly involved in wars against the Ottoman Empire. [Alexander Mikaberidze, 387-388].

Tormasov Alexander P-(1751-1819) Born in a Russian noble family and a general in Russian army. During 1788-1791, participated in the Russo-Ottoman war, commanding a cavalry brigade. During 1792-1794, he fought against Polish insurgents. Appointed commander-in-chief of troops in Georgia in June 1808 and replaced Gudovich in September 1808. He negotiated with Qa'em Maqam I at the fort of Askaran in early 1810, and defeated Sardar Iravani at Akhalkaki and Abbas Mirza at Megri in September 1810. (Mikaberidze, 401-402).

Tsitsianov Pavel D-(1754-1806) A Ltd. Gen. in Russian army, born in prominent noble Georgian family. Appointed Governor of Georgia and the Inspector of the Caucasian Line in 1812. Called by the derogatory name *ishpokhdor* by Iranians, he was responsible arresting and exiling the Georgian royal family and opening the first Russo-Iranian war in 1803 by attacking and capturing Ganjeh. Assassinated in 1806 outside the wall of Baku while attempting to negotiate of that khanate with its local ruler. [Mikaberidze, 406-407].

Zubov Count Valerian A- (1771-1804) A Russian general who led the invasion of south eastern Caucasus in 1796 in retaliation for Aqa Muhmmad Khan'ss conquest of Georgia in 1795. Known as *qezel iyaq* (golden leg) by Iranians. His older brother. Prince Platon A. Zubov (1767-1822) was the last of Catherine II's favorites and the most powerful man in Russia during the last years of her reign. The older Zubov was instrumental in giving his younger brother the command of the invading army. The Russian army evacuated the area after the death of Catherine II in 1797.

NOTES

Introduction

i   Eugen Weber, "History is what Historians Do," *New York Times*, July 22, 1984.
ii   Nader's loot was worth 700 million rupees. It took thousands of camels and mules, as well as three hundred elephants, to haul it back to Iran. See Michael Axworthy, *The Sword of Persia* (London: 2006), 211–13.
iii Ibid., 249.
iv   Axworthy, 236–8; Jones Hanway, *History of Nader Shah*, trans. Isma'il Dawlatshahi (Tehran: 1365/1986), 154–62.
v   For a discussion of this period's prosperity, see: Parviz Rajabi, *Karim khan-e Zand va azaman-e ou* (Tehran: 1367/2008), 155–211.
vi   Mirza Saleh Shirazi, *Safarnameh Mirza Saleh Shirazi* (Tehran: 1363/1984), 31–119.
vii Geoffrey Parker, *The Military Revolution: Military Innovation and the Rise of the West* (Cambridge: 1996), 1–2.
viii Paul Bushkovitch, "The Politics of Command in the Army of Peter the Great," in David Schimmelpenninck van der Oye and Bruce W. Menning, eds., *Reforming the Tsar's Army* (Cambridge: 2004), 25–273.
ix   For Russian population and territorial growth see: Nicholas V. Riasanovsky, *A History of Russia*, 4th edn. (Oxford: 1984), 276–7; Gary Marker, "The Age of Enlightenment 1740–1801," in Gregory L. Freeze, ed., *Russia: A History* (Oxford: 1997), 141; Muriel Atkin, *Russia and Iran, 1780–1828* (Minnesota: 1980), 99.
x   Bushkovitch, "The Politics of Command," 190.

Chapter 1

i   John Malcolm, *The History of Persia*, vol. 2 (London: 1829), 201.
ii   Information on the general history and roots of the Qajar tribe is from the following: Ali Qoli Mirza E'tezad Saltaneh, *Eksir al-tavarikh* (Tehran: 1370/1986), 1–25; Abdal-Razzaq Donboli, *Ma'aser Sultaniyyeh* (Tehran: 1383/2004), 31–5; Mirza Fazollah Khavari-shirazi, *Tarikh dh al-qarneyn*, vol. 1 (Tehran: 1380/2001), 19–21; Muhammad Taqi Sepehr, *Nasekh al-tavarikh*, vol. 1 (Tehran: 1338/1959), 7–10.
iii Abbas Amanat, *Iran: A Modern History* (New Haven and London: 2017), 166.

iv   Malcolm, *History of Persia*, vol. 2, 203–4.
v   Abdollah Mostofi, *Tarikh-e edari va ejtema'i-ye Qajariyeh* (Tehran: 1321/1942), vol. 1, 11–12.
vi   James B. Fraser, *An Historical and Descriptive Account of Persia* (Edinburgh: 1834), 270; Malcolm, *History of Persia*, vol. 2, 205; Mirza Ahmad Azod al-Dowleh, *Tarikh-e Azodi* (Tehran: 1376/1997), 163.
vii Mostofi, *Tarikh-e edari*, vol. 1, 14.
viii Some of the other Ashaqeh-bash clans were: Shambayati, Ishllu, and Ziyadllu or Ziyadoghllu. Some of the other Yukhari-bash clans were: Sepanllu, Kuhanllu, and Qiyaqllu. See: Ann Lambton, *Qajar Persia* (Austin, TX: 1987), 3.
ix   Reza Qoli Hedayat, *Fehrest al-tavarikh* (Tehran: 1373/1994), 331; H. Fasa'i, *The History of Persia Under Qajar Rule*, trans. H. Busse (New York: 1972), 104; Azod al-Dowleh, *Tarikh-e Azodi*, 110.
x   Gavin Hambly, "Agha Muhammad Khan and the Establishment of the Qajar Dynasty," in *The Cambridge History of Iran*, vol. 7 (Cambridge: 1991), 106–7.
xi   Hedayat, *Fehrest*, 294.
xii ó Ali Akbar Dehkhoda, *Loghat nameh Dehkhoda*, 2:1:1 (Tehran: 1325/1946); Muhammad Mo'in, *Farhang-e Mo'in*, vol. 1 (Tehran: 1382/2003), vol. 1.
xiii Dehkhoda, *Loghat nameh Dehkhoda* and Mo'in, *Farhang-e Mo'in*. Nafisi argues that in original Turkic, there was no difference in spelling between the two and one spelling was used for both man and eunuch. Dictionary evidence contradicts his assertion. See: Sa'id Nafisi, *Tarikh ejtema'i va siyasi Iran dar dowreh-ye mo'aser*, vol. 1 (Tehran: 1344/1965), 42.
xiv *Asnad va mokatabat-e tarikhi Iran (Qajar)*, vol. 2 (Tehran: 1366/1987), document 1.
xv   Azod al-Dowleh, *Tarikh-e Azodi*, 164.
xvi Mostofi, *Tarikh-e edari*, vol. 1, 5; Azod al-Dowleh, *Tarikh-e Azodi*, 166.
xvii E'tezad Saltaneh, *Eksir*, 21–8; Muhammad Fathollah Saravi, *Tarikh-e Muhammadi* (Tehran: 1371/1992), 5–59.
xviii Amanat, *Iran: A Modern History*, 161.
xix Information on this round of fighting is from the following: E'tezad Saltaneh, *Eksir*, 25–7; Saravi, *Tarikh-e Muhammadi*, 260–83; Sepehr, *Nasekh al-tavarikh*, vol. 1, 35–85; Hedayat, *Fehrest*, 286-324.
xx   George Bournoutian, *From the Kur to the Aras* (Leiden and Boston: 2021), 14–15; Sean Pollack, *Empire by Invitation? Russian Empire Building in the Caucasus in the Reign of Catherine II*, Dissertation, Department of History, Harvard University (Cambridge, MA: 2006), 241.
xxi Hedayat, *Fehrest*, 290–1; Saravi, *Tarikh-e Muhammadi*, 163; E'tezad Saltaneh, *Eksir*, 51.
xxii Sepehr, *Nasekh al-tavarikh*, vol. 1, 44–5 and 190–1.

xxiii	For Aqa Muhammad's conquest of Azarbaijan, see: Saravi, *Tarikh-e Muhammadi*, 190–8; Sepehr, *Nasekh al tavarikh*, vol. 1, 57–9.
xxiv	Ibrahim Khalil, the khan of Qarabagh, offered two of his relatives. These two attempted to flee while Aqa Muhammad was laying siege to Kerman in 1794. They were both caught and executed; see Ali Reza Rahvar-lighvan and Parviz Zare'-shahmers, *Tarikh-e Qarabagh* (Tehran: 1376/1997), 90–1.
xxv	Pollack, *Empire*, 264–82.
xxvi	Information on the defeat and capture of Lutf Ali Khan Zand is from the following: Sepehr, *Nasekh al-tavarikh*, vol. 1, 70; Hedayat, *Fehrest*, 17–19; Saravi, *Tarikh-e Muhammadi*, 220–4.
xxvii	Amanat, *Iran: A Modern History*, 166.
xxviii	E'tezad Saltaneh, *Eksir*, 46; Khavari-shirazi, *Tarikh dh al-qarneyn*, vol. 1, 39.
xxix	Khavari-shirazi, *Tarikh dh al-qarneyn*, vol. 1, 13.
xxx	Touraj Atabaki, *Azerbaijan: Ethnicity and Autonomy in Twentieth-Century Iran* (London: 2007), 24–6.
xxxi	Rahvarlighvan and Zare'-shams, *Tarikh-e Qarabagh*,75; also see Moritz Deutschmann, *Iran and Russian Imperialism* (London and New York: 2016), 39.
xxxii	The *meliks* of Qarabagh were five clans that often competed and fought each other. See Rahvar-lighvan and Zare'-shahmers, *Tarikh-e Qarabagh*, 73–5.
xxxiii	Auguste Bontems, *Safarnameh-ye Bontems* (Tehran: 1375/1997), 76.
xxxiv	*Asnadi az ravabet Iran ba mantaqeh-ye Qafqaz* (Tehran: 1371/1993), document 24.
xxxv	George Bournoutian, *Russia and the Armenians of Transcaucasia* (Costa Mesa, CA: 1992), 70–1.
xxxvi	P. Ami Jaubert, *Mosaferat dar Armanestan va Iran* (Tehran: 1347/1968), 133–4.
xxxvii	James Morier, *A Second Journey through Persia, Armenia and Asia Minor* (London: 1818), 22.
xxxviii	Bournoutian, *From the Kur to the Aras*, 248.
xxxix	Pollack, *Empire*, 267; Khanak Ishqi, *Siyasat-e nezami Russiya dar Iran* (Tehran: 1353/1974), 22–3; Atkin, *Russia and Iran*, 10–13.
xl	Ishqi, *Siyasat-e nezami*, 299–30; Pollack, *Empire*, 250.
xli	Pollack, *Empire*, 199–202.
xlii	Ibid., 215.
xliii	Ibid., 217–18; Ishqi, *Siyasat-e nezami*, 24; Atkin, *Russia and Iran*, 13.
xliv	*Trikh-e Armanestan*, trans. A. Germanik (Tehran: 1360/1981), 311–16.
xlv	Ibid., 272.
xlvi	Atkin, *Russia and Iran*, 39; E'tezad Saltaneh, *Eksir*, 46–55.
xlvii	Rahvar-lighvan and Zare'-shahmers, *Tarikh-e Qarabagh*, 91.
xlviii	Saravi, *Tarikh-e Muhammadi*, 276–7.

xlix Information on the conquest of the Caucasus by Aqa Muhammad Khan is from the following sources: Saravi, *Tarikh-e Muhammadi*, 271–82; Sepehr, *Nasekh al-tavarikh*, vol. 1, 77–8; Hedayat, *Fehrest*, 20–1; E'tezad Saltaneh, *Eksir*, 46–55; Abbas Qoli Aqa Bakikhanov, *The Heavenly Rose-Garden*, trans. William Floor and Hasan Javadi (Washington, DC: 2009), 89–100; Adigozal Bey, *Karabagh-Nameh* in *Two Chronicles on the History of Karabagh*, trans. George A. Bournoutian (Costa Mesa, CA: 2004), 186–92; Jamil Quzanlu, *Tarikh-e nezami Iran* (Tehran: 1315/1936), 680–2.
l Saravi, *Tarikh-e Muhammadi*, 272.
li Malcolm, *History of Persia*, vol. 2, 197; Pollack, *Empire*, 367–9.
lii Pollack, *Empire*, 364–6.
liii Gholam Hosein Zargari-nezhad, *Roozshomar va tahavolat-e Iran dar asr-e Qajar*, vol. 1 (Tehran: 1388/2009), 817.
liv Ibid., 370–1.
lv Malcolm, *History of Persia*, vol. 2, 198; Sepehr, *Nasekh al-tavarikh*, vol. 1, 82–3; Atkin, *Russia and Iran*, 39–41.
lvi John F. Baddeley, *The Russian Conquest of the Caucasus* (London: 1908), 58; Bakikhanov, *Heavenly Rose-Garden*, 152–3.
lvii Muriel Atkin, "The Pragmatic Diplomacy of Paul I: Russian Relations with Asia, 1798–1801," *Slavic Review* 38, no. 1 (1979): 62.
lviii Amanat, *Iran: A Modern History*, 169.
lix Malcolm, *History of Persia*, vol. 2, 200.
lx Ibid.
lxi Mirza Jamal Javanshir, *Tarikh Karabagh*, in *Two Chronicles on the History of Karabagh*, trans. George A. Bournoutian (Costa Mesa, CA: 2004), 101–3.
lxii For the shah's movements and assassination see: Sepehr, *Nasekh al-tavarikh*, 83–5; Hedayat, *Fehrest*, 323–6.
lxiii E'tezad Saltaneh, *Eksir*, 80.
lxiv For estimates on the shah's military see: Grant R. Watson, *Tarikh Iran dar doreh-ye Qajariyeh* (Tehran: 1348/1969), 98; Malcolm, *History of Persia*, vol. 2, 190–1.
lxv Watson, *Tarikh-e Iran*, 115–18; Muhammad Panahi-semnani, *Fath Ali Shah Qajar* (Tehran: 1378/1997), 25–35; Sepehr, *Nasekh al-tavarikh*, vol. 1, 52.

Chapter 2

i Khavari-shirazi, *Tarikh dh al-qarneyn*, vol. 1, 14.
ii Malcolm, *History of Persia*, vol. 2, 308.
iii Jaubert, *Mosaferat*, 185.
iv James Morier, *A Journey through Persia, Armenia and Asia Minor to Constantinople in the years 1808 and 1809* (London: 1812), 193.

v   Malcolm, *History of Persia*, vol. 2, 399.
vi   John Malcolm, *Sketches of Persia: From the Journals of a Traveller in the East*, vol. 2 (London: 1828), 140.
vii   For names and brief biographies of Fath Ali Shah's wives, sons, and daughters see: Azod al-Dowleh, *Tarikh-e Azodi*, 336–65.
viii   Abbas Amanat, "The Kayanid Crown and Qajar reclaiming of Royal Authority," *Iranian Studies* 34, no. 1/4 (2001): 23–6.
ix   Mostofi, *Tarikh-e edari*, vol. 1, 29.
x   Mostofi, *Tarikh-e edari*, vol. 1, 30–2.
xi   Azod al-Dowleh, *Tarikh-e Azodi* 162.
xii   James Morier, *A Second Journey*, 203.
xiii   Malcolm, *History of Persia*, vol. 2, 414.
xiv   Amanat, *Iran: A Modern History*, 168; also see Malcolm, *History of Persia*, vol. 2, 190–4.
xv   Azod al-Dowleh, *Tarikh-e Azodi*, 168.
xvi   Shaul Bakhash, "The Evolution of Qajar Bureaucracy, 1779–1879," *Iranian* Studies 14, no. 1/2 (1981): 139; on Aqa Muhammad's bureaucracy see: Mostofi, *Tarikh-e edari*, vol. 1, 11–13.
xvii   Bakhash, "The Evolution," 140; Sepehr, *Nasekh al-tavarikh*, vol. 1, 145.
xviii   Morier, *Journey through Persia*, 217.
xix   Ibid., 195.
xx   Ibid., 277.
xxi   Malcolm, *Sketches of Persia*, vol. 2, 137–8, 152.
xxii   Ibid., 126.
xxiii   William Ouseley, *Travels in Various Countries of the East*, vol. 3 (London: 1819), 129.
xxiv   Ibid., 371; Morier, *A Second Journey*, 197–8.
xxv   Azod al-Dowleh, *Tarikh-e Azodi*, 165.
xxvi   Abbas Amanat, "Ebrahim Khan Shirazi," in *Encyclopedia Iranica*, vol. 8 (1998), 66–70; Khavari-shirazi, *Tarikh-e dh al-qarneyn*, vol. 1, 146–53; Azod al-Dowleh, *Tarikh-e Azodi*, 113–14; Hedayat, *Fehrest*, 336–7.
xxvii   Mehdi Bamdad, *Tarikh-e rejal-e Iran*, vol. 1 (Tehran: 1347/1968), 35–6.
xxviii Bakhash, "The Evolution," 141.
xxix   Mostofi, *Tarikh-e edari*, vol. 1, 29.
xxx   Malcolm, *History of Persia*, vol. 2, 324; Shaul Bakhash, "Center–Periphery Relations," *Iranian Studies* 14, no. 1/2 (1981): 30–3.
xxxi   Ervand Abrahamian, "Oriental Despotism: The Case of Qajar Iran," *International Journal of Middle East Studies* 5, no. 1 (1974): 3–31.
xxxii   Ervand Abrahamian, *Iran Between Two Revolutions* (Princeton: 1982), 33.
xxxiii Ibid., 33–4.
xxxiv   Ann Lambton, *Qajar Persia*, 51.
xxxv   Ibid., 78.
xxxvi   Ibid., 80.

xxxvii Malcolm, *History of Persia*, vol .2, 36; the second estimate is by the Gardane missions, quoted in Charles Issawi, ed., *The Economic History of Iran, 1800-1914* (Chicago: 1971), 25.
xxxviii Hamid Algar, *Religion and State in Iran 1785-1906* (Berkeley: 1969), 21-5.
xxxix Hamid Algar, *Roots of the Islamic Revolution in Iran* (New York: 2001), 21.
xl Ibid., 22.
xli Malcolm, *History of Persia*, vol. 2, 311.
xlii Algar, *Religion and State in Iran*, 79; also see Cyrus Masroori, "Russian Imperialism and Jihad: Early 19th-Century Persian Texts on Just War," *Journal of Church and State* 46, no. 2 (2004), 263-79.
xliii Algar, *Religion and State in Iran*, 41-50; Azod al-Dowleh, *Tarikh-e Azodi*, 168.
xliv Muhammad Fatollah Saravi, *Tarikh-e Muhammadi* (Tehran: 1371/1992), 285.
xlv Bontems, *Safarnameh-ye Bontems* 61-2.
xlvi Issawi, ed., *Economic History of Iran*, 20.
xlvii Ibid., 13.
xlviii For Shiraz's population information see: Morier, *Journey through Persia*, 109; for Isfahan see Ouseley, *Travels*, vol. 3, 24.
xlix Ouseley, *Travels*, vol. 3, 119.
l Malcolm, *History of Persia,* vol. 2, 140.
li Morier, *Journey through Persia*, 284; Morier, *A Second Journey*, 225; Jaubert, *Mosaferat*, 124.
lii Jaubert, *Mosaferat*, 117-21.
liii Morier, *A Second Journey*, 321.
liv Bournoutian, *Russia and the Armenians*, 159-60.
lv Bournoutian, *The 1823 Russian Survey of the Karabagh Province* (Costa Mesa, CA: 2011), 228-9.
lvi General Tsitsianov to Tsar Alexander I, in Bournoutian, *Russia and the Armenians*, 111-12.
lvii Information on the Qajar military is from the following sources: Robert Grand Watson, *Tarikh Iran dar doreh-ye Qajariyeh* (Tehran: 1348/1969), 98; Malcolm, *History of Persia*, vol. 2, 190-1; A. Gardane, *Ma'muriyat-e General Gardane dar Iran* (Tehran: 1362/1983), 72-6; Morrier, *Journey through Persia*, 241-77; Jaubert, *Mosaferat*, 147-8 and 215; Fraser, *Historical and Descriptive Account*, 302-6;Aleksander Kibovskii and Vadim Yegorov, "The Persian Regular Army of the First Half of the Nineteenth Century," *Tseikhgauz*, no. 5 (1996): 1-12; Muriel Atkin, *Russia and Iran*, 111-12; Uzi Rabi and Nugzar Ter-Oganov, "The Military of Qajar Iran: the Features of an Irregular Army from the Eighteenth to the Early Twentieth Century," *Iranian Studies* 45, no. 3 (2012): 333-54; Stephanie Cronin, "Importing Modernity: European

lviii	Military Missions to Qajar Iran," *Comparative Studies in Society and History* 50, no. 1 (2008): 197–226.
lviii	Sepehr, *Nasekh al-tavarikh*, vol. 1, 73.
lix	Atkin, *Russia and Iran*, 39; E'tezad Saltaneh, *Eksir*, 46–55; Malcolm, *History of Persia*, 190–1.
lx	Kaveh Farrokh, *Iran at War, 1500–1988* (Oxford: 2011), 166–7.
lxi	Morier, *Journey through Persia*, 241.
lxii	Bontems, *Safarnameh-ye Bontems*, 53.
lxiii	Jaubert, *Mosaferat*, 95.
lxiv	Ibid., 213–15.
lxv	Information on Russian deserters and their impact is based on the following: Muriel Atkin, "Russian Deserters," 106–7; Stephanie Cronin, "Deserters, Converts, Cossacks and Revolutionaries: Russians in Iranian Military Service," *Middle Eastern Journal* 48, no. 2 (2012): 147–82; Aleksandr Kibovskii, "'Bagaderan'-Russian Deserters in the Persian Army, 1802–1839," http://marksrussianmilitaryhistory.info/Persdes2.html.
lxvi	Cronin, "Deserters, Converts," 159.
lxvii	Fraser, *Historical and Descriptive Account*, 302.
lxviii	Morier, *A Second Journey*, 214.
lxix	Qozanlu, *Tarikh-e nezami-e Iran*, vol. 2 (Tehran: 1315/1936), 752–3.
lxx	Bontems, *Safarnameh-ye Bontems*, 68, 83.
lxxi	Harford Jones Brydges, *An Account of the Transactions of His Majesty's Mission to the Court of Persia in the Years 1807–1811* (London: 1834), 253.
lxxii	Jaubert, *Mosaferat*, 256–62.
lxxiii	Bontems, *Safarnameh-ye Bontems*, 79–83.
lxxiv	Morier, *Journey through Persia*, 277.

Chapter 3

i John McNeill, *Memoir of the Right Hon. Sir John McNeill, G.C.B and his Second Wife Elizabeth Wilson* (London: 1910), 53.
ii Nicholas Riasanovsky, *History of Russia*, 266–77; Gary Maker, "The Age of Enlightenment 1740–1804," in Freeze, ed., *Russia: A History*, 141; Muriel Atkin, *Russia and Iran*, 99.
iii James Morier, *Journey through Persia*, 272.
iv Malcolm, *History of Persia*, vol. 2, 123.
v Maryam Ekhtiar, "An Encounter with the Russian Czar: The Image of Peter the Great in Early Qajar History Writings," *Iranian Studies* 29, no. 1/2 (1996): 57–70.
vi Riasanovsky, *History of Russia*, 275.

vii   Hedayat, *Fehrest*, 325–40; Sepehr, *Nasekh al-tavarikh*, vol. 1, 101–17.
viii   Atkin, "Pragmatic Diplomacy," 6–65.
ix   Sepehr, *Nasekh al-tavarikh*, vol. 1, 101.
x   Jaubert, *Mosaferat*, 133.
xi   Morier, *Journey through Persia*, 275; Morier, *A Second Journey*, 215–16.
xii   G. Drouville, *Safarnameh-ye Drouville* (Tehran: 1337/1958), 165.
xiii   Baqer Qa'emmaqami, *Qa'em Maqam dar jahan-e adab va siyasat* (Tehran: 1320/1941), 19; Drouville, *Safarnameh-ye Drouville*, 175.
xiv   Jaubert, *Mosaferat*, 136–7.
xv   Ibid., 176.
xvi   Drouville, *Safarnameh-ye Drouville*, 175.
xvii   Gavin Hambly, "Iran during the Reigns of Fath Ali Shah and Muhammad Shah," in *The Cambridge History of Iran*, vol. 7 (Cambridge: 1991), 146.
xviii David Marshall Lang, *The Last Years of the Georgian Monarchy, 1658–1832* (New York: 1957), 205.
xix   Ibid., 220.
xx   Ali Akbar Bina, *Tarikh-e siyasi va diplomacy-ye Iran*, vol. 1 (Tehran: 1348/1969), 46–7.
xxi   Bournoutian, *Russia and the Armenians*, 22–3.
xxii   Lang, *Georgian Monarchy*, 230.
xxiii Ibid., 233.
xxiv   Atkin, "Pragmatic Diplomacy," 66.
xxv   Bournoutian, *From the Kur to the Aras*, 128.
xxvi   Moritz Deutschmann, *Iran and Russian Imperialism*, 89.
xxvii For more on Tsitsianov see Alexander Mikaberidze, *The Russian officer Corps in the Revolutionary and Napoleonic Wars, 1792–1815* (New York: 2005), 406–7; Baddeley, *The Russian Conquest*, 62–3; Atkin, *Russia and Iran*, 71–3.
xxviii For British interest in Iran see Denis Wright, *Ingilisha dar miyan Iranian* (Tehran: 1385/2007), 13; for Napoleon's policy toward Iran and India see Napoleon's letter to Gardane, 15 May 1807, in Gardane, *Maimuriyat-e General Gardane*, 51.
xxix   Khavari-shirazi, *Tarikh dh al-qarneyn*, vol. 1, 129; Sepehr, *Nasekh al-tavarikh*, vol. 1, 106.
xxx   *Majmu'eh ahdnamehha-ye tarikhi Iran* (Tehran: 1350/1971), 91–2; Wright, *Inglisha dar miyan Iranian*, 14–15.
xxxi   Bournoutian, *From the Kur to the Aras*, 42–6.
xxxii W. Monteith, *Karas and Erzeroum: With the Campaigns of Prince Paskiewitch in 1828 and 1829* (London: 1856), 35; Bournoutian's research in Russian archives regarding the siege of Ganjeh provides us with a clearer view of the events; see George Bournoutian, "Prelude to War: The Russian Siege and Storming of the Fortress of Ganjeh, 1802–1804," *Iranian Studies* 50, no. 1 (2017): 111; Bournoutian, *From the Kur to the Aras*, 47–59.

xxxiii Monteith, *Karas and Erzeroum*, 35; Bournoutian, "Prelude to War," 118.
xxxiv Bournoutian, "Prelude to War," 111.
xxxv For Javad Khan's letter see *Asnad-e ravabet-e Iran va Russia dar dowran Fath Ali Shah va Muhamad Shah Qajar* (Tehran: 1380/2001), document 29; and Bournoutian, "Prelude to War," 112.
xxxvi Bournoutian, "Prelude to War," 118.
xxxvii Ibid., 118; Russians used the term "Tatar" to refer to Turkic-Muslim people of the region.
xxxviii Donboli, *Ma'aser Sultaniyyeh*, 181–2; Khavari-shirazi, *Tarikh dh al-qarneyn*, vol. 1, 193.
xxxix Bournoutian, *Russia and the Armenians*, 15–16.
xl Ibid., 16.
xli Bournoutian, "Prelude to War," 118.
xlii Monteith, *Karas and Erzeroum*, 36.
xliii Atkin, *Russia and Iran*, 82–3.
xliv Fasa'i, *Persia Under Qajar Rule*, 108; Donboli, *Ma'aser Sultaniyyeh*, 181–2; Khavari-shirazi, *Tarikh dh al-qarneyn*, vol. 1, 193–4; Sepehr, *Nasekh al-tavarikh*, vol. 1, 124.
xlv Javanshir, *Tarikh Karabagh*, in *Two Chronicles*, 111; Bakikhanov, *Heavenly Rose-Garden*, 58; for a secondary source see: Ishqi, *Siyasat-e nezami*, 50.
xlvi Baddeley, *The Russian Conquest*, 65–6.
xlvii For an account of the siege and battle of Iravan in 1804 see: Baddeley, *The Russian Conquest*, 68; Donboli, *Ma'aser Sultaniyyeh*, 183–9; Adigozal Bey, *Karabagh-Nameh* in *Two Chronicles*, 208–12; Fasa'I, *Persia Under Qajar Rule*, 107–9; Khavari-shirazi, *Tarikh dh al-qarneyn*, vol. 1, 200–13; Sepehr, *Nasekh al-tavarikh*, vol. 1, 125–7; Mirza Muhammad Sadeq Marvazi, *Ahang Sorush ya tarikh jangha-ye iran-Rus* (Tehran: 1369/1990), 82–102.
xlviii Bournoutian, *From the Kur to the Aras*, 71–2.
xlix Ibid., 82.
l For example, see his letter of January 1804 to Ibrahim Khan Javanshir, informing him of the fall of Ganjeh, and demanding the return of people and animals which had fled to Qarabagh, and the release of Armenian hostages. Bournoutian, *Russia and the Armenians*, 110.
li *Asnad-e ravabet-e Iran va Russia*, document 27.
lii Ibid., document 26.
liii Monteith, *Karas and Erzeroum*, 37.
liv *Asnadi az ravabet-e Iran ba maantaqeh-ye Qafqaz*, document 30.
lv Bournoutian, *From the Kur to the Aras*, 79–80.
lvi Bontems, *Safarnameh-ye Bontems*, 55–7. Also see: Bournoutian, *From the Kur to the Aras*, 96.
lvii Bournoutian, *From the Kur to the Aras*, 87.
lviii Monteith, *Karas and Erzeroum*, 40; Mirza Adigozal Beg, *Karabagh-Nameh* in *Two Chronicles*, 210–11; Bournoutian, *Russia and the Armenians*, 116.

lix   Monteith, *Karas and Erzeroum*, 37.
lx   Brydges, *An Account*, 81.
lxi   *Asnadi az ravabet-e Iran ba mantaqeh-ye Qafqaz*, document 31.
lxii   Jaubert, *Mosaferat*, 147; Morier, *A Second Journey*, 211.
lxiii   Brydges, *An Account*, 279–81.
lxiv   James Fraser, *Travels and Adventures in the Persian Provinces on the Southern Bank of the Caspian Sea* (London: 1826), 306–7.
lxv   For the text of submission of both see Bournoutian, *From the Kur to the Aras*, 108–11.
lxvi   On Ibrahim Khan Javanshir see Muriel Atkin, "The Strange Death of Ibrahim Khalil Khan of Qarabagh," *Iranian Studies* 12, no. 1/2 (1979): 9–107.
lxvii   Information on various battles in 1805 is based on the following: Sepehr, *Nasekh al-tavarikh*, 136–40; Khavari-shirazi, *Tarikh dh al-qarneyn*, vol. 1, 217–31; Donboli, *Ma'aser Sultaniyyeh*, 199–237; Monteith, *Karas and Erzeroum*, 44–6; Marvazi, *Ahang Sorush ya tarikh jangha-ye iran-Rus*, 103–23; Bakikhanov, *Heavenly Rose-Garden*, 160–1; Javanshir, *Tarikh Karabagh*, in *Two Chronicles*, 116–21; Bournoutian, *From the Kur to the Aras*, 114–17.
lxviii Bournoutian, *From the Kur to the Aras*, 116–17.
lxix   Qozanlu, *Tarikh-e nezami-ye Iran*, vol. 2, 734–5.
lxx   Donboli, *Ma'aser Sultaniyyeh*, 243–5.
lxxi   Bournoutian, *From the Kur to the Aras*, 117.
lxxii   For an account of the siege of Ganjeh in 1805, see Qozanlu, *Tarikh-e nezami-ye Iran*, vol. 2, 740–4; Donboli, *Ma'aser Sultaniyyeh*, 233–4; Marvazi, *Ahang Sorush ya tarikh jangha-ye iran-Rus*, 155–68; Khavari-shirazi, *Tarikh dh al-qarneyn*, vol. 1, 228–30; Bournoutian, *From the Kur to the Aras*, 118.
lxxiii Donboli, *Ma'aser Sultaniyyeh*, 235–6, Bournoutian, *From the Kur to the Aras*, 121–2; Qozanlu, *Tarikh-e nezami-ye Iran*, vol. 2, 748–9; Marvazi, *Ahang Sorush ya tarikh jangha-ye iran-Rus*, 172–6; Khavari-shirazi, *Tarikh dh al-qarneyn*, vol. 1, 226–7.
lxxiv   For an account of the Battle of Baku see Donboli, *Ma'aser Sultaniyyeh*, 247–9; Qozanlu, *Tarikh-e nezami-ye Iran*, vol. 2, 751–3.
lxxv   William Ouseley, *Travels*, vol. 3, 348.
lxxvi   Bamdad, *Tarikh rejal-e Iran*, vol. 3, 430–1.
lxxvii Azod al-Dowleh, *Tarikh-e Azodi*, 141; Drouville, *Safarnameh-ye Drouville*, 173–4.
lxxviii Brydges, *An Account*, 248–9.
lxxix   Ishqi, *Siyasat-e nezami*, 52–3 and 59–60; Atkin, *Russia and Iran*, 101; Fasa'i, *Persia Under Qajar Rule*, 124.
lxxx   Fasa'i, *Persia Under Qajar Rule*, 124.
lxxxi   According to Mirza Abu al-Qasem, Qa'em Maqam II, his father was the brain behind modernizing the military, which makes more sense

considering Abbas Mirza's youth. Baqer Qa'em Maqami, *Qa'em Maqam dar jahan-e adab va siyasat* (Tehran: 1320/1941), 19.

lxxxii On the Iranian military performance, see Jaubert, *Mosaferat*, 147.
lxxxiii For an account of British–Iranian interactions in this period, see: Wright, *Inglisha dar miyan Iranian*, 15–16; Iradj Amini, *Napoleon and Persia: Franco-Persian Relations under the First Empire* (Washington, DC: 1999), 50; *Asnadi az ravabet-e Iran va Faranceh dar dowran fath Ali Shah Qajar* (Tehran: 1376/1997), 19.
lxxxiv Amini, *Napoleon and Persia*, 48.
lxxxv For an account of Vassitovitz's debriefing see Amini, *Napoleon and Persia*, 50–1; for the original letter of the shah to Napoleon, see *Asnadi az ravabet-e Iran va Faranceh*, 19–20.
lxxxvi *Asnadi az ravabet-e Iran va Faranceh*, 16.
lxxxvii For an account of Romieu's mission and Napoleon's letter, see Amini, *Napoleon and Persia*, 63–70.
lxxxviii Ibid., 72–3.
lxxxix Ibid., 147.
xc For an account of the number of combatants and battle formations for each force, see Qozanlu, *Tarikh-e nezami-ye Iran*, vol. 2, 764–5; Monteith, *Karas and Erzeroum*, 52.
xci Sepehr, *Nasekh al-tavarikh*, vol. 1, 140; Hedayat, *Fehrest*, 48–9; Russian sources suggest one of the guards fled the scene: see Bournoutian, *From the Kur to the Aras*, 126.
xcii Sepehr, *Nasekh al-tavarikh*, vol. 1, 141–2.
xciii On the death of Ibrahim Khan Javanshir, see Donboli, *Ma'aser Sultaniyyeh*, 118–19; Atkin, "Strange Death of Ibrahim Khalil Khan," 79–107.
xciv Bournoutian, *From the Kur to the Aras*, 135; Baddeley, *The Russian Conquest*, 76.
xcv For more on Sheikh Ali Khan of Darband and Qobbeh, see: Javanshir, *Tarikh Karabagh*, in *Two Chronicles*, 83–4; Bakikhanov, *Heavenly Rose-Garden*, Appendix I.
xcvi Atkin, *Russia and Iran*, 74–5; Donboli, *Ma'aser Sultaniyyeh*, 287; Bournoutian, *From the Kur to the Aras*, 136.
xcvii Bournoutian, *From the Kur to the Aras*, 140–1.
xcviii Donboli, *Ma'aser Sultaniyyeh*, 237–43.
xcix Qozanlu, *Tarikh nezami-ye Iran*, vol. 2, 773–4.
c Bournoutian, *From the Kur to the Aras*, 146–7.
ci *Asnadi az ravabet-e Iran ba mantaqeh-ye Qafqaz*, 213.
cii *Asnadi az ravabet-e Iran va Faranceh*, 36; Amini, *Napoleon and Persia*, 90–103.
ciii Bontems, *Safarnameh-ye Bontems*, 63–8.
civ Ibid., 81.
cv For Finkenstein see Gardane, *Maimuriyat-e General Gardane*, 42; *Majmo'eh ahdnamehha-ye Iran*, 152–153.

cvi   For Napoleon's letter to Gardane, see Gardane, *Maimuriyat-e General Gardane*, 49–51; for an overview on Gardane's mission, see Amini, *Napoleon and Persia*, 107–17.
cvii   Gardane, *Maimuriyat-e General Gardane*, 61; for the text of the treaty of Finkenstein and its analysis, see: *Majmu'eh ahdnamehha-ye tarikhi Iran*, 152–3; Amini, *Napoleon and Persia*, 110.
cviii   Gardane, *Maimuriyat-e General Gardane*, 87–8.
cix   Bournoutian, *From the Kur to the Aras*, 157.
cx   Gardane, *Maimuriyat-e General Gardane*, 98; *Asnadi az ravabet-e Iran va Faranceh*, 41–2.
cxi   For the Russo-Ottoman war in 1807, see Bournoutian, *From the Kur to the Aras*, 150–1.
cxii   Gardane, *Maimuriyat-e General Gardane*, 53.
cxiii   Ibid., 109.
cxiv   *Asnad-i az ravabet-e Iran va Faranceh*, 43.
cxv   Monteith, *Karas and Erzeroum*, 53.
cxvi   Ishqi, *Siyasat-e nezami*, 53. The author's pro-Russia view suggests Gudovich's overture was sincere, and the shah's rejection was because of British intrigue and French promises. This is while the French at this point were Russia's ally and the British had no presence in Iran.
cxvii   For Abbas Mirza's letter, see: *Asnadi az ravabet-e Iran va Faranceh*, document 20.
cxviii Gardane, *Maimuriyat-e General Gardane*, 106–9.
cxix   *Asnadi az ravabet-e Iran va Faranceh*, document 20.
cxx   For a translation of the letter, see Gardane, *Maimuriyat-e General Gardane*, 115–17.
cxxi   Major Lamy's letter of October 19, in Bina, *Tarikh-e siyasi va diplomacy-ye Iran*, vol. 1, 132.
cxxii   Bournoutian, *From the Kur to the Aras*, 160.
cxxiii Monteith, *Karas and Erzeroum*, 52–4; Bournoutian, *From the Kur to the Aras*, 159–60.
cxxiv   Bournoutian, *From the Kur to the Aras*, 163.
cxxv   Monteith, *Karas and Erzeroum*, 55.
cxxvi   Gardane, *Maimuriyat-e General Gardane*, 128–9 and 132.
cxxvii Bournoutian, *From the Kur to the Aras*, 163.
cxxviii Ibid., 165.
cxxix   For an account of this conflict, see: Qozanlu, *Tarikh nezami-ye Iran*, vol. 2, 83–89; Monteith, *Karas and Erzeroum*, 53–6, Marvazi, *Ahang Sorush ya tarikh jangha-ye iran-Rus*, 165–9, Donboli, *Ma'aser Sultaniyyeh*, 21–5, Sepehr, *Nasekh al-tavarikh*, 169–77, Khavari-shirazi, *Tarikh dh al-qarneyn*, vol. 1, 279–90; Bournoutian, *From the Kur to the Aras*, 161–5.
cxxx   Bournoutian, *From the Kur to the Aras*, 167–8.
cxxxi   For Abbas Mirza's letters to Sheikh Ali Khan and Bonaparte, see Parviz Varjavand, *Iran va Qafqaz, Aran va Shirvan* (Tehran: 1378/1999), 157–65 and 161–3.

cxxxii Gardane, *Maimuriyat-e General Gardane*, 117.
cxxxiii Ibid., 120–126.
cxxxiv Ibid., 133–5.
cxxxv Gardane, *Maimuriyat-e General Gardane*, 127; Fasa'i, *Persia Under Qajar Rule*, 125–7. On John Malcolm's correspondence with Iranian officials in 1808, and his offer of British aid against Russia, see FO/248/9.
cxxxvi Brydges, *An Account*,185.
cxxxvii Ibid., 190.
cxxxviii Monteith, *Karas and Erzeroum*, 57.
cxxxix Brydges, 255–6.
cxl Ibid., 267–9.
cxli Ibid., 269–70.
cxlii Information on the battles of 1809 is from the following: Monteith, *Karas and Erzeroum*, 58–63; Sepehr, *Nasekh al-tavarikh*, 183–93; Khavari-shirazi, *Tarikh dh al-qarneyn*, vol. 1, 298–311; Donboli, *Ma'aser Sultaniyyeh*, 305–27; Bournoutian, *From the Kur to the Aras*, 170–8.
cxliii James Morier, *A Second Journey*, 328.
cxliv Bina, *Tarikh-e siyasi va diplomacy-ye Iran*, vol. 1, 148.
cxlv *Asnad va mokatebat-e tarikhi Iran (Qajar)*, vol. 2, document 36; Bina, *Tarikh-e siyasi va diplomacy-ye Iran*, vol. 1, 149–50.
cxlvi Bina, *Tarikh-e siyasi va diplomacy-ye Iran*, vol. 1, 150–1.
cxlvii Information on the battles of 1810 is from the following: Donboli, *Ma'aser Sultaniyyeh*, 4–7; Sepehr, *Nasekh al-tavarikh*, 199–202; Khavari-shirazi, *Tarikh dh al-qarneyn*, vol. 1, 17–21; Monteith, *Karas and Erzeroum*, 75–76.
cxlviii Monteith, *Karas and Erzeroum*, 71–9; Qozanlu, *Tarikh-e nezami-ye Iran*, vol. 2, 803–4; Donboli, *Ma'aser Sultaniyyeh*, 458–9; Bakikhanov, *Heavenly Rose-Garden*, 164–5; Bournoutian, *From the Kur to the Aras*, 190–1.
cxlix Monteith, *Karas and Erzeroum*, 79.
cl Morier, *A Second Journey*, 185–6; Monteith, *Karas and Erzeroum*, 82; Qozanlu, *Tarikh-e nezami-ye Iran*, 804; Sepehr, *Nasekh al-tavarikh*, vol. 1, 217; Bakikhanov, *Heavenly Rose-Garden*, 165; Bournoutian, *From the Kur to the Aras*, 201–4.
cli Ishqi, *Siyasat-e nezami*, 161–2.
clii For the Battle of Aslanduz and Lankaran, see Monteith, *Karas and Erzeroum*, 82–98; Khavari-shirazi, *Tarikh dh al-qarneyn*, vol. 1, 343–52, Sepehr, 335–8; Donboli, *Ma'aser Sultaniyyeh*, 393–9; Bakikhanov, *Heavenly Rose-Garden*, 166–7; Bournoutian, *From the Kur to the Aras*, 222–7.
cliii Bina, *Tarikh-e siyasi va diplomacy-ye Iran*, vol. 1, 181.
cliv Monteith, *Karas and Erzeroum*, 97–8.
clv Drouville, *Safarnameh-ye Drouville*, 181; Ishqi, *Siyasat-e nezami*, 124.

clvi The Treaty of Golestan is available in many languages online; see also Ishqi, *Siyasat-e nezami*, 218–26.

Chapter 4

i Alexander Griboyedov, *Namehha-ye Alexander Griboyedov dar bareh-ye Iran marbut beh saltanat-e Fath Ali Shah* (Tehran: 1356/1977), 17–18.
ii A concise version of this chapter was published in Maziar Behrooz, "Revisiting the Second Russo-Iranian War (1826–28): Causes and Perceptions," *Iranian Studies* 46, no. 3 (2013): 359–81.
iii Mira Muhammad Hadi Alavi-shirazi, *Safarnameh-ye Mirza Abu al-Hasan Shirazi (Ilchi)* (Tehran: 1363/1984), 29.
iv Ibid., 85–92.
v Mirza Salah Shirazi, *Safarnameh-ye Mirza Saleh Shirazi* (Tehran: 1347/1968), 20 and 150.
vi Ibid., 123–5.
vii Monica Ringer, *Amuzesh va gofteman-e eslah-e farhangi dar dowran-e Qajar* (Tehran: 1381/2002), 41–8.
viii Nile Green, *The Love of Strangers* (Princeton, NJ: 2016), 24.
ix Baddeley, *The Russian Conquest*, 92.
x Ibid., 95.
xi Ibid., 97.
xii Moritz von Kotzebue, *Mosaferat beh Iran: dowran Fath Ali Shah 1817* (Tehran: 1348/1969), 69 and 111. For more on Ermolov's mission see Baddeley, *The Russian Conquest*, 101; Atkin, *Russia and Iran*, 153–4.
xiii Baddeley, *The Russian Conquest*, 155 and 176; for the Russian government blaming Iran for breaching the arrangements of the Treaty of Golestan, see a translation of the text of the Russian war declaration in October 1826 in Nafisi, *Tarikh ejtema'i va siyasi Iran*, vol. 2,, 124–7.
xiv Mirza Jamal Javanshir, *Tarikh Karabagh* in *Two Chronicles*, 128 and Mirza Adigozal Bey, *Karabagh-Nameh* in *Two Chronicles*, 225.
xv Fatopllah Abdallahyev, *Monasebat-e Iran va Russiyeh va siyasat Inglis dar Iran dar aghaz qarn-e nozdahom* (Tehran: 1356/1977), 137.
xvi The letter's date is September 13, 1826 and it is addressed to an unknown member of the British mission in Tehran. See *Nameh-haye parakandeh-ye Qa'em Maqam Farahani*, vol. 1 (Tehran: 1357/1978), 70–5. Both Russian and Soviet narratives of the causes of the second war omit Russian provocations or distort such events as the Russian occupation of Gokcha, which was followed by further expansion into Iranian territory in 1825 and 1826.
xvii Abd al-Razzaq Donboli, *Ma'aser Sultaniyyeh*, 505–7; Fasa'i, *Persia Under Qajar Rule*, 174–6; Muhammad Taqi Lesan al-Mulk Sepehr, *Nasekh al-tavarikh*, vols. 1–2 (Tehran: 1377/1998), 356–67; Jahangir Mirza, *Tarikh-e no* (Tehran: 1327/1949), 7–15.

xviii A good example in this case is Nafisi, *Tarikh-e ejtema'i va siyasi Iran dar dowreh-ye mo'aser*, vol. 2, 1. He blames the Qajar court for preparing for war with Russia in order to retrieve territories lost in 1813.
xix Ibid., 115; Nafisi's work is valuable in that it has extensive translation of a Russian book (in French) which includes translation of documents and letters related to the conflict. See Le General Prince Stcherbatow, *Le Feld Marechal Prince Paskevich* (St. Petersburg: 1890). This work is primarily the writings of Paskevich in two volumes and it includes other primary sources.
xx Homa Nateq, *Az mast keh bar mast* (Tehran: 1357/1979), 13–15.
xxi FO/60/27, Willock to Canning (June 27, 1826).
xxii Ibid.
xxiii FO/60/27, Willock to Canning (Tehran, January 13, 1826).
xxiv Ibid.
xxv P. W. Avery, "An Enquiry into the Outbreak of the Second Russo-Iranian War, 1826-28," in C. E. Bosworth, ed., *Iran and Islam* (Edinburgh: 1971), 21.
xxvi Monteith, *Karas and Erzeroum*, 104.
xxvii Alexandr Kibovskii, "'Bagaderan'-Russian Deserters in the Persian Army, 1802-1838," 2.
xxviii Alexey P. Yermolov, *The Czar's General: The Memoirs of a Russian General in the Napoleonic Wars* (Welwyn Garden City: 2005), 229. For more on Ermolov's encounter and his mission see Atkin, *Russia and Iran*, 152–5.
xxix Monteith, *Karas and Erzeroum*, 105.
xxx Baddeley, *The Russian Conquest*, 101.
xxxi Monteith, *Karas and Erzeroum*, 101.
xxxii Baddeley, *The Russian Conquest*, 99.
xxxiii Ibid., 42–5.
xxxiv Ibid., 49–50.
xxxv Baddeley, *The Russian Conquest*, 135–51.
xxxvi As translated in Nafisi, *Tarikh-e ejtema'i va siyasi Iran dar dowreh-ye mo'aser*, vol. 2, 95.
xxxvii Ermolov mentioned the rebuilding and rearming of the Iranian army with the help of English instructors; see Abdallahyev, *Monasebat-e Iran va Russiyeh va siyasat Inglis dar Iran dar aghaz qarn-e nozdahom*, 109–11.
xxxviii Fraser, *Travels and Adventures*, 308–9.
xxxix Nafisi, *Tarikh-e ejtema'i va siyasi Iran dar dowreh-ye mo'aser*, vol. 2, 95.
xl Ibid., 19.
xli Conversation between Abbas Mirza and General V. Madatov, documented in Adigozal Bey, *Karabagh-Nameh* in *Two Chronicles*, 224.
xlii Monteith, *Karas and Erzeroum*, 120.
xliii For a Persian translation of both letters, see Nafisi, *Tarikh-e ejtema'i*, 105–6.

xliv FO/95/591/2, minutes of conversation of Sir Henry Willock's presentation to the Emperor Nicolas (October 1827, St. Petersburg).
xlv Monteith, *Karas and Erzeroum*, 120.
xlvi *Asnad ravabet Iran va Russia dar dowran Fath Ali Shah and Muhammad Shah Qajar*, document 1.
xlvii Griboyedov, *Namehha-ye Alexander Griboyedov dar bareh-ye Iran marbut beh saltanat-e Fath Ali Shah*, 58.
xlviii Bina, *Tarikh-e siyasi va diplomacy Iran*, vol. 1, 203. Atkin describes Moqri as having an unpleasant climate which the Russians found to be lethal; see Atkin, *Russia and Iran*, 153.
xlix Ermolov's letter to Mirza Abd al-Hasan Khan Shirazi Ilchi, Iranian Foreign Minister, translated and dispatched by Willock, FO 60/27, 71.
l *Nameh-haye parakandeh-ye Qa'em Maqam Farahani*, vol. 1, 72.
li FO/60/27, Willock to Canning (dispatch #1, Tehran, January 13, 1826).
lii Nafisi, *Tarikh-e ejtema'i va siyasi Iran dar dowreh-ye mo'aser*, vol. 2, 73.
liii FO 60/27, Willock to Canning (dispatch #1, Tehran, January 13, 1826).
liv FO/60/27, Willock to Canning (Tehran, May 20, 1826).
lv Segments of a Persian translation of the letter are in Abdallahyev, *Monasebat-e Iran va Russiyeh va siyasat Inglis dar Iran dar aghaz qarn-e nozdahom*, 141.
lvi Monteith, *Karas and Erzeroum*, 110.
lvii Fasa'i, *Persia Under Qajar Rule*, 172.
lviii FO/60/27, Extracts from Mr. Willock's Journal (July 3, 1826).
lix Monteith, *Karas and Erzeroum*, 125.
lx FO/60/27, Willock to Canning (dispatch #2, February 17, 1826).
lxi FO/60/27, Willock copying from Colonel MacNeill's journal (July 10, 1826), 177.
lxii For a discussion of the immigrant khans see: Mirza, *Tarikh-e no*, 6–7.
lxiii FO/60/27, Willock to Canning (Camp Sultanieh, 27 June, 1826), 126; see also Abu al-Qasem Lachini, *Ahvalat va dastneveshtehha-ye Abbas Mirza na'eb Saltaneh* (Tehran: n.d.), 14.
lxiv There is a summary of the hawks' line of argument in Willock's journal: FO/60/27, Extracts from Mr. Willock's Journal (July 23, 1826), 164.
lxv FO/60/27, Extracts from Mr. Willock's Journal (July 9, 1826), 172.
lxvi FO/60/27, Extracts from Mr. Willock's Journal (July 8, 1826), 169.
lxvii FO/60/27, Extracts from Mr. Willock's Journal (dispatch #3, June 25, 1826).
lxviii Fath Ali Shah's letter to Abbas Mirza: FO/60/27, Extracts from Mr. Willock's Journal (July 9, 1826), 171.
lxix Algar, *Religion and State in Iran*, 84.
lxx FO/60/27, Willock from the Journal of Colonel McNeill (July 10, 1826), 177–8.

lxxi	FO/60/27, Willock to Canning (from Camp Sultanieh, June 27, 1826), 131.
lxxii	FO/60/25, Willock's translation of a letter by Fath Ali Shah to General Ermolov, November 28, 307–10.
lxxiii	FO/60/27, Extracts from Mr. Willock's Journal (dispatch #3, June 25, 1826), 145.
lxxiv	FO/60/27, Extracts from Mr. Willock's Journal (July 9, 1826), 173.
lxxv	Nafisi, *Tarikh ejtema'i va siyasi Iran dar dowreh-ye mo'aser*, vol. 1, 122–3.
lxxvi	FO/60/27, Extracts from Mr. Willock's Journal (July 8, 1826), 167.
lxxvii	Monteith, *Karas and Erzeroum*, 122; Nafisi, *Tarikh ejtema'i va siyasi Iran dar dowreh-ye mo'aser*, vol. 1, 119–23.
lxxviii	Jamil Qozanlu, *Jang-e Iran va Rus 1827–28* (Tehran: 1314/1936), 4.
lxxix	Information on the second war was extracted from the following: Khavari-shirazi, *Tarikh dh al-qarneyn*, vol. 1, 609–28; Jahangir Mirza, *Tarikh-e no*, 4–46; Qozanlu, *Jang-e Iran va Rus*, 4–5; Sepehr, *Nasekh al-tavarikh*, 355–413; Monteith, *Karas and Erzeroum*, 132–41; Bey, *Karabagh-Nameh* in *Two Chronicles*, 225–43.
lxxx	Bey, *Karabagh-Nameh* in *Two Chronicles*, 230.
lxxxi	Ibid., 231.
lxxxii	Monteith, *Karas and Erzeroum*, 124–5.
lxxxiii	Bey, *Karabagh-Nameh* in *Two Chronicles*, 235.
lxxxiv	Monteith, *Karas and Erzeroum*, 127.
lxxxv	Ibid., 138.
lxxxvi	For the text of Treaty of Turkmanchay, see *Asnadi az ravaned ejra-ye mo'ahedeh-ye Turkmanchay* (Tehran: 1372/1993), 24–9.
lxxxvii	FO/60/27, Minutes of conversation at Sir Henry Willock's presentation to the Emperor Nicolas (October 28 [16], 1827, St. Petersburg).
lxxxviii	Griboyedov, *Namehha-ye Alexander Griboyedov dar bareh-ye Iran marbut beh saltanat-e Fath Ali Shah*, 62–4.
lxxxix	Laurence Kelly, *Diplomacy and Murder in Tehran: Alexander Griboyedov and Imperial Russia's Mission to the Shah of Persia* (London: 2002), 187–95.
xc	Fasa'i, *Persia Under Qajar Rule*, 189.
xci	Mirza Mustafa Khan Afshar Baha' al-Molk, *Safarnameh-ye Khosrow Mirza beh Petersbough* (Tehran: 1349/1970), 197–8.
xcii	Ibid.
xciii	Ibid.
xciv	A collection of his letters to Muhammad Mirza can be seen in Lachini, *Ahvalat va dastneveshtehha-ye Abbas Mirza na'eb Saltaneh*, 53–75.

xcv "Abbas Mirza's Will," trans. Homa Pakdaman and William Royce, *Iranian Studies* 6, no. 2–3 (1973): 136–51.

Conclusion: Seven Points

i Jaubert, *Mosaferat*, 136–7.

BIBLIOGRAPHY

Books

English

Abrahamian, Ervand. *Iran Between Two Revolutions*. Princeton: 1982.
Algar, Hamid. *Religion and State in Iran 1785–1906*. Berkeley and Los Angeles: 1969.
——. *Roots of the Islamic Revolution in Iran*. New York: 2001.
Amanat, Abbas. *Iran: A Modern History*. New Haven and London: 2017.
Amini, Iradj. *Napoleon and Persia: Franco-Persian Relations under the First Empire*. Washington, DC: 1999.
Andreeva, Elena. *Russia and Iran in the Great Game: Travelogues and Orientalism*. London: 2007.
Atabaki, Touraj. *Azerbaijan: Ethnicity and Autonomy in Twentieth-Century Iran*. London: 1993.
Atkin, Muriel. *Russia and Iran, 1780–1828*. Minnesota: 1980.
Axworthy, Michael. *The Sword of Persia*. London: 2006.
Baddeley, John F. *The Russian Conquest of the Caucasus*. London: 1908.
Bakikhanov, Abbas Qoli Aqa. *The Heavenly Rose-Garden [Golestan Eram]*. Translated by William Floor and Hasan Javadi. Washington, DC: 2009.
Benjamin, Samuel G. W. *Persia*. New York and London: 1901.
——. *The Story of Persia*. New York and London: 1887.
Bolukhas, Suha. *Azerbaijan: A Political History*. London: 2011.
Bosworth, Edmund C., ed. *Iran and Islam*. Edinburgh: 1971.
Bosworth, Edmund, and Carol Hillenbrand, eds. *Qajar Iran: Political, Social and Cultural Changes, 1800–1925*. Edinburgh: 1983.
Bournoutian, George. *From the Kur to the Aras*. Leiden and Boston: 2021.
——. *The Khanate of Erevan under Qajar Rule, 1795–1828*. Costa Mesa, CA: 1992.
——. *The Population of Persian Armenia prior and immediately following its Annexation to the Russian Empire, 1826–32*. Costa Mesa, CA: 1998.
——. *Russia and the Armenians of Transcaucasia*. Costa Mesa, CA: 1992.
——, ed. *Russia and the Armenians of Transcaucasia, 1797–1889: A Documentary Record*. Costa Mesa, CA: 2001.
——. *The 1819 Russian Survey of the Khanate of Shekki (Shakki)*. Costa Mesa, CA: 2016.
——. *The 1820 Russian Survey of the Khanate of Shiravan*. United Kingdom: 2016.
——. *The 1823 Russian Survey of the Karabagh Province*. Costa Mesa, CA: 2011.

———. *The 1829–1832 Russian Survey of the Khanate of Nakhchevan.* Cosa Mesa, CA: 2016.

———. *Two Chronicles on the History of Karabagh* [Translations of Mirza Jamal Javanshir, *Tarikh Karabagh* (History of Qarabagh) and Mirza Adigozal Beg, *Karabagh-Nameh* (The Book of Qarabagh)]. Costa Mesa, CA: 2004.

Brydges, Harford Jones. *An Account of the Transactions of His Majesty's Mission to the Court of Persia in the Years 1807–1811.* London: 1834.

———. *Dynasty of the Kajars.* London: 1833.

Buenes, Alexander. *Travels into Bukhara.* 3 vols. London: 1841.

Cronin, Stephanie, ed. *Iranian–Russian Encounters: Empires and Revolutions since 1800.* London and New York: 2013.

Curtis, John Shelton. *The Russian Army under Nicholas I, 1825–1855.* Durham, NC: 1965.

Curzon, George N. *Persia and the Persian Question.* 2 vols. London and New York: 1892.

Debode, C. A. *Travels in Luristan and Arabistan.* 2 vols. London: 1845.

Elton, Daniel L., ed. *Society and Culture in Qajar Iran.* Costa Mesa, CA: 2002.

Farmanfarmaian, Roxane, ed. *War and Peace in Qajar Persia.* London and New York: 2008.

Farrokh, Kaveh. *Iran at War, 1500–1988.* Oxford: 2011.

Fasa'i, H. *The History of Persia Under Qajar Rule* [*Farsnameh-ye Naseri*]. Translated by H. Busse. New York: 1972.

Flower, George. *Three Years in Persia with Traveling Adventures in Koordistan.* 2 vols. London: 1841.

Fraser, James B. *An Historical and Descriptive Account of Persia.* Edinburgh: 1834.

———. *The History of Nadir Shah.* London: 1742.

———. *The Kuzzilbash: A Tale of Khorasan.* 2 vols. New York: 1828.

———. *Narratives of Journey into Khorasan in the Year 1821 and 1822.* London: 1825.

———. *Travels and Adventures in the Persian Provinces on the Southern Bank of the Caspian Sea.* London: 1826.

———. *Travels in Koordistan, Mesopotamia.* 2 vols. London: 1840.

Freeze, Gregory L., ed. *Russia: A History.* Oxford: 1997.

Golovine, Ivan. *Russia under the Autocrat Nicholas the First.* 2 vols. London: 1846.

Green, Nile. *The Love of Strangers.* Princeton, NJ: 2016.

Hunczak, Taras, ed. *Russian Imperialism from Ivan the Great to the Revolution.* Oxford and New York: 2000.

[this sitation is correct]Issawi, Charles, ed. *The Economic History of Iran, 1800–1914.* Chicago: 1971.

Kashani-Sabet, Firoozeh. *Frontier Fiction: Shaping the Iranian Nation, 1804–1946.* New York and London: 1999.

Kazemzadeh, Firuz. *The Caucasus Region and Relations with the Central Government.* Washington, DC: 1979.

———. *Russia and Britain in Persia: Imperial Ambitions in Qajar Iran*. London: 2013.
Kelly, Laurence. *Diplomacy and Murder in Tehran: Alexander Griboydov and Imperial Russia's Mission to the Shah of Persia*. London: 2002.
Keppel, George. *Personal Narrative of Travels in Babylonia, Assyria, Media and Scythia in the Year 1824*. 2 vols. London: 1827.
King, Charles. *The Ghost of Freedom: A History of the Caucasus*. New York and Oxford: 2005.
Kinner, John MacDonald. *Geographical Memoir of the Persian Empire Accompanied by a Map*. London: 1813.
———. *Journey through Asia Minor and Koosdistan, 1813–1814*. London: 1818.
Klaproth von, Julius. *Travels in the Caucasus and Georgia, 1807-1808*. Translated by F. Shoberl. London: 1814.
Lambton, Ann. *Qajar Persia*. Austin, TX: 1987.
Lang, David M. *The Last Years of the Georgian Monarchy, 1658–1832*. New York: 1957.
Malcolm, John. *Life and Correspondence of Maj. Gen. Sir John Malcolm*. Edited by John William Kaye. 2 vols. London: 1856.
———. *The History of Persia*. 2 vols. London: 1829.
———. *Sketches of Persia: from Journals of a Traveler in the East*. 2 vols. London: 1828.
Markham, C. B. *A General Sketch of the History of Persia*. London: 1874.
Matthe, Rudi, and Elena Andreeva, ed. *Russians in Iran: Diplomacy and Power in the Qajar Era and Beyond*. London and New York: 2018.
McNeill, John. *Memoir of the Right Hon. Sir John McNeill, G.C.B. and his Second Wife Elizabeth Wilson*. London: 1910.
———. *Progress and Position of Russia in the East*. London: 1836.
Mikaberidze, Alexander. *The Russian Officer Corps in the Revolutionary and Napoleonic Wars, 1792–1815*. New York: 2005.
Monteith, W. *Karas and Erzeroum: With the Campaigns of Prince Paskewitch in 1828 and 1829*. London: 1856.
Morier, James. *A Journey through Persia, Armenia, and Asia Minor to Constantinople in the years 1808 and 1809*. London: 1812.
———. *A Second Journey through Persia, Armenia and Asia Minor*. London: 1818.
Oliver, G. A. *Travels in the Ottoman Empire, Egypt and Persia Undertaken by Order of the Government of France during the First Six Years of the Republic*. 2 vols. London: 1801.
Ouseley, William. *Travels in Various Countries of the East, more Particularly Persia in 1810, 1811, 1812*. 3 vols. London: 1819–20.
Parade at Persepolis. Tehran: 1971.
Parker, Geoffrey. *The Military Revolution: Military Innovation and the Rise of the West*. Cambridge: 1996.
Pollack, Sean. *Empire by Invitation? Russian Empire Building in the Caucasus in the Reign of Catherine II*. Dissertation, Department of History, Harvard University: 2006.

Porter, Robert K. *Narrative of the Campaign in Russia During the Year 1812.* London: 1814.
——. *Travel in Georgia, Persia, Armenia, Ancient Babylonia.* 2 vols. London: 1822.
Price, William. *Journal of the British Embassy to Persia.* London: 1825.
Rambaud, Alfred. *History of Russia from the Earliest Times to 1882.* 3 vols. Boston: 1880.
Riasanovsky, Nicholas V. *A History of Russia.* 4th edn. Oxford: 1984.
Schimmelpenninck, David, and Bruce W. Menning, eds. *Reforming the Tsar's Army: Military Innovation in Imperial Russia from Peter the Great to the Revolution.* Cambridge: 2004.
Sheil, Mary. *Glimpses of Life and Manners in Persia.* London: 1856.
Stocqueler, Joachim H. *Fifteen Months Pilgrimage through Untrodden Tracts of Kurdistan and Persia.* 2 vols. London: 1832.
Stone, David. *A Military History of Russia: From Ivan the Terrible to the War in Chechnya.* London: 2006.
Sykes, Percy M. *A History of Persia.* London: 1921.
Tancoigne, J. M. *A Narrative of a Journey into Persia and Residence at Tehran.* London: 1820.
Tapper, Richard. *Frontier Nomads of Iran: A Political History of the Shahsevan.* Cambridge: 1997.
Watson, Robert G. *A History of Persia from the beginning of the 19th Century to the Year 1858.* London: 1866.
Yermolov, Alexey P. *The Car's General: The Memoirs of a Russian General in the Napoleonic Wars.* Welwyn Garden City: 2005.

Persian

Afshar, Mustafa. *Safarnameh-ye Khosrow Mirza* [The Travel Chronicle of Khosrow Mirza]. Edited by Muhammad Gulbun. Tehran: 1349/1970.
Afshari, Parviz. *Sadr 'azamha-ye selselah-ye Qajar.* [Chief Ministers of Qajar Dynasty]. Tehran: 1373/1994.
Ahmadi, Hosein, ed. *Asnadi az ravabet-e Iran va Faranseh dar dowran Fath Ali Shah Qajar* [A History of Franco-Iranian Relations during the reign of Fath Ali Shah Qajar]. Tehran: 1376/1997.
——. *Teleshan: az dowran Safavieh ta payan jang dovvom Iran va Rus* [The Talesh: From the Safavid Period to the End of the Second Russo-Iranian War]. Tehran: 1380/2001.
Alavi-Shirazi, Mirza Muhammad Hadi. *Safarnameh-ye Mirza Abu al-Hasan Khan Shirazi (Ilchi) beh Russiya* [Travel Chronicles of Mirza Abu al-Hasan Khan Shirazi (Ilchi) to Russia]. Edited by Muhammad Golbon. Tehran: 1363/1984.
Aqeli, Baqer. *Sharh-e hal-e rejal-e siyasi va nezami-ye mo'aser-e Iran* [The Biography of Iran's Politician and Military Notables in the Modern Period]. 2 vols. Tehran: 1380/2001.

Asef, Muhamad Hashem (Rostam al-Hokama). *Rostam al-tavarikh*. Edited and annotated by Muhammad Moshiri. Tehran: 1357/1978.
Asnadi az ravabet-e Iran ba mantaqeh-ye Qafaqz [Documents on the Relationship Between Iran and the Caucasus]. Tehran: 1372/1993.
Azod al-Dowleh, Mirza Ahmad. *Tairkh-e Azodi*. Tehran: 1376/1997.
Baharami-Damavandi, Akram. *Tabirz az didgah-e sayahan-e khareji dar qarn-e hevdahom* [Tabriz from the Perspective of Foreigners in the Seventeenth Century]. Tehran: 1356/1977.
Bamdad, Medi. *Tarikh rejal-e Iran* [History of Iran's Notables]. 5 vols. Tehran: 1347/1968.
Bayati, Mehdi. *Pansad sal tarikh-e javaherat-e saltanati dar Iran* [Five Hundred Year History of Royal Jewels in Iran]. Tehran: 1348/1969.
Bina, Ali Akbar. *Tarikh-e siyasi va diplomacy Iran* [A Political and Diplomatic History of Iran]. 2 vols. Tehran: 1348/1969.
Dehkhoda, Ali Akbar. *Loghat nameh Dehkhoda*, vol. 2, part 1. Tehran: 1325/1946.
Donboli, Abd al-Razzaq. *Ma'aser-e sultaniyyeh* [The Heritage of Sultaniyyeh]. Edited by Gholam Husayn Zargari-nejad. Tehran: 1383/2004.
E'temad al-Saltaneh, Muhammad Hasan. *Sadr al-tavarikh*. Edited by Muhammad Moshiri. Tehran: 1349/1970.
——. *Tarikh-e monazam-e Naseri* [An Orderly History of Naseri Period]. Edited by Muhammad Isma'il Rezvani. Tehran: 1364/1985.
E'tezad al-Saltaneh, Ali Qoli Mirza. *Eksir al-tavarikh*. Edited by Jamshid Kianfar. Tehran: 1370/1986.
Farahani, Abu al-Qasem (Qa'em Maqam II). *Monshe'at Qa'em Maqam*. Compiled by Farhad Mirza Mo'tamed al-Dowleh. Edited by Jahangir Qa'em Maqami. Tehran: 1337/1958.
——. *Namehha-ye parakandeh-ye Qa'em Maqam-e Farahani*. Compiled by Jahangir Qa'em Maqami. Tehran: 1357/1979.
——. *Namehha-ye siyasi va tarikhi-ye sayyed al-vozara Qa'em Maqam Farahani*. Edited by Jahangir Qa'em Maqami. Tehran: 1358/1980.
Farhang-e estelahat-e dowreh-ye Qajar: goshoon va nazmiyeh [A Dictionary of Military and Police Terms of the Qajar Period]. Tehran: 1380/1991.
Farmanha va raqamhay-e dowreh-ye Qajar [Royal Decrees and Letters of the Qajar Period]. Tehran: 1371/1992.
Foshahi, Muhammad Reza. *Gozaresh kutah az tahavolat-e fekri va ejtema'i dar jame'eh-ye fe'udali-ye Iran* [A Brief Account of Intellectual and Social Changes in Iran's Feudal Society]. Tehran: 1354/1975.
Ha'eri, Abd al-Hadi. *Nokhostin ruyaruyi-e andisgaran-e Iran ba du raviyeh-ye bourgeoisie-e gharb* [The First Encounters of Iranian Thinkers with Approaches of the Western Bourgeoisie]. 2 vols. Tehran: 1372/1993.
Hedayat, Reza Qoli. *Fehrest al-tavarikh* [Catalog of History]. Tehran: 1373/1994.
Ishqi, Khanak. *Siyasat Nezami Russiya dar Iran 1790–1815* [Russia's Military Policy toward Iran 1790–1815]. Tehran: 1353/1974.

Jahangir Mirza. *Tarikh-e no* [New History]. Edited by Abbas Iqbal. Tehran: 1327/1948.
Kazemi-musavi, Ahmad. *Khaqan-e saheb qaran va umala-ye zaman* [The Emperor of the Century and the Ulama]. Tehran: 1397/2018.
Khalili, Muhammad. *Chistan-e Qajar* [The Riddle of Qajar]. Mashhad: 1390/2011.
Khavari-shirazi, Mirza Fazlollah. *Tarikh dh al-qarneyn* [History of Two Centuries]. 2 vols. Tehran: 1380/2001.
Khormowji, Muhammad Ja'far. *Haqayeq al-akhbar Naseri* [Naseri History]. Tehran: 1363/1984.
Lachini, Abu al-Qasem, ed. *Abbas Mirza nayeb al-saltaneh* [Prince Regent Abbas Mirza]. Tehran: n.d.
——. *Ahvalat va dastneveshtehha-ye Abbas Mirza na'eb salataneh* [The Life and Handwritten Documents of Prince Regent Abbas Mirza]. Tehran: n.d.
Marvazi, Mirza Muhammad Sadeq. *Ahang sorush ya tarikh jangha-ye Iran-Rus* [The Sound of Oracle: A History of the Russo-Iranian Wars]. Compiled and annotated by Amir Hushang and Hosein Azar. Tehran: 1369/1990.
Mo'ayer al Mamalek, Doust Ali. *Rejal-e asr-e Naseri* [The Notables of the Naseri Period]. Tehran: 1390/2011.
Mo'in, Muhammad. *Farhang-e Mo'in*, vol. 1. Tehran: 1382/2003.
Mostofi, Abdollah. *Tarikh-e edari va ejtema'i-ye Qajarieh ya sharh-e zendegi-ye man* [A Social and Administrative History of the Qajars or a Narrative of my Life]. 3 vols. Tehran: 1321/1942.
Musavi-Tabari, Mostafa. *Abbas Mirza Qajar: sharh-e siyasat va khadamat* [Abbas Mirza Qajar: An Account of Policies and Service]. Tehran: 1353/1974.
Nader Mirza. *Tarikh va jughrafi-ye dar al-saltaneh-e Tabriz* [A History and Geography of the Court of Tabriz]. Tehran: 1323/1944.
Nafisi, Sa'id. *Tarikh ejtema'i va siyasi Iran dar dowreh-ye mo'aser* [A Political and Social History of Iran during Contemporary Period]. 2 vols. Tehran: 1344/1965.
Najmi, Naser. *Abbas Mirza*. Tehran: 1374/1995.
Nasiri, Muhammad Reza, ed. *Asnad va mokatebat-e tarikhi Iran: Qajariyeh* [Historical Documents and Correspondence of Iran during the Qajar Period]. 2 vols. Tehran: 1366/1987.
Nateq, Homa. *Az mast keh bar mast* [From Us to Us]. Tehran: 1357/1979.
Niknam, Laleh and Fariborz Zowqi. *Tabriz dar gozar tarikh* [Tabriz in the Passage of History]. Tabriz: 1374/1995.
Panahi-Semnani, Muhammad A. *Fath Ali Shah Qajar*. Tehran: 1376/1997.
Peyma'i, Nader. *Tarikh-e Azarbaijan* [History of Azarbaijan]. Washington, DC: 2005.
Pur-Safar, Ali. *Hokumatha-ye mahali-ye Qafqaz dar asr-e Qajar* [Local States in the Caucasus during the Qajar Period]. Tehran: 1377/1998.
Qa'emmaqami, Baqer. *Qa'em Maqam dar jahan-e adab va siyasat* [Qa'em Maqam in the World of Literature and Politics]. Tehran: 1320/1941.

Qa'emaqami, Jahangir, ed. *Monshe'at-e Qa'em Maqam* [Collection of Letters of Qa'em Maqam]. Tehran: 1337/1958.
—, ed. *Nameh-haye parakandeh-ye Qa'em Maqam Farahani* [Scattered Letters of Qa'em Maqam Farahani], vol.1. Tehran: 1357/1978.
Qaziha, Fatemeh, ed. *Asnadi az ravabet-e Iran va Russiya dar dowran Fath Ali Shah va Muhammad Shah Qajar* [Documents on the Relationship between Iran and Russia during the reign of Fath Ali Shah and Muhamad Shah Qajar]. Tehran: 1380/2001.
—, ed. *Asnadi az ravand ejra-ye mo'ahedeh-ye Turkmanchay* [Documents on the Implementation of the Treaty of Turkmanchay]. Tehran: 1372/1993.
Qozanlu, Jamil. *Jang Iran va Rus 1827–28* [Russo-Iran War 1827–28]. Tehran: 1314/1935.
—. *Tarikh nezami Iran* [A Military History of Iran]. 2 vols. Tehran: 1315/1936.
Rahvar-lighvan, Ali Reza and Parviz Zare'-shahmers. *Tarikh-e Qarabagh* [A History of Qarabagh]. Tehran: 1376/1997.
Ra'isnia, Rahim. *Tarikh-e omumi-ye mntaqeh-ye Shervan dar ahd-e Shervanshahan* [A General History of Shervan during the Period of the Shervanshahs]. Tehran: 1380/2001.
Rajabi, Parviz. *Karim khan-e Zand va zaman-e uo* [Karim Khan Zand and His Time]. Tehran: 1367/2008.
Safa'I, Ibrahim. *Yek sanad tarikhi-ye dowran Qajar* [A Historical Document from the Qajar Period]. Tehran: n.d.
Saleh, Gholam Hosein Mirza, ed. *Asnad-e rasmi-ye dar ravabet siyasi-ye Iran ba Inglis va Rus va Osmani* [Official Documents Concerning Iran's Relations with England, Russia and the Ottoman Empire]. 2 vols. Tehran: 1365/1986.
Salour, Husayn Qoli Mirza (Itemad al-Saltaneh). *Aqa Muhammad Khan-e Qajar: dastan zendegi-ye avalin padeshah Qajar* [Aqa Muhammad Khan Qajar: The Life Story of the First Qajar King]. Tehran: 1390/2011.
Saravi, Muhammad Fathollah. *Tarikh-e Muhammadi (Ahsan al-tavarikh).* Edited by Gholamreza Tabataba'i-majd. Tehran: 1371/1992.
Sari' al-Qalam, Mahmud. *Eqtedar gara'i-ye Irani dar ahd-e Qajar* [Iranian Authoritarianism during the Qajar Period]. Tehran: 1390/2001.
Sasani, Khan Malek. *Dast-e penhan-e siyasat-e Inglis dar Iran* [The Hidden Hand of English Politics in Iran]. Tehran: 1362/1983.
—. *Siyasatgozaran-e dowreh-ye Qajar* [The Policymakers of the Qajar Period]. Tehran: 1335/1959.
Sepehr, Lesan al-Mulk, Muhammad Taqi. *Nasekh al-tavarikh* [Historical Manuscript]. 3 vols. Tehran: 1377/1998.
Shahidi, Seyf al-Reza. *Karnameh-ye siyasi-ye Qa'em Maqam Frahani*. Tehran: 1386/2007.
Shamim, Ali Asqar. *Iran dar dowreh saltanat Qajar* [Iran during the Qajar Reign]. Tehran: 1374/1995.

Shirazi, Ali Reza. *Tarikh-e Zandiyeh* [History of the Zand Dynasty]. Tehran: 1365/1986.
Shirazi, Mirza Saleh. *Safarnameh-ye Mirza Saleh Shirazi* [Chronicles of Mirza Saleh Shirazi's Travels]. Tehran: 1363/1984.
Shushtari, Abd al-Latif. *Tohfehat al-'alam*. Edited by Samad Movahed. Tehran: 1363/1984.
Tabataba'I, Javad. *Ta'amoli dar bareh Iran: maktab Tabrizva moqadamat-e tajadod* [Reflection on Iran: The School of Tabriz and Preparations for Modernity], vol. 2. Tehran: 1384/2005.
Vahid-Mazandarani, Gholam Ali. *Mojmu'eh ahdnamehha-ye tarikhi Iran* [A Collection of Iran's Treaties]. Tehran: 1350/1971.
Varjavand, Parviz. *Iran va Qafqaz, Aran va Shirvan* [Iran and the Caucasus, Aran and Shirvan]. Tehran: 1378/1999.
Zargari-nezhad, Gholam Hosein. *Roozshomar va tahavolat Iran dar asr-e Qajar* [Chronology and Developments of Iran in the Qajar Period], vol. 1. Tehran: 1388/2009.

Persian translations

Abdollahyev, Fatollah. *Gushehha-yi az monasabat-e Russiya va Iran va siyasat Engelestan dar Iran-e qarn nuzdahom* [Aspects of Russo-Iranian Relations and the Role of England in Ninteeenth-Century Iran]. Translated by Gholam Husein Matin. Tehran: 1356/1977.
Bontems, Auguste. *Safarnameh-ye Bontems* [The Letters of a French General during his Short Trip to Turkey and Iran in the Year 1807]. Translated by Masureh Ettehadiyeh. Tehran: 1375/1997.
Churchill, George. *Farhang-e rejal-e Qajar* [Biographical Notices of Persian Statesmen and Notables]. Translated by Gholam Husayn Mirza Saleh. Tehran: 1369/1990.
Drouville, G. *Safarnameh-ye Drouville* [Voyage en Perse], Translated by Javad Mohi. Tehran: 1337/1958.
Gardane, A. *Ma'muriyat-e general Gardane dar Iran dar doreh-ye emperaturi-ye aval-e Faranceh* [Mission du general Gardane en Perse sous le Premier Empire]. Translated by Abbas Iqbal. Tehran: 1362/1983.
Jaubert, P. Ami. *Mosaferat dar Armenstan va Iran* [Voyage en Armenie et en Perse]. Translated by Ali Naqi E'temad-Moqadam. Tehran: 1347/1968.
Kuznetsova, N. A. *Oza' siyasi va ejtema'I Iran dar payan-e sadeh 18 ta nimeh-ye nokhost-e sadeh 19 miladi* [Iran's Socio-Political Condition during the Late Eighteenth and Early Nineteenth Century]. Translated by Cyrus Izadi. Tehran: 1358/1980.
Minorsky, N. *A History of Sharvan and Darband*, Translated by Mohsen Khadem. Tehran: 1375/1996.
——. *Studies in Caucasian History*. Translated by Mohsen Khadem. Tehran: 1375/1996.

Namehha-ye Alexander Griboyedov dar bareh-ye Iran marbut beh dowran saltanat Fath Ali Shah Qajar [Letters of Alexander Griboyedov on Iran during the reign of Fath Ali Shah Qajar]. Translated by Reza Farzaneh. Isfahan: 1356/1977.
Pakravan, Amineh. *Abbas Mirza*. Translated by Qasem Saghuri. Tehran: 1376/1997.
———. *Abbas Mirza va Fath Ali Shah: nabardha-ye dah saleh-ye Iran va Rus*. Translated by Safiyeh Ruhi. Tehran: 1376/1997.
Pollack, Jacob Edward. *Safarnameh-ye Pollack* [Persian, das Land und seine 1865]. Translated by Keykavous Jahandari. Tehran: 1368/1989.
Ringer, Monica M. *Amusesh, din, va gofteman-e eslah-e farhangi dar dowran-e Qajar* [Education, Religion, and the Cultural Discourse of Cultural Reform in Qajar Iran]. Translated by Mehdi Haqiqat-khah. Tehran: 1381/2002.
Soltykoff, Alexis. *Mosaferat beh Iran* [Voyage en Perse]. Translated by Mohsen Saba. Tehran: 1336/1957.
Tarikh-e Armanistan. Translated by A. Gemanik. Tehran: 1360/1981.
Watson, Robert Grant. *Tarikh Iran: Dowreh-ye Qajarieh* [History of Iran during the Qajar Period]. Translated by Vahid Mazandarani. Tehran: 1348/1969.
Wright, Denis. *Ingilisha dar miyan Iranian* [The English among the Persians]. Translated by Lotf Ali Khonji. Tehran: 1385/2007.
———. *Iranian dar miyan Inglisha* [Iranians among the English]. Translated by Karim Imami. Tehran: 2007.

Articles

English

"Abbas Mirza's Will." Translated by Homa Nateq and William Royce. *Iranian Studies* 6, no. 2–3 (1973): 137–51.
Abrahamian, Ervand. "Oriental Despotism: The Case of Qajar Iran." *International Journal of Middle East Studies* 5, no. 1 (1974): 3–30.
Amanat, Abbas. "Amin al-Dawla Abdallah Khan." *Encyclopedia Iranica*, vol. 1 (1985): 939–41.
———. "Dawlatshah, Muhammad-'Ali Mirza." *Encyclopedia Iranica*, vol. 7 (1994): 147–9.
———. "Ebrahim Kalantar Shirazi." *Encyclopedia Iranica*, vol. 8 (1998): 66–70.
———. "Fath Ali Shah Qajar." *Encyclopedia Iranica*, vol. 9 (1999): 407–21.
———. "The Kayanid Crown and Qajar Reclaiming of Royal Authority." *Iranian Studies* 34, no. 1–4 (2001): 17–30.
Atkin, Muriel. "The Pragmatic Diplomacy of Paul I: Russian Relations with Asia, 1796–1801." *Slavic Review* 38, no. 1 (March 1979): 60–74.
———. "Russian Intrusion into the Guarded Domain: Reflections of a Qajar Statesman on European Expansion." *Journal of the American Oriental Society* 113, no. 1 (1993): 35–56.

———. "The Strange Death of Ibrahim Khalil Khan of Qarabagh." *Iranian Studies* 12, no. 1–2 (1979): 79–107.
Avery, P. W. "An Enquiry into the Outbreak of the Second Russo-Persian War, 1826–1828." In *Iran and Islam*, edited by C. E. Bosworth, 17–45. Edinburgh: 1971.
———. "Nadir Shah and the Afsharid Legacy." In *The Cambridge History of Iran*, vol. 7, edited by P. Avery, G. R. G. Hambly and C. Melville, 3–33. Cambridge: 1991.
Axworthy, Michael. "The Army of Nader Shah." *Iranian Studies* 40, no. 5 (December 2007): 635–47.
Azizi, Muhamad Hossein. "Government-Sponsored Iranian Medical Students Abroad, 1811–1935." *Iranian Studies* 34, no. 3 (June 2010): 349–65.
Bakhaash, Shaul. "Center–Periphery Relations in Nineteenth-Century Iran." *Iranian Studies* 14, no. 1–2 (1981): 29–51.
———. "The Evolution of Qajar Bureaucracy, 1779–1879." *Middle Eastern Studies* 7, no. 2 (May 1971): 139–68.
Banani, Amin. "Administrative Development in Qajar Iran." *Iranian Studies* 4, no. 2–3 (1971): 118–19.
Behrooz, Maziar. "From Confidence to Apprehension: Early Iranian Interaction with Russia." In *Iran and Russia*, edited by Stephanie Cronin, 359–81. London and New York: 2013.
———. "Revisiting the Second Russo-Iranian War (1826–28): Causes and Perceptions." *Iranian Studies* 46, no. 3 (2013): 359–81.
Bournoutian, George. "Ebrahim Khalil Khan Javanshir." *Encyclopedia Iranica*, vol. 8 (1998): 71–3.
———. "Husayn Quli Khan Qazvini Sardar of Erevan: A Portrait of a Qajar Administrator." *Iranian Studies* 9, no. 2–3 (1976): 63–79.
———. "Prelude to War: The Russian Siege and Storming of the Fortress of Ganjeh, 1803–1804." *Iranian Studies* 50, no. 1 (2017): 107–25.
Busse, H. "Abbas Mirza." *Encyclopedia Iranica*, vol. 1 (1985): 79–84.
———. "Abol Fath Khan Javanshir." *Encyclopedia Iranica*, vol. 1 (1985): 285–6.
Cowe, S. P. "Ejmiatsin." *Encyclopedia Iranica*, vol. 8 (1998): 278–81.
Cronin, Stephanie. "Deserters, Converts, Cossacks and Revolutionaries: Russians in Iranian Military Service 1800–1920." *Middle Eastern Journal* 48, no. 2 (2012): 147–82.
———. "Importing Modernity: European Military Missions to Qajar Iran." *Comparative Studies in Society and History* 5, no. 1 (2008): 197–266.
Ekhtiyar, Maryam. "An Encounter with the Russian Czar: The Image of Peter the Great in Early Qajar Historical Writings." *Iranian Studies* 29, no. 1–2 (1996): 57–70.
Hairi, Abd al-Hadi. "The Legitimacy of the Early Qajar Rule as Viewed by the Shi'i Religious Leaders." *Middle Eastern Studies* 24, no. 3 (1988): 271–86.
Hambly, Gavin. "Agha Muhammad Khan and the Establishment of the Qajar Dynasty." In *The Cambridge History of Iran*, vol. 7, edited by P. Avery, G. R. G. Hambly and C. Melville, 104–41. Cambridge: 1991.

——. "An Introduction to the Economic Organization of Early Qajar Iran." *Iran* 2 (1964): 69–81.
——. "Iran during the Reigns of Fath Ali Shah and Muhammad Shah." In *The Cambridge History of Iran*, vol. 7, edited by P. Avery, G. R. G. Hambly and C. Melville, 144–73. Cambridge: 1991.
Javadi, H. "Abd al-Vahhab Motamed al-Dowla." *Encyclopedia Iranica*, vol. 1 (1985): 170–1.
——. "Abu'l-Hasan Khan, Ilchi." *Encyclopedia Iranica*, vol. 1 (1985): 308–10.
Kashani-Sabet, Firoozeh. "The Diminishing Domains of Qajar Iran." *International Journal of Middle East Studies* 29, no. 2 (1997): 205–34.
Khodarkousky, Michael. "Of Christianity, Enlightenment, and Colonialism: Russia in the North Caucasus 1550–1800." *Journal of Modern History* 71, no. 2 (1999): 394–430.
Kibovskii, Aleksandr. "'Bagaderan' – Russian Deserters in the Persian Army, 1802–1839." Translated by Mark Conrad. *Tseikhgauz* 5 (1996). http://marksrussianmilitaryhistory.info/Persdes2.html.
Kibovskii, Aleksandr, and Vadim Yegorov. "The Persian Regular Army of the First Half of the Nineteenth Century." Translated by Mark Conrad. *Tseikhgauz* 5 (1996): 20–5. http://marksrussianmilitaryhistory.info/PERSIA.html.
Mansoori, Cyrus. "Russian Imperialism and Jihad: Early 19th Century Persian Texts on Just War." *Journal of Church and State* 16, no. 2 (Spring 2004): 263–79.
Matthee, Rudi, "From Splendor and Admiration to Ruin and Condescension: Western Travelers in Iran from the Safavids to the Qajars." *British Institute of Persian Studies* LIVI (2016): 3–22.
——. "Historiographical Reflections on the Eighteenth Century in Iranian History: The Decline and Insularity, Imperial Dreams, or Regional Specificity?" In *The History and Historiography of 18th Century Iran*, edited by Michael Axworthy, 21–42. Oxford: 2018.
Melville, Firuza. "Khsosrow Mirza's Mission to St Petersburg in 1829." In *Iranian–Russian Encounters*, edited by Stephanie Cronin, 69–95. London and New York: 2013.
Meredith, Colin. "Early Qajar Administration: An Analysis of its Development and Function." *Iranian Studies* 4, no. 2–3 (1971): 59–84.
Nava'i, A. H. "Fath Ali Khan Qajar." *Encyclopedia Iranica*, vol. 9 (1999): 406–7.
Oberling, P. "Aga Muhammad Khan Qajar." *Encyclopedia Iranica*, vol. 1 (1985): 602–6.
Pakdaman, Homa, and Pope William. "Abbas Mirza's Will." *Iranian Studies* 4, no. 2–3 (1973): 136–51.
Perry, John. "The Zand Dynasty." In *The Cambridge History of Iran*, vol. 7, edited by P. Avery, G. R. G. Hambly and C. Melville, 63–104. Cambridge: 1991.
Qa'em Maqami, J. "Aslanduz" *Encyclopedia Iranica*, vol. 2 (1987): 770.

Rabi, Uzi, and Nugzar Ter-Oganov. "The Military of Qajar Iran: The Features of an Irregular Army from the Eighteenth to the Early Twentieth Century." *Iranian Studies* 45, no. 3 (2012): 333–54.
Savory, Roger. "The Qajars: The Last of the Qezelbash." In *Society and Culture in Qajar Iran*, edited by Elton L. Daniel, 3–32. Costa Mesa, CA: 2002.
Tucker, Ernest. "Nadir Shah and the Ja'fari Madhab Reconsidered." *Iranian Studies* 27, no. 1–4 (1994): 163–79.

Persian

Hazhir, Abd al-Husayn, "Dra rah-e vali'ahdi-ye Abbas Mirza" [Abbas Mirza's Path to Becoming Crown Prince]. *Mehr* 9 (1315/1934): 707–9.
Khalupur, Cyrus. "Gusheh'i nashenakhteh az dowran-e Fath Ali Shah Qajar" [An Unknown Aspect of the Reign of Fath Ali Shah Qajar]. *Iran Shenasi* 3 (1376/1997): 515–22.
Rashtiyani, Gudarz. "Diplomacy dar miyan-e du jang: sefarat general Yermolov beh Iran va dastavardha-ye an" [Diplomacy In Between Two Wars: The Mission of General Eermolov to Iran and its Achievements]. *Motale'at Euroasiya* 12 (1392/2003): 55–74.

British National Archives

FO/25/36
FO/60/25
FO/60/2
FO/60/26
FO/60/27
FO/94/159
FO/95/61
FO/95/159/i
FO/95/159/ii
FO/95/175
FO/95/591
FO/96/672
FO/95/673
FO/248/1
FO/248/5
FO/248/9
FO/248/13
FO/248/16
FO/248/22
FO/248/31
FO/284/32

FO/248/32
FO/248/47
FO/248/55
FO/248/73
FO/248/76
FO/351/1
FO/352/2
FO/352/2A
FO/352/3
FO/366/315
FO/591/2
FO/802/390
FO/881/1427

Index

Abbas I, Shah, 8
Abbas Mirza Qavanllu-Qajar, 17, 44, 79
   1807, 85
   appearance, 51
   appointed prince regent, 26, 51
   Battle of Aslanduz, 98, 101
   Battle of Ganjeh, 137
   Battle of Khanshin, 82–3
   Battle of Nakhjavan, 92–3
   Battle of Qarabagh, 69–70
   Battle of Sultanabad, 100
   Battle of Uch Kelisa, 63
   battles of 1806, 82–5
   birth, 51
   blame game, 108
   British influence, 120–1
   challenges from brothers, 73–5
   Council of Sultanieh, 120–5
   courting of the ulama, 122
   death, 132
   envoy to Ermolov, 114–5
   Ermolov and, 109, 110, 112
   failure, 137
   first Battle of Iravan, 46–7
   first siege of Iravan, 61, 62–7
   frustration in fighting the Russians, 52–3
   governorship of Azarbaijan, 35
   Griboyedov mission massacre, 131
   Griboyedov negotiations, 110
   Gudovich letter, 91, 94
   interwar years, 120
   letter to Sheikh Ali Khan of Darband, 94
   and Menshikov, 123–4
   military command, 46, 47, 51, 73–4
   peace treaty, 101–2
   position, 121
   reforms, 31, 52, 67, 75–6, 112, 121, 135, 136
   relationship with the ulama, 136
   role, 137
   Russia policy, 51–3, 121–2
   Russian retreat from Ganjeh, 72
   second Russo-Iranian War, 125–8, 130, 137
   second siege of Iravan, 93
   siege of Ganjeh, 71
   strategic situation, 1806-11, 73–5
   title, 51
   Tormazov letter, 98–9
Abd al-Vahhab, Neshat-e Isfahani (Mo'tamed al-Dowleh), 117
Abol Qasem Farahani, 119
Abrahamian, Ervand, 35–6
Abu al-Hasan Khan, 34
Abu al-Hasan Shirazi (Ilchi), 80, 103, 109
Abu al-Qasem (Qa'em Maqam II), 106–7, 115, 137, 165
Adel Shah Afshar, 8–9
Adineh Bazaar, 19
Afghanistan, 56–7, 80
Afshar tribe, 2
Ahmad Khan Abdali, 3–4
Akhalsikh, siege of, 100
Alexander I, Tsar, 5, 53, 55, 60, 75, 103, 111, 112, 113, 117, 128, 130
Ali Khan Saliyani, 159
Ali Murad Khan, 14
Ali Qoli Khan Shahsavan, 25, 159
Allahyar Khan Develu-Qajar (Asef al-Dowleh), 119, 159–60
Amanallah Khan Khamseh-Afshar, 92, 93, 160
Amanat, Abbas, 6
Amir Khan Develu-Qajar (Sardar), 126–7, 160
Anglo-Iranian agreement, 96–7, 134
Anzali, attack on, 72
Aq Oghlan, 83
Aqa Muhammad Khan, 4, 6
Aqa Muhammad Shah, 8–14, 27, 134
   and annexation Georgia, 54
   appearance, 9–10
   army, 40, 42–7

assassination, 24, 28, 33
attitude to the Russians, 24–5
birth, 8
castration, 9
conquest of the Caucasus, 15–25
coronation, 38
crown, 31
cruelty, 9
defeat of the Zand, 12, 14–5
education, 30
employment of close relatives, 34–5
governorships, 35
kills half-brothers, 10
legacy, 10–1
military skill, 9, 42–3
personal administration, 31–2
personality, 9–10
pre-coronation tribal title, 11–2
relationship with the ulama, 38
sack of Tiflis, 59
strategy, 25, 42–3, 134–5
struggle for supremacy, 13–4
succession, 11
temperament, 9
treasure, 10
Aqa Sayyed Muhammad (Mojahed) Isfahani, 119
Aras, River, 15, 16, 19–20
Ardabil, 128
Arkaran, Battle of, 70
Armenian Orthodox Church, 17
Armenian population, 17–8, 19, 39, 58–9, 65
Asadollah Khan Nuri, 32, 165
Asef al-Dowleh, 127–8
Asgar Khan Afshar Urumi, 88–9, 160
Askaran, 99
Aslanduz, Battle of, 45, 101
Atkin, Muriel, 6
Austerlitz, Battle of, 81
Avery, P. W., 108, 121
Azad Khan, 3
Azarbaijan, 14, 15–6, 35, 39, 73, 76

Badkubeh, siege of, 72–3
Baghdad, 2
Baku, 81, 83
Bash Aparan, 124, 125, 126
Black Sea, 21, 78

Bonaparte, Napoleon, 56, 67, 76, 76–80, 86, 87, 88, 94, 100, 103, 136
Bontems, Auguste, 38, 86, 86–7
border incursions, 105–6, 133–4
Bournoutian, George, 6
British mission, 32–3
Bruguieres, Jean-Guillaume, 54
Brydges, Harford Jones, 45–6, 66, 67, 95, 95–9, 114

Caspian Sea, 14, 18, 70, 72
casualties, 83, 59, 138
Catherine II, Tsarina, 5, 18–9, 50
Caucasus, the
conquest of, 15–25
Russian invasion of, 22–5, 50
Cheragh Ali Khan, 50
Christian populations, 17–8, 38
chronology, 139–57
crisis of 1825, 106

Daghestan, 2
Darband, 59
Darband-Qobbeh, 22–3
Decembrist rebellion, 106, 117, 130
deterrence, Iran's lack of, 137–8
Devellu, 93
diplomacy and intrigue, first Russo-Iranian War, 76–80, 85–91

East India Company, 56
Egypt, 135
Enlightenment, the, 4–5
Ermolov (Yermolov), Aleksey P., 104–5, 124–5, 136, 171
and Abbas Mirza, 112, 114–5
contempt for Muslims, 111, 116–7
escalates hostilities, 112–3, 116
Iran mission, 109–11
lack of preparedness, 125
policy disagreement, 111
southeastern Caucasus policy, 108–18, 128–30
Etchmiadzin, 63, 127
eunuchs, 9
Europe, 4–5

Farajallah Khan Shahsavan, 84, 93, 160
Fatah Ali Khan Fumeni, 34, 114, 128, 137

Index

Fath Ali Khan Shav, 121
Fath Ali Shah, 6, 27–9, 54, 128–9
  accession, 25
  appearance, 27, 28
  army, 40, 47
  attempt to improve relations with Russia, 50–1
  birth, 27
  blame game, 107
  challenges to reign, 25–6
  children, 51
  coronation, 25
  Council of Sultanieh, 122–5
  court procedures, 27–8
  crown prince, 11
  curiosity about outside world, 32–3
  decrees favoring the Armenian population, 17
  diplomacy and intrigue, 76–80
  education, 30
  employment of close relatives, 34–5, 35
  Ermolov's visit, 109–10
  fall of Ganjeh, 57
  first siege of Iravan, 61
  and Gardane mission, 88, 90, 95
  governor of Fars, Yazd, and Kerman, 15
  governorships, 35
  Griboyedov mission massacre, 131
  harem, 28
  imperial titles, 30
  mediation proposal, 123
  ministers, 32
  peace treaty, 101
  reforms, 32
  relationship with the ulama, 38
  Romieu's impression of, 78–9
  Russia policy, 122–5
  Russia recognizes, 102
  second Russo-Iranian War, 105
  set up central command at Takht-e Tavus, 70
  Shi'i religious establishment pressure, 117
  style of reign, 27–8
  succession, 102, 132
  temperament, 27
  thrones, 28–9
Fazlollah Khavarishirazi, 15

Finkenstein, Treaty of, 86, 86–7, 90
first Russo-Iranian War, 6
  1806–11, 73–6
  Abbas Mirza appointed commander, 51
  Abbas Mirza's policy, 51–3
  aftermath, 101–2
  anti-Russian rebellions, 99–100
  attack on Anzali, 72
  Battle of Arkaran, 70
  Battle of Aslanduz, 45, 101
  Battle of Ganjeh, 46
  Battle of Khanshin, 82–3
  Battle of Lankaran, 101
  Battle of Nakhjavan, 91–3
  Battle of Qarabagh, 67, 67–70
  Battle of Shah Bulaghi, 70–1
  Battle of Sultanabad, 100
  Battle of Uch Kelisa, 63
  battles of 1806, 80–5
  British overtures, 95
  ceasefire request, 85
  deterioration of relations, 53–7
  diplomacy and intrigue, 76–80, 85–91
  fall of Ganjeh, 57–60
  first Battle of Iravan, 43, 46–7
  first siege of Iravan, 60–7
  France and, 76–80, 87–91
  Gardane mission, 85, 87–91, 91, 94–5
  Gudovich replaced, 94
  hostilities resume, 91–2
  Iranian strategy, 134–5
  joint Ottoman–Iranian attack, 100
  Jones Brydges mission, 95–9
  lack of preparedness, 53
  peace proposals, 75, 98–9
  peace treaty, 101–2
  prelude, 1801-1803, 49–51
  prisoners of war, 67
  Russian command changes, 68
  Russian reinforcements, 68
  Russian retreat from Ganjeh, 71–2
  second siege of Iravan, 75, 92–4
  siege of Akhalsikh, 100
  siege of Badkubeh, 72–3
  siege of Ganjeh, 70–2
  strategic situation, 1806-11, 73–6
  strategic situation, spring 1805, 68
  trigger, 55

France, 54, 56–7, 68, 75, 76, 76–80, 85–91, 99, 136
Franco-Iranian treaty, 1807, 88
Fraser, James, 112
French–Iranian relations, 76–80
Friedland, Battle of, 86

Ganjeh, 20, 98
    Battle of, 46, 127, 137
    fall of, 57–60
    siege of, 70–2
Gardane, Alfred du, 47, 85, 87, 87–91, 91, 94–5, 96
George III, King, 96
Georgia, 18, 50, 53–5, 57, 82, 83, 85, 105
Georgievsk, Treaty of, 18, 19, 54
Gilan, 13, 34, 70
Giorgi XII, 54
Glazenap, Alexander P, 83
global context, 135
Gokcha crisis, 113–5, 118–9, 122, 124, 129, 130, 136
Golestan, Treaty of, 101–2, 103, 106, 107, 109, 110, 114, 116, 129, 130
Golestan Palace, 28, 29
Gorgestan, 16
Great Britain
    imperialism, 136
    interest in Iran, 55–7
    Iran policy, 107–8
    Jones Brydges mission, 95–9
    overtures, 95
    policy, 76
    pro-British faction, 80
    second Russo-Iranian War influence, 106, 107–8, 120–1
    treaty, 1801, 76
Green, Nile, 104
Griboyedov, Alexander, 103, 108–9, 110, 130–1
Griboyedov mission massacre, 130–1
Gudovich Count Ivan Vasilyevich, 21, 54, 59, 68, 75, 83, 85, 88, 89–90, 91, 92–4, 94, 171

Haji Ibrahim Khan (Kalantar) I'timad Dowleh, 52
Haji Muhammad Hosein Khan Sadr-e Isafahani, 32

Hamzeh Khan Anzali, 127, 160–1
harems, 28
Hasan Khan Sari Aslan, 92
Hedayatollah Khan Fumeni, 13
Hidden Imam, the, 37
Hosein Ali Mirza Farman Farma, 66
Hosein Qoli Aqa, 58
Hosein Qoli Khan Badkubeh, 72, 81, 161
Hosein Qoli Khan Qavanllu-Qajar Qazvini (Sardar Iravani), 17, 40, 38, 68, 73, 83, 84, 92, 100, 125–6, 161–2
Hosein Qoli Mirza (Jahansuz), 12, 27
Hulagu Khan, 7

Ibrahim Khalil Khan Javanshir of Qarabagh, 14, 19–20, 24, 67–8, 68–9, 82, 162
Ibrahim Khan, 31
Ibrahim Khan Badkubeh, 81
Ibrahim Khan Shirazi (Kalantar-I'timad al-Dowleh), 14, 24, 30–1, 34, 54, 56, 162
Il-Khan period, 7
Imami Shi'a ulama, the, 37
imperial titles, 29–30
imperialism, 135, 136
Independent Georgia Corps, 105
India, 55–7, 76, 87, 134
Industrial Revolution, 4–5
interwar years, 103–5, 120
Irakli II Bagration, 18
Irakli/Erekli II, 16, 19, 20, 21, 53, 54
Iran, 86
    anti-British alliance with France, 87
    Bontem's impression of, 86–7
    borders, 29
    lack of preparedness, 53
    relationship with Russia, 53–7
    reunification of, 6, 8–14, 133–4
    strategic situation, 1806-11, 73–5
Iran–Iraq War, 138
Iraq, 29
Iravan, 39, 68
Iravan, first Battle of, 43, 46–7
Iravan, first siege of, 60–7
    Armenian population, 65
    battle of Uch Kelisa, 63
    defences, 64
    garrison, 64

initial engagement, 62
Iranian advance, 62
Iranian forces, 62
Iranian mobilization, 61
lessons of, 65–7
Muhammad Khan's negotiations, 61–2
preparations, 60–1
Russian advance, 61
Russian dispositions, 64
Russian forces, 60
Russian raids, 65
Russian retreat, 65, 67
the siege, 63–7
Iravan, second siege of, 75, 92–4
Isa (Bozorg) Farahani Qa'em Maqam I, 31, 32, 33, 37–8, 51–3, 67, 73, 120, 165
Isfahan, 1
Iskandar Mirza, 85, 99
Isma'il, Shah, 30
Isma'il Khan Sardar Damghani, 40, 71, 83, 84, 162–3
Istifanov, Major, 85

Ja'far Isfahani, 34
Ja'far Qoli Khan, 25
Jahangir Mirza, 127
Jaubert, Amedee, 41, 44, 51, 76, 79
Javad Khan Ziyadllu (Ziyadughllu) Qajar, 20, 57–9, 163
Jewish population, 38
jurisprudence, 37

Kalb Ali Khan Kangarllu-Qajar, 24, 163–4
Karim Khan, 3–4, 9, 11, 12, 13, 34
Kartel'i-Khakhet'I, 16, 54
Kerman, siege of, 15
Khak-e Ali, Battle of, 25
khanates, 16
Khanshin, Battle of, 82–3
Khark Island, 76
Khoda A farin, 82
Khosrow Mirza, 127, 131
Khoy, 39
Knorring Karl. F., 54, 171
Kotlyarevskii Pyotr S, 54, 171
Kurds, 14, 39

Lake Gokcha, 106–7, 113–5
land ownership, 36

Lankaran, 69
Battle of, 101
siege of, 126
Lazarev Ivan P (Lazarian), 54, 172
Lisanevich Dimitri T70, 80, 82, 172
looting, 21, 44–5
Lutf Ali Khan Zand, 4, 9, 14–5

Macdonald, George, 107
Madatov Valerian "Rostam" G, 126–7, 172
Mahdi, the, 37
Mahdi Qoli Khan, 70
Makintsev, Samson Y., 43
Malcolm, John, 9–10, 22, 27, 28, 33, 36, 50, 56, 88, 95, 134
Malik Mahmud Hotak, 1
Manuchehr Khan Gorji (Mo'tamed al-Dowleh), 120, 164
Marx, Karl, 35
Mehdi Qoli Khan Devellu-Qajar, 56, 62, 68, 164
Mehdi Qoli Khan Javanshir, 82
Menshikov, Prince, 108, 118, 123, 123–4, 129, 130
Mesopotamia, 39
military revolution, European, 4–5
Morier, James, 44, 49–50, 95–6
Mostafa Khan Afshar Baha' al-Molk, 131–2
Mughan plain, 21, 22
Muhammad Ali Mirza Dowlatshah, 74, 97, 98, 109
Muhammad Hadi Alavi-shirazi, 103–4
Muhammad Hasan Khan, 3, 8, 11, 12
Muhammad Hosein Khan Qavanllu-Qajar, 19, 20, 61–2, 63, 68, 166
Muhammad Hosein Khan Sadr-e Isfahani, 80, 96, 166
Muhammad Khan of Iravan, 70
Muhammad Khan Zand, 25
Muhammad Mirza, 126, 127, 132
Muhammad Reza Qazvini, 80, 86
Muhammad Shafi' Qadimi-Mazandarani (Sadr-e 'Azam), 31, 32, 33, 34, 63, 78, 79–80, 166
Musa Monajem Bashi, 72
Musaddeq, Muhammad, 138
Mustafa Khan Devellu-Qajar, 14, 166
Mustafa Khan of Shirvan, 167
Mustafa Khan of Talesh, 19, 98, 164

Nader Mirza Afshar, 26
Nader Shah Afshar, 2–3, 8, 29, 31, 33, 36
Nafisi, Sa'id, 107
Nakhjavan, Battle of, 91–3
Nakhjavan City, 39
Nateq, Homa, 107
Nebolsin Peter F, 82–3, 84, 91–3, 93, 172
Nesselrode, Karl, 111
Nicolas I, Tsar, 106, 113, 117, 123, 124, 130

Oliver, Guillaume-Antoine, 54
Ossep Vassitovits, 77
Ottoman Empire, 2, 18, 21, 55, 56, 68, 75, 77, 81–2, 89, 90, 93, 99, 100, 112, 116, 135, 136
Ouseley, Gore, 100, 101

Pambak, 39
Paskevich, Ivan F., 127, 131, 137, 172
Paul, Tsar, 50, 53
Paulucci, Filippo, 68, 172
Persia, 1
Persian language, 30
Peter I, Tsar, 5
Pir Qoli Khan Shambayati-Qajar, 65, 70, 83, 167
plague, 84
population, 38–9
Portnagene, Semen A., 92
Potemkin, Grigory A., 18–9
prisoners of war, 67, 126
public opinion, 37–8

Qa'em Maqam I, 76, 91, 99, 101–2, 105, 109, 120, 137
Qajar dynasty, 5
  branches, 8
  cultural perspective, 118
  factionalism, 129
  origins, 4, 7–8, 29–30
  pro-British faction, 80
  reunification of Iran, 6, 8–26
Qajar military, 40–7
  artillery, 2, 20, 41, 41–2, 66
  attack on Anzali, 72
  Battle of Arkaran, 70
  Battle of Khanshin, 82–3
  Battle of Nakhjavan, 92–3
  Battle of Qarabagh, 67–70
  Battle of Shah Bulaghi, 70–1
  battles of 1806, 80–5
  camps, 45–6
  cavalry, 41, 42, 45
  chain of command, 40, 44
  defects, 40, 41, 44–7, 65–6
  dispositions, 1806, 80–1
  equipment, 41
  first siege of Iravan, 62–7
  intelligence-gathering, 40, 45
  lack of security, 45–6
  logistical support, 40
  looting, 44–5
  mobilization, 46–7
  modernization, 89, 97, 102
  officers, 40, 46
  organization, 40
  performance, 41
  quality, 42, 75, 97, 112
  reforms, 31, 43–4, 67, 75–6, 76, 87, 112, 135
  Romieu's impression of, 78
  royal bodyguards, 41
  seasonal nature, 41
  second siege of Iravan, 92–4
  siege of Badkubeh, 72–3
  siege of Ganjeh, 70–2
  strength, 40, 47, 92
  tactics, 40, 41, 42
  training, 44
  Tribal Council, 44
  tribal-military habits, 44–7
  uniforms, 43
  upkeep, 40
  weapons, 41, 42
Qajar state
  bureaucrats, 30–1, 32
  early, 29–35
  employment of close relatives, 34–5
  governorships, 35
  imperial titles, 29–30
  lack of secrecy, 33
  land ownership, 36
  reforms, 32
  revenue, 36
  social classes, 35–6
  taxes, 36
  ulama–state relations, 36–8
Qarabagh, 17, 80, 82

Qarabagh, Battle of, 67, 67–70
Qasem Ferdowsi Tusi, 30
Qezelbash, the, 2, 8, 30

Reutt, Iosif A, 126, 173
Reza Qoli Mirza, 3
Reza Qoli Nava'i (Monshi al-Mamalek), 32, 78, 167
Roberts, Michael, 4–5
Romieu, Alexander, 77–9
royal bodyguards, 41
Rtischev Nicolas E, 68, 100, 172
Russia, 17
    advantages, 134
    aggression, 53
    annexation of Georgia, 53–5, 57
    anti-British foreign policy, 50
    border incursions, 105–6
    Caucasus policy, 18–9, 21
    Decembrist rebellion, 106, 117, 130
    expansion, 18
    fall of Ganjeh, 57–60
    French mediation request, 88–91, 91
    imperial ambition, 130
    imperial expansion, 49, 53
    initial encounters with, 13–4
    interwar years, 103–4
    invasion of the Caucasus, 22–5, 50
    Iranian attitude towards, 49–50
    Khosrow Mirza mission, 131–2
    military revolution, 5
    Napoleon invades, 100
    other fronts, 68
    peace proposals, 75
    regional hegemony, 55
    relationship with Iran, 53–7
    Romieu's impression of, 78–9
    southeastern Caucasus policy, 108–18, 128–30
    strategic situation, 1806-11, 75–6
    terror policy, 59–60
Russian army, 60–7
    artillery, 79
    attack on Anzali, 72
    Battle of Arkaran, 70
    Battle of Khanshin, 82–3
    Battle of Nakhjavan, 91–3
    Battle of Qarabagh, 67–70
    Battle of Shah Bulaghi, 70–1
    battles of 1806, 80–5
    command changes, 68
    desertions, 43, 67
    dispositions, 1806, 80
    firepower, 43, 65, 78, 79
    logistical support, 65
    officers, 43, 131
    quality, 43, 52
    raids, 45
    retreat from Ganjeh, 71–2
    Romieu's impression of, 79
    second siege of Iravan, 75, 92–4
    siege of Badkubeh, 72–3
    siege of Ganjeh, 70–2
    strength, 77, 80, 91
Russian War College, 5
Rustavi, Battle of, 20

Sadeq Khan Az al-Dinllu, 101, 167
Sadeq Khan Marvazi, 115–6
Sadeq Khan Shaqaqi, 14, 25, 167–8
Safavi Sufi Order, 7–8
Safavid Empire, 1–2, 29, 30, 36
Saleh Shirazi, 104
Salim III, Sultan, 12
Salim Khan Shakki, 67–8, 68–9, 168
Sardarabad, 92
Sayyed Muhammad Amin Vahid, 86
scribal class, 30–1
second Russo-Iranian War, 6
    aftermath, 130–2
    anti-Russian rebellions, 125, 130
    Battle of Ganjeh, 137
    blame game, 106–7, 128–9
    border incursions, 105–6
    British influence, 106, 107–8, 120–1
    causes, 128–30
    conflict, 125–8
    Council of Sultanieh, 118–25, 136
    crisis of 1825, 106
    Gokcha crisis, 113–5, 118–9, 122, 124, 129, 130, 136
    hostilities escalate, 116–8
    joint border commission, 112
    mediation proposal, 123
    mistreatment of the Muslim population, 116–7
    peace party, 119–20
    peace treaty, 128, 129, 130

prelude to, 105–8
prisoners of war, 126
Russian southeastern Caucasus policy, 108–18, 128–30
surrender of Tabriz, 127–8
war party, 119, 120
Selim Khan Shakki, 84
Shafi' Mazandarani, 52–3, 86, 96, 101
Shah Bulaghi, Battle of, 70–1
Shahrokh, 3–4
Sheikh Ali Khan of Qobbeh and Darband, 22–3, 72, 73, 94, 99, 168–9
Sheikh Haidar, 7
Shi'a–Sunni divide, 2–3, 99
Shi'ism, 30
Shiraz, 4, 14, 30
Shirvan, 83–4
Shusha, 39
Shusha, Battle of, 69–70
Shusha, siege of, 20, 126–7
social classes, 35–6
sources, 6
state revenue, 36
strategy, 42–3
Suleiman Khan Qavanllu-Qajar (E'tezad al-Dowleh), 14, 25, 169
Sultanabad, Battle of, 100
Sultanieh, Council of, 105, 118–25, 136
supernatural attacks, 81
Surkhay Khan II of Daghestan, 16, 169
Surkhay Khan of Lezgi, 72, 73
Suvorov Alexander Vasilyevich, 19, 173
Sweden, 68, 89, 90

Tabriz, 31, 32, 39, 53, 79, 101, 105, 109, 120, 127–8
tactics, 40, 41, 42–3
Takht-e Tavus, 20, 70
Talesh, 24, 101, 125
taxes, 36
Tehran, 22, 24, 38–9, 88, 101, 109–10, 130–1
Tiflis, 20, 54, 57
 sack of, 9, 59
 siege of, 20–1, 22
Tilsit, Treaty of, 87

Timur, 7
Tipu Sultan, 56
Tormazov, Alexander P., 68, 75, 94, 98–9, 173
Tsitsianov Pavel D, 55, 173
 assassination, 81
 Battle of Shah Bulaghi, 71
 battles of 1806, 80–5
 correspondence with the khans of Qarabagh and Shakki, 67–8, 68–9
 dispositions, 1806, 80
 fall of Ganjeh, 57–60
 first siege of Iravan, 60–7
 Muhammad Khan's negotiations with, 61–2
 reinforcements, 68
 siege of Ganjeh, 71
Turkmanchay, Treaty of, 128, 130–1
Turko-Mongol military tradition, 21

Uch Kelisa, 92
Uch Kelisa, battle of, 63
ulama, the, 122, 136
ulama–state relations, 36–8
Umm Khan of Avar, 16, 169

Valadikafkaz, 54
velayats, 16
Verninac, Raymond, 54

war weariness, 85
weapons, 41, 42
Weber, Eugen, 6
Wilhelmov, General, 115–6
Willock, Henry, 107–8, 113, 116, 118, 120–1, 122, 123, 123–4, 129, 136
World War I, 138
World War II, 138

Yusef Monshibashi, 72

Zaman Shah Durani, 26
zamburaks, 2
Zand, the, 9, 12, 13, 14–5
Zavalishin, General, 80, 81
Zubov, Count Valerian A, 22, 23, 50, 134, 173